Political and Social Economy
*Edited by C. Addison Hickman and
Michael P. Shields*

Other Books in This Series:

An Economic Analysis of Democracy

Randall G. Holcombe

SOUTHERN ILLINOIS UNIVERSITY PRESS

Carbondale and Edwardsville

To Mom and Ed

LIBRARY OF CONGRESS CATALOGING IN PUBLICATION DATA
Holcombe, Randall G.
    An economic analysis of democracy.

    (Political and social economy)
    Bibliography: p.
    Includes index.
    1. Public administration—Decision making.
2. Finance, Public—Decision making.   3. Voting.
4. Democracy.   I. Title.   II. Series.
JF1525.D4H65   1985   330.12   84-23584
ISBN 0-8093-1211-5

Contents

Figures

Tables

Preface

The goal of this book is to develop an economic model of the way in which a representative democracy allocates resources. Readers familiar with earlier writing on the subject will undoubtedly notice the similarity between the title of the present volume and the title of Anthony Downs's book *An Economic Theory of Democracy*. The similarity extends to more than the title. Both books endeavor to use economic theory to describe political decisions made by representative democracies. Downs's book, published in 1957, has had great influence over the thinking of economists and political scientists, and deservedly so, but in the decades that have passed since then, many others have done work in the same area. The present volume is able to take advantage of the cumulative research that has appeared since the time that Downs wrote, and many of the key elements in the theory presented here are built on a foundation of that research.

Under ideal circumstances, decades of research would point toward a single model of public sector resource allocation that could then be compiled into a reference book on the subject. New ideas have been developing rapidly, however, and research over the past decade has often been in the nature of building new models that question the appropriateness of their predecessors. The result has been an abundance of models examining many individual details of democratic decision making, such as bureaucracy, referenda, logrolling, special interest politics, and so forth. Regrettably, it is not always clear whether the models are consistent with one another, and to the extent that they are, what is implied about the way that representative democracies allocate resources. This book tries to fill that void by offering a consistent general model of resource allocation by representative democracy.

Not everyone will agree with the model's development or conclusions, because although the main building blocks of the model have their origins in the works of others, not all existing work on the subject is in agreement. My own efforts in developing the model and drawing out its logical implications make this book an independent statement about the nature of representative democracy and its implications for resource allocation. As such, the book can be judged on its own merits, independently of the other literature in the area. But since it is so closely tied to some important current issues in the theory of public choice, it can also be viewed as a part of a larger debate. Whenever possible, I have tried to adhere closely to existing work in the area to make it as easy as possible for readers familiar with the related literature to spot similarities and differences in my model.

The ideas developed in this book have been influenced by a number of individuals who deserve mention. James M. Buchanan read and commented on some early manuscripts that evolved into this book, but deserves credit over and above his comments on this specific work for the influence he has had over my general thinking on the subject. My many references to his work give some indication of his influence, direct and indirect, over the content of this volume. Gordon Tullock also deserves prominent mention, again for comments rendered on earlier material, and also for the influence that his work has had on the views expressed in this book. A number of other people have given me insightful comments, either on written work or when I have presented papers on the subject. Juergen Backhaus and John Stehle are two of the many that should be mentioned. I am also grateful to my wife Lora for her comments, support, and encouragement as I was working on the manuscript. Since none of these individuals had the opportunity to comment on the final draft, I alone must be held responsible for the book's shortcomings.

I am pleased to be working again with the Southern Illinois

University Press. They published my earlier book, *Public Finance and the Political Process*, and this book is, in a sense, a sequel to the earlier one. Many of the fundamental ideas in chapters 2 and 3 are based on concepts I discussed in the earlier book, making this book a natural extension of those ideas. But while *Public Finance and the Political Process* dealt with many models and concepts in public finance, the present book has a more narrow focus aimed at generating a single model of resource allocation by representative democracy. With this book, as with the previous one, I have always found the Southern Illinois University Press easy to work with, but I am especially happy to have them publish this book, given its close relationship to the earlier one.

The manuscript was typed at the Manuscript Preparation Center at the School of Business, Auburn University, and Bess Yellen deserves much credit for directing the staff's fast and efficient typing and for proofreading. Parts of the manuscript were typed by Juana M. Taylor, Priecilla Holifield, Loraine M. Hyde, and Dawn Hyde. I am also grateful to the Earhart Foundation for providing financial support for part of this project. Their assistance enabled me to complete the manuscript more rapidly than otherwise would have been possible.

An Economic Analysis
of Democracy

1 / Introduction

The American institutions are democratic, not only in their
principle but in all their consequences.   Alexis de Tocqueville[1]

Democratic political institutions are the foundation of
American society. The Constitution of the United States reflects the fact that the founders of the nation established a
government to protect individual rights. The powers of the
government are specified in the Constitution, and the Constitution itself prohibits the government from expanding its activities beyond those enumerated in the Constitution. First and
foremost, the purpose of the Founding Fathers was to establish
a government that protected the rights of its citizens. But although this was the purpose, the method used to carry out this
purpose was—and still is—democracy. The Founding Fathers
might have established some type of ruling elite; after all, until
the founding of the United States, a true democracy had not
existed in the world since the ancient Roman democracy. Although a ruling elite with powers carefully limited by a constitution might have been an acceptable protector of individual
rights, the Founding Fathers wanted the individual entrusted
with the running of the government to be the choice of the
nation's citizens. The underlying philosophy, new to the world
at that time, was that the government should serve its citizens
rather than the other way around.

Perhaps the reliance on democracy, combined with governmental powers closely circumscribed by the Constitution, was an

1

effort to avoid an outcome similar to the Roman case. The Roman Senate had virtually voted Caesar into the position of emperor,[2] so in the Roman case, a democracy voted itself out of existence. The reliance on approval from the general citizenry for governmental leaders could be viewed as a method for keeping one individual group from becoming too powerful. While this idea undoubtedly has some merit, the political philosophy of a government designed to serve its citizens is probably a more important causal factor. In the seventeenth and eighteenth centuries and in all of history before that time, the world was accustomed to viewing citizens of a state as subjects of a monarch, and the very idea that the citizens should control their government, rather than the government controlling its citizens, was a revolution in political thought. This is the characteristic that caused Alexis de Tocqueville to remark that American institutions are democratic in their principle.

Tocqueville went on to remark that American institutions are also democratic in their consequences, and it is the consequences of democracy that will be discussed here. A reading of the Constitution reveals a government established to protect the rights of its citizens, with democracy being a means toward that end, but Tocqueville's quotation at the beginning of the chapter suggests that Americans view their government as an institution designed to implement the will of the majority. If this was evident in Tocqueville's time, it is certainly evident today. There is a distinction here important enought to merit some emphasis. Democracy in America, originally established as a means to limit the power of government, has evolved into an end in itself. Rather than being viewed as a tool for safeguarding the rights of its citizens, democracy has become a mechanism for furthering the will of the majority.

Some reflections on the institution of democracy suggest why this will always tend to be the case. When governmental leaders are selected by majority rule, the approval of a majority of the voters is a prerequisite for elective office. Once elected, these officials must be periodically reelected to keep their posts, which means enacting policies which please a majority of the voters. The incentives implied in a democracy naturally lead the government to pursue policies that further the interests of a majority. In competition for elected office, a winning political campaign must present the candidate as being better able to further the interest of a majority than the alternative candidates. When political leaders are selected by majority rule, a government cannot escape being democratic in principle.

This leads to the question about the consequences of democracy. Modern democracies are, of necessity, representative democracies. For a nation of millions of people, it is obviously infeasible to have a direct democracy. Even in an electronic age where national referenda are possible, there must be some way to limit the agenda of a government, and that method is to allow access to the agenda only to elected representatives. At this point, the collective decision-making process becomes more complex because rather than directly furthering the will of the majority, the democratic government carries out the will of a majority of representatives, who themselves are selected by a majority of their constituents. This book examines the decision-making process of a representative democracy from an economic viewpoint. The incentives facing the participants of democratic government are examined, and the consequences of the actions that respond to those incentives are deduced using economic analysis.

This introductory chapter has two primary purposes. First, it will give an overview of the argument to be presented in detail through the rest of the book. The value in this is that as the details are presented in succeeding chapters, the reader will already have an idea about where the details will lead and, so, will be better able to see the parts of the argument as pieces of a coherent whole. The second goal of this chapter is to briefly review several decades of previous research on the subject to explain how the argument in this book relates to other work in the area. The analysis presented here is a natural extension of previous work and deals with some unresolved questions in the area of public choice. The book can be read simply for its own content, but its arguments take on an added significance when considered against the background of earlier work. With this introduction, a brief overview of the book's analysis follows.

Overview

The ultimate conclusion of the book will be that a representative democracy does not allocate resources in a way that serves the best interests of its citizens.[3] This conclusion would be quite understandable if the government in question were forced upon its citizens. In the U.S. case, at least, it appears that the governmental form was freely chosen by its citizens, and the theoretical challenge is to explain how a government freely chosen by its citizens can act in a way that is not in the best interest of those citizens. Apart from any connection with historical reality, any meaningful theory of government that shows that the government can act against the best interests of its citizens must rest on a foundation theory that the offending institution could have been chosen voluntarily by the governed citizens. It is of relatively little importance to point out that a government imposed upon people could work against those people's best interest. Of far more significance are the cases where governments voluntarily chosen by people can work against their interests.

This is true for two reasons. First, it illustrates that the institutional structure created with one end in mind has been designed in such a way as to allow unintended consequences. The second reason is that in a voluntarily chosen government, reform may be possible if the causes of inefficiency are clearly understood. Institutions may be poorly designed, or perhaps the problem may not be amenable to governmental solutions at all. Identifying an aspect of society that is less than ideal does not necessarily imply that a government program can result in improvements. But it seems important to set the analysis on a foundation of governmental institutions that, at least conceptually, could be agreed upon by the citizenry. This way, any inefficiencies that arise in the public sector cannot be the result of institutions forced upon a nation's citizens.

Chapter 2 addresses this issue by developing a model that shows how, conceptually, individuals could agree that they would be better off united through a government, and that a representative democracy would be the likely choice of governmental form. This government would not have unlimited powers, however. The model in chapter 2 has some correspondence with the American case, where a limited government was formed using representative democracy.

Any government, if it is to survive, must provide flexibility to deal with new and unforeseen circumstances as they arise. In a representative democracy, elected representatives have the power to legislate change, subject to the constraints given by the government's constitution. This mechanism of change creates a bias in the way that the rules of a nation will evolve, because those who make the rules are always within the government. When reviewing any potential change, any individual will tend to view more favorably changes that benefit the individual, and so over time the rules of government will evolve to favor those in the government. After all, those in the government make the rules. The result is government growth, as over time the rules change to allow the government to command an increasing share of national output.

In order to understand the activities of the government in detail, a model of governmental decision making must be developed. The foundations of such a model are in chapter 3, titled "The Median Voter Model." The median voter model has been a cornerstone of collective choice theory, and chapter 3 examines the model's strengths and weaknesses. The median voter model concludes that the outcome of a democratic decision is the outcome most preferred by the voter with the median preference. The model seems to have a great deal of relevance to single-dimensioned political decisions but does not appear to generalize to multidimensional issues. Chapter 4 picks up at this point to discuss multidimensional political issues.

A major problem that arises with multidimensional issues is that there in general is no stable equilibrium outcome. Several issues, considered separately, may each have a stable median voter outcome, yet when the issues are considered simultaneously in a multidimensional framework, no one outcome dominates all others. Issues voted on by the general public, like which candidate to elect or how much to spend for public schools, will tend to be single-dimensioned issues. These types of issues are depicted well by the median voter model. The issues voted on by representative bodies, on the other hand, tend to be multidimensional in character. The reason is that with a small number of voters, and with votes being a matter of public record, it is easy to exchange votes across issues. Logrolling and vote trading mean that the outcome of one issue affects the outcome on other issues, so that even issues that appear on the surface to be single-dimensioned are in fact simultaneously determined. The theoretical problem is that within the context of the median voter model, there is no stable equilibrium outcome to this type of multidimensional voting.

Observation of the real world shows that political processes produce very stable outcomes, however. Incumbency is an advantage in an election, and political programs, once started, tend to endure. The institutional structure of politics appears to contain stability-producing mechanisms, and the book's model is built around a model of stability in a distributive game.

Government activity might be pictured in this way. The government collects taxes, and deposits tax revenues in the treasury. Then Congress decides how those revenues should be divided. The collection of taxes is independent of government spending, so the allocation of government spending might be pictured, at its simplest, as a distributive game. Consider a simple example where three representatives are to decide by majority rule how to divide government revenues. Under majority rule, two representatives could form a coalition to divide the revenues between them. Using the elements of the set in parentheses to denote the shares to each representative, this division would appear as (½, ½, 0). With this outcome, however, the third representative could offer to increase the share of one of the other representatives to form a new coalition, perhaps with a distribution of (0, ⅔, ⅓). Two out of three representatives are better off under this distribution, so majority rule would select it over the first outcome. This, in turn, would encourage similar behavior by the first representative, leading to a distribution of (⅓, 0, ⅔), which would invite the second representative to propose (⅔, ⅓, 0), and so on. There is no stable equilibrium in this situation.

A stable outcome could arise if the representatives were concerned with the variation in the distribution as well as its size. In the game described above, the expected value of the outcome of one play is ⅓ for each representative, but with considerable variance. If representatives were interested in producing a constant flow of government spending in addition to a large flow, a stable solution emerges. Since the expected value is ⅓ for all, they could unanimously agree on an outcome of (⅓, ⅓, ⅓), which would distribute the same amount of wealth to each representative in the long run, but with minimum variation in the flow. Chapter 4 argues that this device is the stability-producing mechanism in a representative democracy. A democratic government will tend to divide its budget so that something is given to everybody, in order to promote stability in government. This is the principle of universalism.

Chapter 5 considers the use of taxes as a redistributive mechanism. While the rhetoric of redistribution emphasizes taxation, in practice most changes in the redistributive formula occur on the expenditures side of the equation. There are several possible explanations for this. One is that the government acts as an interest group for its own programs and would rather redistribute by adding to government spending than by implementing tax cuts. Another explanation, which chapter 5 considers in detail, is that changes in the tax structure will be ineffective as a redistributive mechanism. This conclusion relies on the theory of tax shifting and argues that workers have many possibilities of changing jobs and work effort to adjust to changes in the tax structure. The ultimate burden of taxation will fall on factors that are relatively fixed. Since employees are interested in their after-tax wages rather than before-tax wages, they will bargain for a certain posttax wage. If the tax structure were to become more progressive, employers would have to compensate individuals in high-income jobs for the additional tax burden if they wanted to retain their employees. They could, however, pay low-income employees less and still leave them with the same posttax wage. Thus, the economy will adjust to changes in the tax structure, leaving the after-tax distribution relatively constant. This explains why redistributive programs tend to rely on government spending rather than taxation and supports the argument of chapter 4 where the government is depicted as collecting taxes from the general public and then distributing the proceeds through the political process.

Chapter 6 explains how this distributive government works.

The general public will be rationally ignorant of most of the government's activities. Special interest groups, in contrast, have an incentive to be informed and to be politically active on those issues that affect their group. Therefore, elected representatives will be hearing primarily the demands of special interests. In order to keep their jobs, representatives must be reelected, which requires them to pursue a vote maximizing legislative strategy. If the existing representatives do not act in order to maximize votes, challengers will arise who will campaign using the vote maximizing strategy and will be able to unseat the incumbents. Since the general public will be uninformed on most issues but special interests will be well informed, the successful representative will be the one who caters to special interests.

This implies more than simply voting in accordance with the desires of special interests. Representatives control the legislative agenda, and determine the type of legislation that will be considered. Special interests will lobby representatives to have legislation favoring the special interest group placed on the agenda. In exchange for the representative's service, the special interest groups can offer political support to the representative. Since most individuals are unaware of most of the government's activities, sponsoring special interest legislation will provide the representative with a net gain in political support.

A representative could sponsor legislation in the general public interest, but this strategy has several drawbacks. First, the general public will be largely unaware of the representative's efforts in their behalf, particularly since even special interest legislation will be advertized as if it is in the general public interest. Second, the benefits of general public interest legislation will be very diluted, and will extend beyond the representative's own constituents. The representative will be benefitting those who cannot vote for him or her, and even the representative's constituents will receive diluted benefits rather than the concentrated benefits that could be delivered with special interest benefits. This will dilute voter loyalty as well. Considering the drawbacks to sponsoring legislation in the general public interest, probably the greatest factor discouraging public interest legislation is that time and effort expended to promote public interest legislation takes away time the representative could have used to sponsor special interest legislation. The representative with an eye turned toward reelection has an incentive to promote special interest legislation and let somebody else worry about the general public interest. With all representatives facing the same incentives, however, there is nobody else. The result is that legislation tends to favor special interests and ignore the general public interest.

The legislator's challenge in this type of system is getting special interest legislation passed. A group of representatives will all have different special interest programs that they favor, so that if each program were voted on in isolation, each one would get only one or two votes. The solution is logrolling and vote trading to form a majority coalition that will approve all of the special interest programs. Who will be included in the majority coalition? This is the problem mentioned earlier, that is discussed in detail in chapter 4. If the majority coalition excludes some, then the outcome will be unstable. In a government that, in essence, collects taxes from the general public and distributes the proceeds according to the decision of a majority of the representatives, the expected value of the distribution will be the same in each period, as noted earlier, but the variance will be minimized when all representatives are included as members of the majority coalition. The principle of universalism applies, and each representative is able to distribute benefits to special interests of the representative's choosing. The result is a government is essentially distributive in nature. The government collects taxes from the general public in order to distribute benefits to special interests, while ignoring the general public interest.

The general principles of this model are developed in chapter 5, and chapter 6 is devoted to extending the model and making it more realistic. One question that arises during the course of the discussion is what limits this activity. In chapters 6 and 7, the answer given is simply that the government faces a budget constraint. Chapter 8 examines the government's budget constraint in more detail. There are basically two types of constraints that limit government spending. The first type is a fiscal constraint that is the upper bound on tax revenues that can be raised. This idea has been popularized as the Laffer curve. The idea is that beyond some limit, the government cannot increase its tax revenues by raising tax rates. A second type of constraint exists if the political institutions do not allow approval of increases in government spending. In a representative democracy, a majority of the representatives must approve spending, and there may be a limit beyond which a majority will not approve additional spending. This limit is called the boundary of the feasible majority set. These concepts are discussed in chapter 8, but it is unclear whether government spending is limited by fiscal constraints or the feasible majority set. Perhaps both constraints are in effect on different margins.

This model depicts government as being inefficient, and the existence of inefficiency implies that there are gains that could be realized by reorganizing government spending to make it more efficient. There is the potential for a political entrepreneur to propose a change that could benefit everyone and still leave some entrepreneurial profits. These incentives undoubtedly exist and undoubtedly are acted upon in some cases. Chapter 9 discusses the possibilities and also considers why the property rights system implied in a representative democracy is a hindrance to efficiency. Ownership of money in the public treasury is uncertain, and the representatives who ultimately assign ownership are legally barred from directly appropriating this money for themselves. It is in their interests to assign ownership to special interests rather than approving programs in the general public interest. Although government activity is inefficient, the institutional structure of a representative democracy provides each individual participant with an incentive to act in a manner that produces a distributive government.

Chapter 10 investigates the causes of government growth. It begins with a discussion of Arrow's contributions to social choice theory, and extends that discussion to a general paradigm for examining government growth. The theoretical framework draws heavily on the material developed in chapter 2. Beginning with a limited representative democracy, the argument is that over time the rules of society evolve to favor those who have the power to change the rules; namely, those in government. The evolution causes an increasing share of resources to be controlled by government as time passes. Any hope for controlling government growth is predicated on understanding the process by which government grows.

The Development of Public Choice Models

On the one hand, this book can be read on its own as an essay on the institutional structure of representative democracy. The model is developed beginning at its foundations, so the argument can be comprehended in isolation, without considering its relationship to other works in the area. On another level, however, the argument is firmly embedded in a body of literature on public choice and is better viewed as an extension of previous work. The purpose of this section is to explain the relationship of the book's argument to earlier public choice models.

One of the most important models in public choice is the median voter model. Conceived by Hotelling[4] and extended by Bowen, Black, and Downs,[5] the median voter model develops a methodology for aggregating preferences by majority rule and of explaining the characteristics of the equilibrium outcome of a decision made by majority rule. Although the theory was not developed by Downs, the widespread acceptance of the model was largely due to the influence of Downs's book, which explained the model, defended its use, and placed it within the larger context of governmental decision making. The reader will notice the close similarity between the title of the present volume and Downs's *An Economic Theory of Democracy*. The similarity extends beyond the titles, because both books have as their objective the use of economic analysis to understand how resources are allocated by representative democracy. The present volume, written more than a quarter of a century later, is able to take advantage of the theoretical developments made in the intervening time, but is an extension of the median voter model developed by Bowen, Black, and Downs.

By the early 1970s, the median voter model was generally accepted as a model descriptive of decision making under majority rule. Although the model was developed in a simple one-dimensional framework, it was developed in a number of different settings. The general conclusion that majority rule would select the outcome most preferred by the median voter was developed in a referendum setting, for decision making by committee, and in a setting of representative democracy.[6] Because of the apparent generality of the model, writers in the early 1970s were willing to apply the model's conclusion to any decision made in a democracy, and many articles in prominent economics journals were willing to assume that a median voter equilibrium existed in the public sector for purposes of empirical analysis.[7] This is certainly meant not as a criticism but simply as an observation of the state of the art application of public choice theory at that time.

During the decade of the 1970s, several important developments in public choice theory caused analysts to be more skeptical about the robustness of the median voter model.[8] An important catalyst was Niskanen's *Bureaucracy and Representative Government*,[9] which argued that the government tends to produce more than the median voter would most prefer. The setting in Niskanen's model was somewhat different from that in the median voter model, but theorists clearly sensed the power of Niskanen's argument that individuals in government have an incentive to maximize their budget. Budget maximization in bureaucracy was seen as the analog to profit maximization in the private sector.

This idea was integrated into the median voter model, perhaps a bit awkwardly, in what has been referred to as agenda control. The origins of the concept of agenda control predate Niskanen's book,[10] but the idea did not really capture the attention of public choice theorists until Niskanen's concept of budget maximization had migrated from bureaucracy to voting models.[11] The basic model of agenda control applies to referendum voting and argues along the following lines. Most referenda, for example, for public school financing, are choices between two discrete alternatives, and if a budget maximizer were to control the alternatives offered, it would be possible to manipulate the alternatives such that the median voter is given a two-point offer that would force the median voter to select an alternative larger than that the voter most desires.[12] The agenda control model is interesting from a theoretical standpoint because it is a median voter type model that has an outcome different from the median voters' preference.

The model fits awkwardly into public choice theory for the following reason. Referenda are held on relatively few issues. Most issues are decided by elected representatives without a referendum. In the referendum model, the referendum actually acts as a constraint on the budget maximizer's activity, so actually, expenditures should be lower in the agenda control referendum model than if the referendum were not held. If there is any validity to the agenda control model, then the important issues really lie outside the model. Why are agenda setters budget maximizers, and what is the equilibrium level of government spending when referenda are not used? Despite its shortcomings, the agenda control model did serve as a starting point for integrating the idea of budget maximization into voting models, and it also clearly focused on the importance of controlling the agenda to the outcomes of voting models. The concept of agenda control was one factor that undermined some confidence in the robustness of the median voter model.

Another important development was a proof by McKelvey that under seemingly reasonable conditions, a multidimensional median voter model would not have a stable equilibrium outcome.[13] The median voter model of Bowen, Black, and Downs was developed in a single dimension, and McKelvey showed that a set of preferences that would produce a median voter equilibrium in one dimension would, under the same voting rules, fail to produce an equilibrium when extended to multiple dimensions. McKelvey's proof, combined with the developing notion of agenda control, upset the existing notions of public sector equilibrium. The median voter model that in 1970 was an accepted description of equilibrium under majority rule was a decade later viewed as woefully inadequate.[14] These theoretical developments to some made the outcomes of political decisions appear to endlessly cycle, and the possibility of a majority rule equilibrium appeared remote.

This conclusion of endless cycling appears to clash with reality, because political outcomes in the real world seem to be very stable; much more stable than the private sector, for instance. In light of the theoretical developments of the 1970s, this has prompted researchers to look for the causes of stability in politics.[15] The general conclusion on this question is that the institutional structure of majority rule constrains outcomes to be stable even when preferences alone would allow cycles to occur. This general conclusion leaves considerable latitude regarding the nature of the resulting equilibrium, however.

The present book is an extension of this body of public choice theory. Its foundation is the median voter model, but it considers the concept of agenda control and McKelvey's demonstration of cycles in multidimensional issue space. With regard to agenda control, individual representatives are depicted as having control over the agenda for the issues that directly affect the special interest groups whose interests the representatives promote. The representative may choose which special interest to represent, and once this decision is made, the representative is free to bring to the floor any notion to further the well-being of the special interest. Getting the issue passed once it is on the agenda, however, is another matter, which is examined in detail in later chapters. McKelvey's demonstration of cycles in multidimensional issue space is considered in a game theoretic model that invokes the notions of universalism and reciprocity as stability-producing devices. The way in which stability is generated is directly related to the notion of agenda control and the characteristics of the resulting equilibrium.

Thus, while the book can be read in isolation as an economic analysis of democracy, it can also be viewed as an extension of public choice theory that deals with some currently unresolved questions. It considers the issues of agenda control and cycles in multidimensional issue space using the median voter model as a foundation. These issues raise important questions about the nature of public sector equilibrium, and the chapters that follow try to provide some answers.

2 / The Origins of Democracy

The ideals of democratic government were widely known before they were widely practiced. Historically, democracy can trace its origins back to ancient Greece, where Greek democracy was at its height in the fifth century B.C., before the Peloponnesian War.[1] Had the classical Greek democracy survived, that would have provided strong evidence about the superiority of democratic political institutions—superiority in a Darwinian sense, at least. But it did not, and several observers of democracy have suggested that democracy may sow the seeds of its own destruction.[2] Whether true or not, this view has the virtue of presenting democracy as a dynamic, rather than static, form of government. In a static sense, one might examine a democracy at some point in time to try to understand its operation, but equally important is the examination of the way in which a democracy evolves over time.

The purpose of this chapter is to analyze the origin and evolution of democratic government, but from a theoretical, rather than historical, perspective. Two types of models might be devised. In the first, which might be called the British model, a country is ruled by a dictator (or king), who is unable to maintain dictatorial control. As the balance of power shifts away from the dictator, the dictator may be able to prevent being overthrown by establishing some democratic institutions whereby the dictator agrees to share some power with a democratically elected parliament in exchange for being able to retain office. In the British model, a dictatorship evolves toward democracy because the dictator wants to keep from being overthrown. In the second model, which might be called the American model, a group of people with no prior independent government form a democracy in order to further the best interests of the group. While the British and American democracies have many similarities in the real world, there are important analytical differences in using one model or the other for purposes of theoretically examining the evolution of democracy. In the British model, democratic institutions may not be optimal because they were not designed to be optimal. They were designed only to shift some political power from the dictator. In the American model, on the other hand, political institutions are designed, *de novo*, solely for the benefit of the group to be governed. By modeling the origins of democracy in this way, the model is developed in a manner most favorable for democracy. As the efficiency of democratic government erodes, a model constructed in this way is most clearly able to illustrate the causes of the erosion. For this reason, the present chapter explicitly builds its framework on the foundation of the American model of democracy.[3]

The Social Contract Theory of the State

Conceptually, the American model might be most favorably viewed as the writing of a social contract to provide a democratic government. In the early 1970s, Buchanan, Nozick, and Rawls, whom Scott Gordon called the new contractarians,[4] made significant contributions to the social contract theory.[5] Nozick argues that in the absence of force, voluntary agreements among individuals in a society of peaceful anarchists would eventually lead to a minimal government. In Nozick's view, the moral limits of this government would be the provision of protective services, which suggests the question of how the government has expanded beyond the limits of Nozick's minimal government.[6] Nozick's model is distinguished from the other two because it is not a model of a social contract, strictly speaking. The resulting minimal government arises from voluntary contracts but is not a single contract. For present purposes, Nozick's model is significant because it describes a process by which voluntary agreements produce a government that improves the welfare of the governed.

Rawls's model of government also produces a government that improves the welfare of the governed, but the government in Rawls's model is produced by a social contract that is unanimously approved. Rawls invents a "veil of ignorance" behind which individuals develop the social contract. Behind the veil, nobody knows what position they will occupy in the society, so the social contract is able to be written without the conflict of individuals trying to design the rules to favor their individual interests. After the contract is written, the veil is lifted, and individuals take their places within the society.

Rawls's veil of ignorance is a good analytical device for developing an efficient social contract. Since everybody is ignorant about the positions that they will occupy in the society, the components of the social contract would be unanimously approved only if each component enhanced the social welfare. While one might quarrel with some of the details of Rawls's model,[7] the veil of ignorance does create a mechanism whereby the framers of the social contract will draw up the terms of contract with the general interest of the society taking precedence over individual special interests.

The social contract theory of the state lacks realism because there never has been an instance where a social contract had been written and unanimously approved.[8] However, in the American case, the theory approximates reality to some degree. The American Constitution is a general document that has as its main purpose the limitation of the powers of government, with the details of governmental operation to be left to elected representatives. To the extent that the Constitution does not contain the specific rules under which different classes of individuals will interact, but merely specifies how those rules are to be made by elected representatives, the veil of ignorance seems to be at least partly in place. The Constitution does lay out general rules that apply to every citizen but, for the most part, does not differentiate among income, occupation, or other classes of people, for instance. Those laws, which will govern the day-to-day operation of the nation, are to be determined by elected representatives.

Viewed idealistically as a social contract, the Constitution specifies two types of citizens: those who will be elected representatives and will determine the laws and those outside the government who will live under the laws. The veil of ignorance is largely intact here, because when the social contract is being written, before elections are held, nobody knows who will win the elections and serve in the government. And even if this is not entirely true, the Constitution specifies periodic elections, so that a person elected for one term may not be reelected, and therefore may be outside the government in the next term. With a democratic election of government officials, the framers of the social contract find themselves behind a veil of ignorance as the contract is written, and also to some extent after it is enacted, since even though the outcome of the last election is known, the outcome of the next election is uncertain, but at least partly contingent on the extent to which the elected official acts in the public interest. To some degree, Rawls's theory of the social contract is descriptive of the writing of the American Constitution, and the Constitution is written in a manner to try to promote legislation that furthers the public interest.

The purpose of this discussion is twofold. First, it is intended to set up a theoretical framework for democratic government that is as conducive as possible for economically efficient decisions. Beginning the theory from the benchmark of efficiency, it is then possible to develop a model of those forces within a democracy that pull it away from efficiency. Second, this discussion is intended to draw a parallel between the theoretical model that is being developed and the particular case of the American government. The parallels are not always exact, but it does appear that the American government began in as ideal a setting as could be possible in the real world, free from outside constraints and from the internal constraints of special interests.[9]

The Continuing Contract

Once the social contract has been approved, individuals take their places in society and the veil of ignorance is removed. This is the point at which the social contract theory meets its most severe test because, similarities to the American case notwithstanding, no advocate of the social contract theory claims that an actual social contract was ever actually agreed to by a society. Rather, the contract is conceptual in nature, and citizens are in conceptual agreement with the contract. At this point the social contract theorist must convince skeptics that a nation's citizens actually are in conceptual agreement with a conceptual social contract.

Buchanan's *Limits of Liberty* makes an argument that this conceptual agreement does exist. Without the social contract, society would exist in a state of anarchy, a Hobbesian jungle where no individual rights were observed, and therefore individuals live under constant threat of aggression from their fellows. A structure of rights would protect individuals from one another and so allow capital accumulation, exchange, and therefore specialization and division of labor. The contract makes everyone better off. Buchanan describes conceptual agreement with the social contract in the following way. The alternative to the status quo is to move to a state of anarchy, and from anarchy to renegotiate the social contracts. Individuals must then envision the range of outcomes that they would expect to see emerge from renegotiation. If their present well-being falls within that range, then individuals are said to be in conceptual agreement with the existing social contract.

This device of conceptual agreement separates Buchanan's social contract theory from Rawls's in two ways. First, the device makes Buchanan's theory a positive theory of the social contract rather than a normative theory like Rawls's.[10] A social contract exists if the conditions of conceptual agreement are met. Second, the terms of Buchanan's social contract are likely to be different from the terms of Rawls's social contract. For Rawls, the terms of the contract are agreed upon behind a veil of ignorance where everyone is ignorant about their stations in life. For Buchanan, everybody knows their station in life and must compare that condition with renegotiation from a state of anarchy.

The difference arises because the exact outcome of a renegotiation cannot be certain. Each individual will view a range of outcomes as possible, and if the status quo falls within that range, the individual would be in agreement with the contract, viewing the status quo as a possible outcome of renegotiation. But since individuals are not behind the veil of ignorance, all individuals will already know their positions in the society, and those individuals in the government who make the rules can alter the rules in ways that benefit themselves. The outcome may be within the range of renegotiation, satisfying the criterion of conceptual agreement, and yet the outcome will be biased in favor of those who make the rules.[11] An analogy might be drawn here to the home field advantage in sports, with individuals outside the government being the visiting team. They figure that although the outcome falls within the range of likely outcomes, they would probably do at least as well, and maybe better, under renegotiation of the contract. In sports, observers may consider the rules to be fair, even while recognizing an advantage for the home team. In the same way, conceptual agreement with the social contract might occur despite the appearance of favor shown to those in the government. The analogy illustrates that in government, as in sports, the institutions could show some bias without being outside the limits of what might generally be agreed upon as fair.[12]

The Evolution of the Contract

At this point, it is possible to sketch a general argument regarding how the social contract might be expected to evolve. There are three elements that combine to make up the argument of this section. The first is the bias that can be expected to appear in the contract, as just discussed. The second is the nature of anarchistic equilibrium in a developing society, and the third is the nature of production possibilities and probable outcomes of renegotiation from an anarchistic equilibrium.

The problem regarding the bias in the social contract would seem to be a necessary component of any society, at least as long as the model of economic man is used to describe human nature.[13] A dynamic society must have some provision for modifications of social rules to apply in new and unforeseen circumstances; and in real-world affairs that are not conducted behind a veil of ignorance, some group of people must have the responsibility for initiating change. The group could hide behind a fiction that the rules are not changing, even as they change, such as is the case with the courts,[14] or the group could be an explicit legislative body,[15] but some group of people within a society will have the responsibility for altering social rules as social circumstances change. That group of people will be the group of people within the government, and one would expect that over time, as the rules are changed, the modifications will tend to favor the people who did the modifying—namely, those in government.

There are several reasons to believe that this bias will exist even if the people in government generally try to behave in the public interest. The first is the natural tendency for people to make judgments favorable toward themselves. Sports fans frequently notice questionable calls of officials that go against their team, but rarely notice questionable calls in the other direction. The same is true in politics, but the politicians have the power to make policy changes favorable to themselves, despite believing that the changes are in the public interest. A good example is the presidential campaign checkoff on U.S. income tax forms that allows each taxpayer to, at negligible cost to himself, donate a dollar of tax revenues to presidential campaigns. The negative aspects of having the government determine who qualifies for these funds, and therefore help determine the person who will preside over the government, should be obvious.[16] Furthermore, the fact that those already in government have an advantage in qualifying for this aid should also be obvious, yet it appears that the congressional proponents of the presidential campaign checkoff believed that they were acting in the public interest. It is always easier for one to observe favorable social consequences for policies that benefit the observer relative to policies that do not.

The second reason is related to the first. Altruists in government feel that they know what is best for the nation, and so will be inclined to grant themselves more power to do more good. The most altruistic individuals will pursue the careers that they feel can most benefit society, so those in government will automatically be biased toward increasing the scope of governmental oversight. The increased power that goes to the government today is available for abuse by the politicians of tomorrow. These conclusions have been derived from the assumption that those in government are pursuing the social good; the bias favoring the government would obviously manifest itself when we realistically note that individuals will consider their own self-interests as well. The inescapable conclusion is that when some individuals have the power to alter the rules, the rules will tend to be biased in favor of the rule makers.

At the moment that the social contract is written, this bias will be minimal, because a contract written behind a veil of ignorance will tend to have checks and balances that limit the amount that the contract can be manipulated. As the contract evolves slowly over time, the bias will tend to be more pronounced. The effect will be intensified because of changes in the nature of anarchistic equilibrium and changes in the society's production possibilities which will widen the range of potential renegotiation.

An efficient social contract will have the effect of allowing the society to develop, because social interaction can now occur more productively. The result will be specialization, the division of labor, and a society where each individual is more dependent upon the other members of society.[17] All of this has the effect of making anarchy less desirable for individual members of a society. As a society becomes more interdependent, individuals could expect to do worse if that interdependence were eliminated. Two hundred years ago, for example, people might have been worse off if the social contract were eliminated, but since most families were largely self-sufficient, anarchy then would not be as difficult as today, when most people would not be able to survive without the cooperation of their fellows in society. Thus, as a society develops, the condition of anarchy from which a new social contract would be written becomes worse and worse as an alternative for the members of the society.

As a society develops and the prospects for survival under anarchy diminish, the production possibilities of the society increase. The same factors which make the prospects under anarchy more bleak—specialization and increasing interdependence among society's members—makes the economy more productive and increases everybody's actual well-being. But as production possibilities increase and at the same time prospects under anarchy decrease, this widens the bargaining range under which outcomes of a social contract renegotiated from anarchy could emerge. When a society is close to anarchy, the bargaining range of the social contract is, obviously, narrow. The farther a society moves from anarchy, the wider this bargaining range becomes.

The increasing bargaining range, coupled with the fact that the contract will tend to be biased toward the government, means that as the society evolves, this social contract which has conceptual agreement as Buchanan defines it will be less and less like a social contract that meets the veil-of-ignorance test posited by Rawls. Even though there is conceptual agreement with the contract, the contract has a bias toward the government.

The social contract theory lends some light to the subject of government growth, but it only provides a framework, devoid of institutional details. Most of those details will be filled in in later chapters. The remainder of this chapter will consider only two issues relevant to the foundations of democracy: first, the reasons why a social contract would be expected to produce a government, and second, why that government would be expected to operate democratically.

Efficiency Motivations for Government

A social contract theory of the state must justify the state on grounds of efficiency. Individuals behind a Rawlsian veil of ignorance who unanimously agree to the social contract must do so because they view themselves better off with the contract than without it. Even individuals in conceptual agreement with the contract as Buchanan has defined it find the social contract within the bounds of their expectations if renegotiation were to take place from anarchy. In a sense, Buchanan's test for agreement is even stronger than Rawls's, because while Rawls's individuals unanimously argee that they are better off with the contract than without it, Buchanan's individuals are both better off with the contract and view the existing contract as placing their welfare within the bounds that it would be with a renegotiated contract. The important point here, though, is that the individuals within a society unanimously agree that the social contract improves their welfare. Quite clearly, the social contract is justified on purely Paretian terms, with the acceptance of the social contract representing a Pareto superior move. If a government is part of the terms of the social contract, then the social contract theory justifies government because it is economically efficient.

Government can obviously be justified by criteria other than economic efficiency, and some other criteria explicitly reject economic efficiency as a criterion.[18] In this category are the Rand and Nozick type arguments on the moral bounds of the state.[19] The general argument is that people will invest resources to protect their property and may sometimes require force to do so. In addition to the threats of theft, attack from foreign governments, and so forth, are legitimate disputes that can arise between individuals. Protection of property requires police and military forces and a court system. Both Rand and Nozick, through somewhat different routes, reason that this will lead to a monopoly provider of these services, which is a government. In this view, the role of the government is to protect individual rights, and in doing so, the government is granted a monopoly over the use of force.

This theory morally limits the role of government to the protection of individual rights, and so rejects the social contractarian theory. Individuals, after all, might agree to a government that did more than simply protect individual rights. The social contract theory could embody this government that protects individual rights, however. Logic almost dictates that this minimal state would be a part of the social contract, because individuals behind a veil of ignorance would be expected to agree to an institutional structure that would guarantee the rights of the individual. The caveat is necessary because some might view the rights of the individual to be subordinate to the state, and because some might believe that other institutions could serve the function better than government.[20]

Despite these caveats, one might imagine the minimal state that protects individual rights to be a part of the social contract, since the members of society view the creation of a minimal state to be a Pareto superior move. One might also imagine quite a bit more state activity based on efficiency grounds as well. Economists have worked out in detail the conditions under which the market will fail to allocate resources optimally, and each instance may call for government intervention to make the economy perform more efficiently.[21] In each case, the individuals behind the veil of ignorance would want to compare the outcome of private sector resource allocation with the outcome of public sector resource allocation, since it will not necessarily be true that just because the market is not perfect by theoretical standards, the government could do any better.[22] Still, it is conceivable that behind the veil of ignorance, individuals could foresee net benefits that would result from the collective provision of some goods.

The social contract theory does not by itself predict what the terms of the social contract will be, but it is easy to envision a government that protects individual rights and that produces some public goods receiving the unanimous approval of its citizens. On efficiency grounds, then, the social contract includes a provision for a protective and a productive state.

Optimality in Public Goods Production

Many goods have public goods characteristics because they produce significant spillover benefits, or because it is excessively costly to exclude consumers. These goods will be underproduced in the private sector, generating an efficiency argument for public sector production. The arguments are well known, and so will not be explored in detail here. For the optimal amount of the public good to be produced, Samuelson noted that the sum of all individuals' marginal valuations for the good should equal the marginal cost of the good,[23] or where V_i is the marginal valuation of the ith individual out of a population of n, and the marginal cost of the good is MC,

$$\sum_{i=1}^{n} V_i = MC. \tag{2.1}$$

If the good is financed by taxes, then where the marginal tax price of the ith individual is T_i, $\sum_{i=1}^{n} T_i = MC$, so optimality requires that

$$\sum_{i=1}^{n} V_i = \sum_{i=1}^{n} T_i. \tag{2.2}$$

This simple condition will be useful in the next chapter, when democratic outcomes can be compared to this ideal of economic efficiency.

Another significant question must be addressed when considering optimality in public goods production: tax collection. Equation (2.2) gives the condition for the optimal amount of tax collection, but it does not specify how these taxes are to be collected. There are two issues here. The first is what share of the total tax bill each individual should pay, and the second is whether payments should be voluntary or coerced.

The issue of assigning tax shares is a difficult one, and there is no clear answer to the problem. At first glance, Lindahl tax shares, where

$$T_i = V_i \text{ for all } i \qquad (2.3)$$

seem appealing. On the surface, they seem to be the public sector analog to setting price equal to marginal utility in the private sector, but closer inspection reveals that this is not the case. First of all, individuals cannot marginally adjust in the public sector the way that they can in the private sector, so that individual conditions like equation (2.3) are meaningless for efficiency purposes. Only the aggregate condition in equation (2.2) matters. Still, Lindahl prices might have some appeal based on an equity argument within the context of a social contract model.

This justification for Lindahl prices disappears under closer examination as well. Lindahl prices do have the redeeming quality that in a real-world political setting, they provide unanimous agreement regarding the amount of the good to be produced. To compare the concepts of two classic writers in public finance, Lindahl prices produce Wicksellian unanimity on the quantity of a good to be produced.[24] This feature makes Lindahl prices desirable on one ground: that a decision rule of unanimity ultimately will generate the optimal amount of output if transactions and bargaining costs are ignored. The weakness in applying this argument is that rarely is a unanimous decision rule used. Of course, if Lindahl prices can be calculated ahead of time, any decision rule will produce the optimal level of output, but that is a big if.

Efficiency arguments for Lindahl prices appear weak, and equity arguments vanish under close examination as well. At first, setting public sector prices equal to marginal benefits seems fair, but there may be a significant difference in marginal and inframarginal benefits among individuals. Individuals with high total benefits may be near their bliss points and have low marginal benefits, while individuals with low total benefits may place a high value on the good at the margin.[25] Take an example of a television broadcast signal, with the group determining how much wattage to broadcast. Someone living right next to the transmitter may be able to receive a good signal at very low output, so that after a certain point the individual receives high total utility from the clear signal, and no marginal utility from additional wattage. Another individual who lives some distance away may receive a poor signal, and so less total utility, but may value marginal additions to the signal very highly. In this case, the individual who receives the poorer signal would have the higher Lindahl price. If population density is constant and tower location is arbitrarily chosen, a fairness criterion behind the veil of ignorance would seem to suggest a higher tax price for the nearby individual who receives the best signal, but Lindahl prices charge that person the lower tax.

Lindahl prices would be hard to defend on equity grounds, and also are on weak footing on efficiency grounds, although an argument can be made for trying to approximate Lindahl prices in order to try to reduce political disagreements. User charges, as analogs to market prices, will be efficient when they can be applied, but public goods with significant spillovers and exclusion costs preclude user fees, so at this point no particular tax rule can be shown to be efficient and equitable. The only efficiency condition is the equating of marginal cost with the sum of the individual marginal valuations.

The second issue with regard to taxes is whether they should be voluntary or compulsory. This issue can best be addressed by alluding to the free rider problem. When individuals cannot be excluded from consuming a good, they have an incentive to understate the value they place on the good in order to reduce their payments. Indeed, the reason for producing such a good in the public sector in the first place is that the private sector will underproduce the good, so presumably if the social contract called for public provision, it would also call for compulsory payment in order to circumvent the free rider problem. In this way, it is possible for individuals to unanimously agree to be coerced to pay their taxes. All individuals view themselves as better off if they and everybody else are forced to contribute as opposed to the case where all payments are voluntary.

Democratic Government

At this point, the social contract model has been extended to include a government that protects individual rights and produces goods in the public sector, all financed by a levy of compulsory taxes. Up to this point, however, there has been no mention of the organizational form of the government. This section will extend the model to encompass a democratic government.

The first point to recognize is that democratic governments do not give unlimited power to the majority. Rather, the government is given certain powers, and democracy is a method of selecting the individuals who can exercise the government's power, and also perhaps a method of selecting among alternative legislative options within the predetermined bounds of government activity. Within the social contract framework, there is a step that logically precedes the selection of a democratic government; namely, determining the powers that the government will have and also the bounds of government activity. A democratic government, as much as any other form, needs to have bounds placed on its power to prevent a tyranny of the majority, as Tocqueville called it. The details of the bounds placed on government by the social contract will not be speculated upon here. It is sufficient to recognize that any government that protects individual rights must be bounded in its power, or the government itself will be a violator of individual rights. In this light, it is interesting to note that in contemporary societies there is much concern over governments' violations of the rights of their citizens.

The model has suggested a social contract which provides for a government with limited powers that will protect individual rights and produce some goods and services. The next question is how the government will make decisions, and who will act as an agent of the government. It is important to note that even a democratic government does not simply agree to carry out the will of the majority. Rather, the government has certain powers and objectives specified in the social contract, and those who represent the government act as agents of the parties to the social contract. In order for the government to operate, the parties to the contract must have some collective decision rule to determine government actions, such as how much to invest in government roads and schools, if they are a part of the social contract and are to be decided collectively. In addition, since the principle of specialization and gains from trade extends to the government, the parties to the contract need some decision rule to determine who will represent them and act in the name of the government. Within the social contract framework, the most obvious decision rule is unanimity.

The individuals writing a social contract behind a veil of ignorance will want to be assured that when the veil is lifted and the society begins to operate according to the terms of the contract, the government will be acting in their best interests. One way to do this is to require a unanimous decision rule so that no decisions can be made without the individual's consent. In this case, every action will have to be in everybody's best interest. The social contract framework is set up so that only Pareto superior moves can be made. However, once the principle of representative government is embodied in the contract, the necessity for Pareto superior moves vanishes, since a representative, even if unanimously approved, may undertake actions that harm the welfare of some. Still, representative government is the rule rather than the exception because making decisions directly entails very high decision-making costs. Individuals could unanimously agree to allow representatives to make the bulk of the government's decisions because the reduction in decision-making costs would outweigh the potential costs of some decisions being made contrary to an individual's preference.

One could imagine a dictator or dictating group being chosen to exercise the powers of government, but even then the citizens of a nation would be likely to foresee that they would desire the option of periodically reviewing the performance of government leaders and, perhaps, choosing a new group. The desirability of periodic elections seems obvious enough that it does not require elaboration. The only remaining question is how the representatives are to be elected. Again, unanimity suggests itself within the social contract framework, in order to assure a Pareto optimal choice.

Buchanan and Tullock, in *The Calculus of Consent*,[26] have persuasively argued that individuals could unanimously agree to a decision rule of les than unanimity. Their argument follows the lines of the argument used earlier regarding representative government. There are two types of costs an individual must consider when making collective decisions. First are what Buchanan and Tullock call external costs. These are the costs that are borne because a collective decision is made that goes against the best interest of the individual. These costs can be avoided entirely by requiring unanimous decisions, in which case every individual reveals that every approved action is expected to further the individual's well-being. The smaller the percent of the group that must agree, the more likely it is that any individual in the group will find a particular decision to be against his or her best interest, so external costs are high when a small number of individuals can take action for the group, and reduce as a larger consensus is required, dropping to zero when unanimous agreement is required. This cost is labeled E in figure 2.1, where the cost is plotted against the percent of the group required to agree to take action for the group.

The other cost to be considered is the cost of arriving at a collective decision. If one individual can unilaterally act for the group, there are no collective decision-making costs, since no group decision is required. Decision-making costs increase as more people are required to agree, generating the decision-making cost curve D in figure 2. When these two costs are considered together, D + E gives the total cost of a decision rule and shows that the lowest cost decision rule is the requirement that n percent of the group agree. This presentation summarizes the ingenious explanation of Buchanan and Tullock about how everyone in the group can be better off with a less than unanimous decision rule. While it is true that some decisions will be

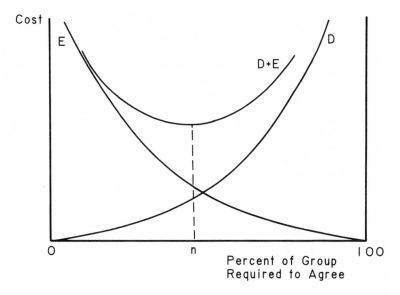

Fig. 2.1   Selection of the optimal voting rule

made that are not in the individual's best interest, the individual is more than compensated by lower decision costs when compared to unanimity.

From the formulation in figure 2.1 it is easy to see that higher external costs will increase n, while higher decision costs will decrease n, all other things constant. This provides an explanation for the variety of decision rules seen in the real world. Although majority rule is widely used in politics, other rules, such as a 60 percent or two-thirds majority, are sometimes used and are specified in the federal and state constitutions. In this framework, such decisions would be those with high external costs. The important point here, though, is to see that behind the veil of ignorance, the social contract could be written to provide for less than unanimous agreement on most issues because the parties to the contract would find a unanimous decision rule to be too costly.

When external costs are very low the decision rule could be

small, and certainly could be less than a simple majority for some issues. A good example of this case would be a hypothetical coffee club with, say, twenty members. The members agree to pay dues to purchase coffee, and then coffee will be available when members want it. The club would be likely to institute a decision rule of less than a simple majority on when to make coffee. At the extreme, the club might agree that any member could make coffee any time; however, this could allow one member to impose high external costs on the group. For example, the coffee club might be in an office, and one individual could make a pot of coffee just before quitting time. Most of the pot would be wasted, since there would not be much time to finish the pot. To lower the external costs, the group might unanimously agree that any time any four members want coffee, a pot can be made. In this example, n = 20 percent, because only 20 percent of the group must agree to take action for the group. Note that a decision not to make coffee is a different issue from a decision to make coffee. Only 20 percent need to agree to make coffee, but over 80 percent must agree in order to prevent coffee from being made.

Another example of a voting rule of less than 50 percent approval is the Supreme Court's rule on which cases they will hear. Only four of the nine justices must favor consideration of a case for it to be heard, so that a minority can agree to take action for the majority. Perhaps this example better shows the application of a voting rule of less than 50 percent, since it applies to a significant decision at the national level.

These examples illustrate how decision rules of less than a simple majority can work. Both examples concern relatively unimportant issues, and that must be the case for external costs to be lower than decision costs. On more important issues, a more inclusive decision rule would be likely. Thus, the Supreme Court may agree to hear a case with less than a majority approval, but the outcome of the case requires a majority. Likewise, the U.S. Congress, which makes decisions mostly by simple majority, makes some decisions using a more inclusive rule. The main point of this section, though, is to illustrate how parties to a social contract could unanimously agree to a representative government that makes decisions using a rule less inclusive than unanimity.

Majority Rule

The model depicted in figure 2.1 shows how a less-than-unanimous decision rule can be optimal, but within this model, simple majority rule is one among many possible alternatives, and 50 percent plus one does not stand out in the model as a magic number. The purpose of this section is to offer a simple explanation of why majority rule will be chosen behind the veil of ignorance as the optimal rule for most decisions. The simplest case to consider is the election of representatives to political office. Behind the veil of ignorance, individuals can determine the decision rule, but they cannot know how they will cast their future votes, since both the future choices and their particular circumstances are presently unknown. Since the decision rule must be unanimously agreed upon at this stage, however, some form of the Pareto principle must apply.

The rule of unanimity is the only decision rule that can guarantee a Pareto superior move in every decision, but the fact that everybody's welfare can be enhanced by a less inclusive rule has already been established. In a choice where there are gainers and losers, the choice could still enhance everybody's welfare if the benefits to the gainers were large enough so that the gainers could use some of their gains to compensate the losers. If the value of the gain to the gainers exceeds the value of the loss to the losers, this compensation could be paid. If the compensation were paid, everybody would be better off and a Pareto superior move would have been made. If the compensation could be paid but is not, the change could be called a potential Pareto superior move. All that is lacking is the compensation to the losers, which could be paid by the gainers.

The problem with actually compensating the losers is that the result requires unanimous approval, with all of the decision costs that the group was trying to avoid by using a less inclusive rule. The problem with not paying compensation is that the people in the minority find themselves worse off. This problem is not so great behind the veil of ignorance, because individuals foresee that a large number of future issues will be decided, and everyone can anticipate being a gainer sometimes and a loser others. Over a large number of decisions, these situations could be expected to net out. Particularly considering the decision costs of reaching unanimous agreement, individuals behind the veil of ignorance would be likely to settle for the decision rule most likely to produce a potential Pareto superior move while avoiding the costs of reaching agreement on compensation to create an actual Pareto superior move. Thus, the optimal decision rule is one that produces an outcome where the gainers potentially could compensate the losers out of their gains, even though the compensation will not actually occur.

Consider now the situation where two (or more) candidates are running for office. What is the optimal decision rule? At this constitutional stage, behind the veil of ignorance, there is no way to know the particular circumstances of future elections. The candidates are unknown, and individuals cannot know whom they will prefer or the intensity of their preferences. In fact, some peoples' preferences will be more intense than others, but behind the veil of ignorance, there is no way to anticipate whose preferences will be more intense or which candidate they will prefer. Thus, *ex ante*, the expected intensity of each person's preferences will be the same. To maximize the expected value of the outcome of an election when the expected intensity of all voters' preferences is the same, the optimal choice is the preference of the majority. If in fact individual voters on each side of the issue had equally intense preferences, it would be conceptually possible for the gainers to compensate the losers under majority rule. Therefore, behind the veil of ignorance, simple majority rule emerges as the optimal decision rule. This explains why simple majority rule is so much more common than any other decision rule.[27]

The same general principle will apply to issues other than electing representatives as well. In referenda in general, when there is no a priori reason to believe that one group will have more intense preferences, simple majority rule is most likely to produce a potential Pareto superior outcome. In issues such as the coffee club example earlier in the chapter, there may be reason to believe that the minority that wants coffee has more intense preferences than the majority that does not, so a less inclusive decision rule is applied. Some states require more than a simple majority to pass a bond issue referendum, and this is likely to be due to the expectation that those voters who are opposed have more intense preferences than those in favor. The general principle is that when those in favor of an issue can be expected to have more intense preferences, a decision rule of less than 50 percent is optimal; when those against an issue can be expected to have more intense preferences, a decision rule of more than 50 percent is optimal; when there is no a priori reason to believe that either group will feel more intensely about the issue, a simple majority rule is, *ex ante*, optimal.

Sometimes decision rules of more than 50 percent are used because individuals have some rights to an outcome beyond the will of the majority. For example, a two-thirds majority is necessary in Congress to impeach a president or to override a presidential veto. These rules suggest that the president has a right to the office and a right to veto legislation over and above the preferences of members of Congress. This is an example of the power of Congress being bounded by the Constitution. As noted earlier, a democracy does not decide every issue democratically. The laws prohibit, for example, the burning down of an unpopular person's house even if a majority would prefer the house to be burned. The point is that some instances of a more inclusive voting rule, such as unanimity in a jury, may be designed to limit the power of government rather than to produce an optimal rule in an economic sense. It may be optimal to burn the person's house down, but the social contract will allow it only if the house is purchased from the person. In this way, the minority is actually compensated, despite the higher transactions costs.

The social contract will certainly put bounds on the applicability of majority rule, and the most important parts of the social contract will be those specifying the rights of the individual and the extent and limits of the authority of the state. In those areas where the government does have the authority to take action, a representative government will usually be most efficient, and a simple majority rule will usually be the optimal constitutional decision rule.

Conclusion

At the foundation of this chapter is the social contract theory of the state, but the use of the social contract model is not meant to imply that there is actually a social contract. Whether a social contract actually exists or not is irrelevant to the arguments just made. The purpose in using a social contract model is to develop a model of an optimal democratic state that operates in the best interest of all of its citizens. The argument is not so strong as to say that a state must be democratic to act in the best interests of its citizens; rather it is merely to suggest that the features of representative government and simple majority rule that are common to modern democracies are institutions that might seem optimal to individuals who could choose their form of government. From this optimal beginning, it will be possible to understand some aspects of democratic decision making and to trace some of the causes of inefficiency in democracy.

The purpose of this chapter, then, has been to model representative democracy as an optimal form of government—a form which will be in the best interest of the members of a society—and the social contract model was used as a device to illustrate the conceptual agreement of a nation's citizens to a government of representative democracy. The model suggested three key features which could be viewed as optimal characteristics of a government: explicit limitations on the power of government and the bounds of government activity, direction of government activity by elected representatives, and the use of simple majority rule as the dominant decision rule. The remainder of the book develops a model of this type of government.

The social contract model in this chapter outlines the type of development that can be expected even when a government is designed under ideal circumstances. The individuals in the government have the power to modify the rules of the society, and one would expect that as the rules change, they will tend to change in favor of those who change them. Thus, over time, the government becomes more powerful, and the rules change to increasingly favor those in the government.

There are limits to how much the rules can change, but as a society develops, the limits broaden. In a more developed society, all individuals are more interdependent, meaning that an upsetting of the established order will be more costly. In addition, a more developed society will be more wealthy, implying a larger target for transfers. Growing government power, an increasing cost to upsetting the established order, and more wealth available for transfer provide an ideal setting for a government that grows in size as well as power and increasingly engages in distributive activities. A scenario like this could appear very plausible for a government imposed on its people from outside. The purpose of this chapter is to argue that a representative democracy will be a desirable type of government from the viewpoint of its citizens, so that the undesirable by-products of democratic government cannot be blamed on influences outside the realm of the democratic choices themselves.

3 / The Median Voter

Chapter 2 analyzed the foundations of democracy and argued that the institutional features of limited government, representative democracy, and the reliance on simple majority rule are features that can be readily understood in terms of economic efficiency. These features could be expected to enhance the welfare of a nation's citizens, implying that there should be general agreement regarding the desirability of these institutions. Despite the general desirability of limited government by representative democracy, an examination of existing governments of this type shows that in its actual application, this type of government can fall short of perfection. Due to the complexities of the real world, few things work as well in practice as they do in theory, but understanding why is the first step toward designing improvement. In the case of the characteristics of limited government, representative democracy, and majority rule, the most obvious problem would be an expansion of the government beyond its ideal bounds. Even when constitutional limits are observed, these bounds could still be overstepped by the decisions of elected representatives operating within the framework of majority rule, which would make the problem a subset of the effects of representative democracy. This chapter begins examining those issues by analyzing decision making under majority rule.

The process by which democratic decisions are made can be

very complex and is likely to vary from issue to issue. Decisions may be single-dimensional or multidimensional, access to the agenda may be controlled, and sometimes the sharing arrangement for public goods—or taxes—may be incorporated into the issue of how much of the good to produce. One of the interesting aspects of analyzing democratic decisions is that because these characteristics may vary from decision to decision, two majority rule decisions may have very different characteristics depending upon the other institutional details of the setting in which the decision is made. This chapter examines a subset of democratic decisions by limiting the scope of discussion to decisions on single-dimensional issues.

The median voter model has been the cornerstone in the construction of economic models of the political process, and especially when modeling the outcomes of single-dimensional issues. The median voter model is intuitively appealing, and its conclusion is extremely powerful, for it asserts that the outcome of a majority rule decision is the outcome most preferred by a single individual: the median voter. In this way, the median voter model acts as an aggregation mechanism for individual preferences in a democracy, and for democratic decisions, the median voter's demand curve is analogous to the market demand curve in microeconomic theory. The general applicability of the median voter model has been questioned frequently, and one of the goals of this chapter is to examine some of those questions.

This chapter confines itself to single-dimensioned issues for several reasons. The first is to develop a general framework that can be expanded to multiple issues in the next chapter. When considering multiple issues, logrolling and vote trading can become significant factors in determining outcomes, and it will be useful to isolate the model from those complications initially. Another issue that is more easily dealt with in a single dimension is the optimality of the median voter outcome. Yet another reason to confine the issue space to one dimension is that complications may arise to prevent the median voter outcome in one dimension, and these complications will be examined before expanding the model. Finally, there is much empirical evidence on the median voter model—most of it developed in a one-dimensional framework. This chapter is an appropriate time to review that evidence and, in light of some of the difficulties of empirical testing, consider the additional difficulties that would be involved in testing a multidimensional model.

Chapter 2 provided a framework within which majority rule decision making would be optimal. The next step is to analyze the characteristics of decisions made under majority rule. One point that will emerge from this and the following chapters is that positing simply that decisions are made by majority rule is a very incomplete specification of the decision-making process, something like saying that resources are allocated by the market. An elaborate theory of market structure has been developed by economists, and the implications for resource allocation through the market will be very different, depending upon the type of market structure. Resource allocation by a monopoly, for example, will differ from competitive resource allocation, and even within the monopoly case the degree to which price discrimination can take place will affect the allocation of resources. Just as market structure makes a difference when analyzing resource allocation through the market, political structure is important when analyzing resource allocation under majority rule, and all majority rule institutions will not produce the same political outcome. Seen in this light, this chapter and the following chapters are studies in the political structure of majority rule, and slight variations in the structure can have significant effects on the outcome.

The Model with Three Voters

With this in mind, the median voter model developed here can be regarded as a framework upon which to build a more complex model of the political process under majority rule. Later chapters will do some of that construction, but even the most complex models in the book should be considered more as suggestions about a useful way of analyzing the political process rather than as the final word on democratic government. Still even the simplest construction of the median voter model pro-

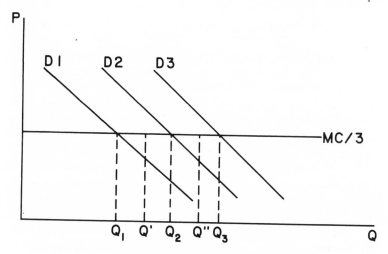

Fig. 3.1   The median voter model

vides much insight into the way in which majority rule decisions are made. This warrants beginning the analysis with a simple model.

Consider the three-person model depicted in figure 3.1. Three individuals have demand curves D1, D2, and D3 for some public sector output and will each share one-third of the cost. With a constant marginal cost, each individual will pay tax price MC/3. The decision on how much of the good to produce will be made by majority rule. At this point, some institutional content must be added to the model. In the committee process described by Duncan Black,[1] the three individuals form a committee in which any member can make a motion to produce some amount of the good. If another motion is made, the committee members vote on the motions to determine the winning motion by majority rule. New motions can be proposed which will always be considered against the existing motion by majority rule. In this setting, there is only one motion that can defeat all others: the motion most preferred by the median voter.

The first individual most prefers Q_1, so would make a motion to produce that amount. The second individual might then propose Q_2, which would defeat Q_1 by two votes to one. Individual 1 most prefers Q_1, but individual 2 most prefers Q_2. Individual 3 would rather have Q_3, but in a choice between Q_1 and Q_2, Q_2 would be chosen, since it is closest to the individual's most preferred level.[2] After the victory of Q_2, individual 3 could propose Q_3, but it also would be defeated by majority rule, since individuals 1 and 2 would vote for Q_2 rather than Q_3. Q_2 is the only motion that can defeat all other motions by majority rule, and it is the preference of the median voter.

A variant of this model that provides the same conclusion was suggested by Howard Bowen.[3] Bowen examined majority rule decision by referendum. Assume that an agenda setter were to propose producing a small amount of the good in figure 3.1 and then proposed marginal increases which would have to be approved by majority rule. For example, the agenda setter first proposes the production Q_1 which would be unanimously favored over no production. A proposal to increase output to Q' would be approved by individuals 2 and 3, as would a marginal increase from Q' to Q_2. However, a proposal to further increase output from Q_2 to Q'' would be defeated, since individuals 1 and 2 would prefer Q_2. Thus, majority rule decision making has led to an output of Q_2—the median voter's preference—in this referendum setting as well as in the committee setting described by Black.

Yet another variant of the model is the representative democracy model suggested by Hotelling and elaborated by Downs.[4] In this model, two candidates are trying to be elected to political office by majority rule, and three voters have demand curves D1, D2, and D3. Voters evaluate the candidates on a single issue—the quantity of the public good to be produced—and the candidates must choose a platform somewhere on the quantity axis. Consider the case where initially one candidate would prefer Q_1 and the other Q_3. In competition for Q_2's vote, the first candidate could move his platform from Q_1 to Q', closer to Q_2, which would win the votes of the first two individuals, and the election. In response to this political competition, the second candidate would move closer to Q_2, prompting the first candidate to move, and so forth, until both candidates proposed output level Q_2. If one candidate proposed Q_2, while the other did not, the candidate proposing Q_2 would be sure to win. The outcome is that both candidates must propose Q_2 to try to win, and again the outcome most preferred by the median voter is selected.

The General Applicability of the Model

The median voter model is an extremely powerful tool for analyzing the outcomes of democratic decisions because it concludes that democratic decisions result in the selection of the median voter's most preferred outcome. Although the model presented in figure 3.1 is extremely simple, it could have been even simpler, because the only points in figure 3.1 that are relevant to the outcome of the model are the voters' most preferred points, Q_1, Q_2, and Q_3. Thus, the model could just as easily have been diagramed in a single dimension along the Q axis rather than in the two-dimensional P-Q plane. The model was developed in two dimensions only in order to show more clearly its economic foundations. Also note that the location of Q_2 is critical, since Q_2 is the majority rule outcome, but the only significance of Q_1 and Q_3 is on which side of the median they fall.

This presentation of the median voter model makes the results appear quite robust, since in three different democratic institutional structures—committee, referendum, and representative democracy—the same conclusion emerges. Instances where this result does not occur will be discussed at length later, but at this time it is important to notice the generality of the result. In this model, political competition selects the median voter's most preferred outcome when democratic decisions are made.

It is also worth mentioning that the result generalizes to any number of voters. If the model in figure 3.1 had included five voters, D1, . . ., D5, then the same logic would have produced the most preferred outcome of D3—the new median voter—to be selected. The same would be true of any number of voters, and Down's development of the model used a density function approach that obviously applied to a large electorate. Figure 3.2 illustrates a Downsian density function of voters arrayed along a single-dimensioned continuum, here using a continuum from political left to political right as the continuum, rather than the

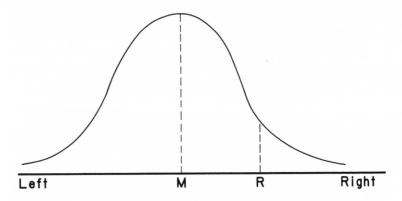

Fig. 3.2   The median voter model with a large number of
voters

quantity, of a public good. Again, democratic institutions will select M, the median voter's most preferred outcome, in an election. Downs took advantage of the fact that the issue space could be considered a single-dimensioned continuum and that each voter's preference could be represented as a single point on the continuum. Much of the modeling of democratic institutions will be done using three voters for simplicity, so it should be noted that the median voter model's results generalize the large numbers of voters.

Even this simple presentation of the model has a great deal of descriptive ability with regard to democratic institutions. For example, many critics of the political system complain that all candidates look alike; that there is little difference in the major party candidates. This is easily explained by the median voter model. In figure 3.1 it was shown that with two candidates, both candidates would have an incentive to propose Q_2, making their platforms identical. Likewise, in figure 3.2, both candidates in a two-candidate election have an incentive to propose platform M on the left-right continuum. The reason is obvious. The candidate who wins the median voter's vote gets that vote plus all of the votes to one side of the median, which makes a majority. Both candidates propose platform M because the candidate who wins the median voter's vote wins the election.

Another observation is that extreme candidates cannot win an election. The median voter model shows why. If one candidate takes an extreme platform like R, the other can propose M and win by a wide margin. American presidential elections seem to support this observation. Goldwater, viewed at the extreme right in 1964, and McGovern, viewed at the extreme left in 1972, both lost decisively. Along these lines, it is interesting to observe that while Reagan was viewed as a right-wing candidate in 1980, Carter was also considered right wing, particularly for a Democrat. It appears that as the sentiments of the median voter change, political parties try to adjust their platforms accordingly. While suggesting that politicians implicitly operate according to the median voter model, it is relevant to recall that with all of the vocal dissent and protest in Nixon's first administration, Nixon claimed to be aiming his policies at the "silent majority." Nixon's concept of the silent majority appears to be exactly the public choice concept of the median voter.

Finally, note that in democracies where one candidate is elected to office by majority rule, there tends to be two main political parties. Until now, the model had assumed only two candidates, but the model can also explain why there are only two major political parties. Within the context of figure 3.2, consider two major parties, both with platforms aimed at the median voter, M. Since both parties are so similar, many voters may feel that they are not well represented, so a third party arises on one side of the median, for example, at point R. This party will then divide the votes to the right of the median with one of the major parties, so that the other party gets all the votes to the left of the median and so receives significantly more votes than either of the other parties. The party furthest left will always win, causing the two parties to the right to cease being viable political parties. Since presumably the purpose of the parties is to elect candidates, and since the existence of the third party thwarts this purpose for two of the parties, either the parties must merge or one of them must cease to exist in order for them to be able to elect candidates. As a result, the existence of three major parties is not a viable long-run situation in a winner-take-all democracy, and the equilibrium number of parties is two.

Up to this point, the median voter model has been developed only in its simplest form, yet it appears to have a great deal of descriptive ability. This simple model's main limitation is that it limits the issue space to a single dimension, but that limitation will not be relaxed until the next chapter. This chapter will continue to analyze the median voter model within the context of a single-dimensioned issue space.

Optimality Conditions of the Model

Some aspects regarding the optimality of majority rule outcomes were discussed in chapter 2. There it was observed that when a referendum is being held to choose between one of two possible outcomes, and when there is no a priori reason for suspecting that the group favoring one outcome has more intense preferences than the other group, the use of simple majority rule will select the outcome with the highest expected value. An example might be an election between two candidates. The model in this chapter is more complex, because even an election between two candidates takes on the characteristics of a continuous, rather than discrete, choice as candidates adjust their platforms to try to maximize their chance of winning an election. The question that arises is whether the median voter outcome will be economically efficient in this continuous case.

Referring to figure 3.1, consider the case where a group of voters is going to decide by majority rule how much of a good should be supplied through the public sector. Figure 3.1 illustrates the case of three voters, but the general case of n voters will be considered to increase the generality of the illustration. In chapter 2, economic efficiency was shown in equation (2.2) to imply that

$$\sum_{i=1}^{n} V_i = \sum_{i=1}^{n} T_i, \qquad (3.1)$$

where there are n voter-taxpayers, and the ith voter has a marginal valuation of the public good of V_i and pays a marginal tax price T_i. Using m to denote the median voter, the median voter's most preferred outcome is where the median voter's marginal valuation is equal to his tax price, or

$$V_m = T_m. \tag{3.2}$$

The condition for efficiency will be satisfied in the median voter model only when equations (3.1) and (3.2) are simultaneously satisfied, implying that

$$V_m / \sum_{i=1}^{n} V_i = T_m / \sum_{i=1}^{n} T_i. \tag{3.3}$$

This means that the median voter's marginal valuation must be the same percentage of the sum of all voters' valuations as his tax share is of the sum of the tax shares. Under these circumstances the median voter model will lead to economic efficiency in the public sector, at least as Samuelson has defined efficiency.

This concept of economic efficiency is overly restrictive, however, in the sense that it excludes some outcomes that in the real world would be more efficient than any other alternative. That is, it is true that if the median voter model describes the result of an election, and if equation (3.3) is satisfied, the result will be Pareto efficient. But if these conditions are not satisfied, there is no guarantee that resources could be allocated any more efficiently than under majority rule. If the median voter result applies, the satisfaction of equation (3.3) is sufficient, but not necessary, for an optimal allocation of resources. The reason is that the transactions costs of finding the more efficient allocation may be larger than the efficiency gain once it is found.

In the 1950s the market failure literature, typified by Bator's classic article,[5] enumerated the cases where the private market would fail to achieve a Pareto optimum in the sense that all conceivable gains from trade were not exhausted. However, if the alternative is to place the activity in the public sector, and if

the median voter model described public sector resource allocation, then if equation (3.3) was not satisfied, public sector resource allocation would fail to achieve Pareto optimality in the
same sense. In both the public sector and the private sector,
individuals always have an incentive to make Pareto superior
moves, but high information or transactions costs could prohibit
the move from being made. In most cases, it would be very costly
to discover how close the real world is to satisfying equation (3.3),
so that in a limited sense majority rule might be viewed as optimal
in the public sector simply because nobody has demonstrated that
another method of public sector decision making would be more
efficient.[6] In this sense, the world as it exists might be viewed as
optimal, but people have an incentive to discover ways to overcome information and transactions costs which would move the
world closer to a narrowly defined Pareto optimum.[7]

The implications for majority rule voting can be summarized as follows: the fairly stringent condition that the median
voter's marginal tax share must be the same fraction of the sum
of all voters' marginal tax shares as his marginal valuation is of
the sum of all voter's marginal valuations must be satisfied for
optimality in the sense that there could be no possible improvement in economic welfare. However, given transactions costs
and information costs in the real world, and given the reason-
ableness of the condition, it is likely that the median voter outcome is as close to optimal as one could expect to come in the
real world, particularly when the problem of aggregating a large
number of individual preferences with some collective decision
rule. In short, the outcome of the median voter model looks
good, if not perfect, from an efficiency standpoint. Problems of
resource allocation in the public sector would probably be minimal if the median voter model were descriptive of reality, so
attention can be focused on those aspects of the political process
where the median voter model is not descriptive of the institutions and outcomes in the public sector. One additional remark:
it may be reasonable to impute the median voter outcome as the
objective of democratic decision making, in which case the median voter outcome would gain additional status as a benchmark
for public sector efficiency. These remarks point to an examination of cases where the median voter result does not apply.

Agenda Control

An excellent departure from the median voter model is the agenda control model, because it uses many of the median voter model's characteristics.[8] Following the median voter models, the median voter is still the decisive voter, so agenda control can be modeled using only the median voter's preferences, but in this model the outcome is a level of government expenditures larger than the amount most preferred by the median voter. The reason is that another agent—the agenda controller—determines the options among which the voters can choose in such a way that the median voter ends up selecting an outcome that is not the voter's most preferred option.

The simplest case of agenda control would occur when only one candidate appears on a ballot for election to office. This occurs frequently in governmental elections in Communist countries, as well as in clubs and scholarly societies. In this case the nominating committee effectively controls the outcome of the election. Even though a write-in candidate could conceivably defeat the single candidate nominated, it is unlikely, and in any event the nominating committee, by controlling the agenda, has a great deal of control over the outcome. A similar strategy would be to nominate two candidates, with one being clearly unacceptable. In this way, despite an apparent choice given to the electorate, the nominating committee has effectively controlled the agenda to cause the voters to vote for the committee's choice.[9]

More complex cases can easily be imagined. When cycles are possible, control over the order in which proposals are considered is important.[10] For example, in the U.S. presidential race in 1976 Reagan and Ford were the top runners in the Republican primary. Reagan argued that Republicans should support him because despite Ford's strength among Republicans, Reagan could beat Carter in the national election, but Ford could not. At least some of Reagan's predictions came true. Ford did beat Reagan in the primary and lost to Carter in the national election. Furthermore, Reagan beat Carter in 1980, although the ceteris paribus conditions were probably violated. In this case, where Ford beats Reagan, Carter beats Ford, and Reagan beats Carter, the order in which alternatives are considered obviously determines the outcome of an election; if the winner of Ford and Reagan runs against Carter, Carter will win; if the winner of Ford and Carter runs against Reagan, Reagan will win, and if the winner of Reagan and Carter runs against Ford, Ford will win. In this case, it is obvious that if an agenda controller can determine the order of the runoff elections, the controller effectively will control the outcome of the election.[11]

Control over the agenda can be a powerful political tool, and many of the implications of control in a multidimensional setting will be examined in later chapters. Meanwhile, after that brief introduction to the concept of agenda control, the present analysis will return to the one-dimensional issue space of the median voter model. Reflecting on the median voter result in the models of Black, Bowen, and Downs, it occurs in each case because the potential agenda consists of all points on the continuum. In the referendum model, if some points are excluded from consideration, the median voter may not have the choice of selecting his most preferred alternative.

In this model of agenda control, a referendum is viewed as a two-point offer, and the median voter's preferences determine the outcome of the referendum. Consider the example depicted in figure 3.3, where the median voter's demand curve is DM and the median voter's tax price is T_m. In the standard median voter model, Q_m would be the outcome, but some slight changes in the assumptions of the model will alter the result. First, assume that a single referendum is to be held to determine how much of the good is to be produced. If the referendum fails, Q_r will be produced. Q_r is called the reversion level by Romer and Rosenthal. An agenda setter will determine what level will be the alternative to Q_r, and the level chosen by the agenda setter will be called Q_a. The questions are: What level will the agenda setter choose, and what will be the outcome of the referendum? Note that this situation appears to have many real-world counterparts, in school financing and state and local bond issues, for example. Voters are offered a two-point offer, and typically if an election is to be held, the reversion level will be significantly below Q_m. For bond issues, as an example, the reversion level frequently will be zero.

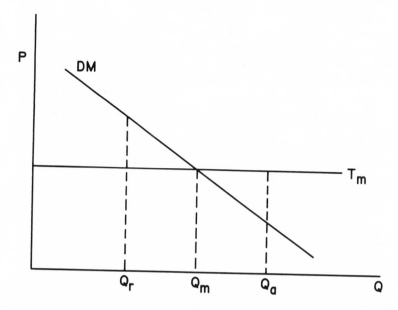

Fig. 3.3   Agenda control in the median voter model

The solution to the problem requires that some preferences be ascribed to the agenda setter, and the agenda control model assumes that the agenda controller wishes to maximize the budget spent on the good. The budget-maximizing assumption for governmental decision makers was developed extensively by Niskanen,[12] who makes a persuasive case. Niskanen argues that a government bureaucrat is unable to take home any profits, so has no incentive for profit maximization. Rather, the bureaucrat is rewarded for the number of people he oversees, and for the size of his budget, both of which give the bureaucrat the budget maximization incentive. Furthermore, the bureaucrat finds it easier to get along with those under him when the agency is expanding, so that individuals in the agency will be receiving promotions and pay raises rather than stagnating or being laid off. This intensifies the bureaucrat's incentive to enlarge the bureau's budget. In addition to income, security, and a congenial environment, bureaucrats may also be interested in power and prestige, but these too tend to increase with the size of the bureau's budget. Thus, Niskanen makes a convincing case that the bureaucratic analog to profit maximization in the private sector is budget maximization in the public sector.

Agenda setters may be elected officials rather than career bureaucrats, and the implications of this will be considered later. Adopting the assumption of a budget maximizing agenda setter, consider the case where the reversion level is below the median voter's preference. The agenda setter could propose the output Q_m to satisfy the median voter, but the budget maximizing agenda setter will choose a larger alternative, Q_a, such that the median voter would barely prefer Q_a to Q_r. In other words, the consumer surplus gained by the median voter because of units from Q_r to Q_m would be only slightly larger than the negative consumer surplus due to units from Q_m to Q_a. The median voter is almost indifferent between Q_a and Q_r, only slightly preferring Q_a, so that the outcome of the referendum is Q_a, a larger expenditure than would be most preferred by the median voter. The relationship between the final equilibrium, Q_a, and the median voter's preference, Q_m, depends upon the reversion level. The smaller the ratio of Q_r/Q_m, the larger will be the ratio of Q_a/Q_m. A lower reversion level implies a higher expenditure level. With a linear demand curve, a reversion level of zero, as for example in a bond issue, would make the agenda control outcome nearly twice as great as the median voter's preference.

While the analytical details of the agenda control model could be examined in more detail, the framework just outlined is sufficient for present purposes.[13] Of more interest here are the implications of the agenda control model. The first thing to note is that in the referendum model just outlined, the referendum does not cause the problem of excessively large government; in fact, it acts as a constraint. Although the resulting level of expenditures is larger than the median voter would prefer, the referendum constrains it to be no larger than Q_a. For the many goods and services that are produced in the public sector without referendum approval, the level of output would presumably be larger than Q_a, implying that the real problem is not agenda control in referenda but rather the budget-maximizing government. The referendum acts as a constraint, keeping the government from producing more than Q_a in this model.

The agenda control model of a referendum may be an intrinsically interesting object of study, but when examined within the context of the general subject of public finance, its implications are small. A very small percentage of governmental output must be approved in referenda, so the fact that referenda may constrain the government in these cases says little about what constrains budget maximizing governments in the absence of referenda. In other words, if the agenda control model of referenda is in the fact descriptive of referenda in general, the implications of this would have less to do with the referenda themselves than about the representative government that controls the agenda. Within the context of figure 3.3, the agenda control model implies that government spending would exceed Q_a without a referendum, and the most significant issues would seem to revolve around what level the representative government would approve without the referendum, and why. The fact that referenda occasionally constrain the budget maximizing government seems to be of minor importance in determining the overall level of government. Stated more bluntly, if the model is true, then its most interesting implications lie outside the model.

Why be concerned with the agenda control model, then? One reason is that it does shed some light on the issue of budget maximization within the government. This issue will be examined in the next section. A second reason is that the model sheds some light on the way that representative bodies determine output levels, since representative bodies in a democracy generally make their decisions by majority rule as well. The model can serve to illuminate, for example, committee recommendations to the entire Congress. In analyzing representative bodies, however, issues will almost always be multidemensional and more complex than this referendum model as a result. Still, the insights gained from the single-dimensioned referendum model, regardless of their appplicability to public referenda, serve to illuminate some more complex issues concerning representative government. Seen from this perspective, the agenda control model's most important applications may extend beyond simple referenda to the representative government that the model characterizes simply as a budget maximizer.

These applications will be left for analysis in later chapters. The next section will discuss some empirical questions related to the median voter model and agenda control.

Empirical Evidence

One of the earliest empirical studies on the median voter model was done by Barr and Davis in 1966.[14] Barr and Davis present a number of regressions results that are consistent with the median voter model, although they have no actual observations about the particular individual who is the median voter. The problem of not being able to observe the characteristics of that particular individual has usually been circumvented, as Barr and Davis did, by making assumptions regarding the relationship between the median voter and characteristics of the the the aggregate population. The title of Robert Inman's article—"Testing Political Economy's 'as if' Assumption: Is the Median Income Voter Really Decisive?"—illustrates the logical extension of this approach. Inman's answer to the question, by the way, is yes.

This approach toward empirically examining the median voter model has been criticized by Romer and Rosenthal,[16] who list a number of other studies with similar problems. Romer and Rosenthal's criticisms fall into two general areas. First, they argue that the empirical specifications of the models do not demonstrate that it is the median voter, as opposed to the mean voter or the voters in some other fractile, who determine election outcomes. For example, a typical question that goes unaddressed in these models is whether the median income offers greater explanatory power than the income of the lower 20 percent of voters. Their second criticism is that even if median characteristics do offer more explanatory power, there is no evidence in the typical model to demonstrate that the outcome is that preferred by the median voter, rather than some multiple of the median preference, as would be predicted in the agenda control model. Romer and Rosenthal interpret the existing empirical work by concluding "that the studies fail to indicate that actual expenditures correspond in general to those desired by the median voter.[17] It appears that their criteria are rather stringent, for it is generally accepted that empirical evidence cannot be used to prove a theory to be true, although a theory could be falsified by empirical testing.[18] Just by examining their list of studies that find evidence consistent with the median voter hypothesis, the fact that they do not list any studies finding evidence inconsistent with the hypothesis seems to be evidence in favor of the model.

Still, their criticisms are well taken, and future empirical research should endeavor to grapple with the problems that Romer and Rosenthal raise. Specifically, studies should be able to differentiate the median voter from the general population,[19] and they should be able to differentiate the Bowen-Black-Downs result from the agenda control result. Regarding this second issue, a later study by Romer and Rosenthal attempted such a differentiation but concluded that "Rather than resolving the question of the simple setter model against the simple median voter model, our results indicate that both may be inappropriate and the endeavors dealing with complexities omitted here are warranted."[20] Romer and Rosenthal, who have been advocates of the agenda control model, have not found evidence to support it versus the standard median voter model, which is probably the most noteworthy aspect of their results. As they suggested in the quotation above, their model was not correctly specified, which again illuminates a path for future research.

Two empirical studies that were not analyzed in their study on "The Elusive Median Voter" probably should be mentioned as works that have tried to avoid some of the problems Romer and Rosenthal cite. The first study, by the present author, attempted to directly estimate the median voter's most preferred level of expenditures in several hundred school referenda in Michigan. The details are described elsewhere,[21] but the basic method is as follows. There were two hundred fifty-seven referenda in the sample, with twenty-four cases of two referenda occurring in one school district. The data included the reversion level, the proposed level (Q_r and Q_a in fig. 3.3), and the percentage of yes votes. For each referendum, the marginal voter would be in the situation depicted in figure 3.3. Assuming a linear demand curve, the marginal voter's reference will be midway between Q_r and Q_a. For example, if a referendum passed by 60 percent, the 60th percentile voter would most prefer the midpoint between Q_r and Q_a,

assuming a linear demand curve. This identifies the most preferred location of one voter. In the twenty-four cases where two
referenda were held, the most preferred location of two voters
could be located. Assuming that voters are distributed normally
along the Q axis, the most preferred location of the median voter
(or any other voter) could be located, because the normal distribution is a two-parameter distribution so the locations of the two
parameters define the whole distribution. The average standard
deviation for these cases was calculated and used as the standard
deviation in the case where only one referendum was held, allowing the median voter's preference to be calculated there as well.
When compared to the actual level of output, the median voter's
preference was not significantly different from the actual level of
output, which supports the median voter model rather than the
agenda control variant.

Another imaginative test of the model was undertaken by
William McEachern.[22] McEachern noted that states of the
United States have three basic referendum rules for approving
debt issue: some states require a referendum approval by a
simple majority of the voters, some states require approval of
more than a simple majority, and some states have no referendum requirement. If the median voter hypothesis is correct in its
broadest form, then the government should propose the median
voter's most preferred level of debt without a referendum.
Therefore, a simple majority referendum should not be a constraint, and there should be no difference between the nonreferendum states and the simple majority referendum states. Where
more than a simple majority is required, this should produce a
constraint because, if two-thirds majority were required, for example, the decisive voter in the referendum would be the 66th
percentile voter rather than the 50th. Debt in those states should
be lower as a result. This is precisely what McEachern found.
Note that if the agenda control hypothesis were true, referenda
should have been a constraint in both cases, so nonreferendum
states would have had larger expenditures than simple majority
referendum states. McEachern's imaginative test makes use of
few assumptions and clearly differentiates between the standard
median voter model and the agenda control model.

It is frequently amazing that two people can look at the same evidence and see such different things. In economics, for example, Marxists and supply siders look at the same economy, and while one group sees an oppressive group of capitalists exploiting workers and calls for nationalization of the means of production as the answer, the other group sees the government as a burden that keeps the economy from reaching its full potential and argues that everybody would be better off with less government. The same thing is, of course, possible with the evidence on the median voter model, as already suggested.[23] However, it appears that the empirical evidence at the present time overwhelmingly aligns with the median voter model.

The implication is not that majority rule always produces the median voter's most preferred outcome, because most empirical tests have several institutional factors in common: the issues are one-dimensional; the units of government are small, which allows intergovernmental competition; and the agenda setters are elected officials. Contrast this with the case where the issue space is multidimensional, there is a single unit of government, and the agenda setters are not elected by the voters, and the political structure is more changed than the market structure when comparing the neoclassical economic theories of monopoly and competition. The empirical evidence that suggests that the median voter model describes some simple instances does not argue that the outcome always emerges in a democracy any more than the observed pricing behavior under competition can be extrapolated to monopolies.

While recognizing that different individuals may interpret the evidence differently, it does appear that the median voter model describes the outcomes of the cases which it models. In committees where all members have access to the agenda, in referenda where the agenda setter is an elected official, and when candidates are running for political office, the model seems to be extremely descriptive, and it will be used for the foundation of the model developed throughout the book. Reflecting on why no evidence of agenda control appears in the typical referendum, an elected agenda setter has an incentive to satisfy the median voter in order to be reelected. If one of Niskanen's bureaucrats were the agenda setter, things might be quite different, but typically this is not the case.

Thinking ahead to possible complications, in multidimensional issues where logrolling and vote trading might be possible, the median voter model may not be descriptive. When Congress votes on bills from committees, the committee members are not elected by Congress—the group that is voting on the bill—and this could cause a problem. In national politics, as compared to state and local politics, the optimal solution may be harder to produce for two reasons. First, governments are not competing with one another,[24] and second, governments do not have other similar governments to be compared with. Even when "voting with your feet" is not possible, other similar governments can provide examples of how one's own government can be run, and if other similar governments are more efficient, the elected officials of the inefficient government can expect to be replaced. At the national level, this comparison is not possible. It appears that the median voter model is descriptive of simple cases, but as later chapters will show, the model's results do not apply to more complex democratic political structures.

Changes in Benefit and Tax Shares

Some writers have argued that manipulating benefit and tax shares is a type of agenda control,[25] but there is an important difference. Agenda control keeps the median voter away from his most preferred outcome, while the manipulation of benefit and tax shares changes the outcome that the median voter would most prefer.[26] Thus, while the agenda control model would be more applicable to a situation with a monopoly agenda setter, the manipulation of benefit and tax shares is a feature of competitive government. The monopoly aspects of the agenda control model should be clear; if the agenda setter had to compete with others as an elected official, then the setter who took advantage of the two-point-offer nature of a referendum could be defeated by a competitor who would offer to propose the median voter's preference. However, an agenda setter could manipulate benefit and tax shares to make the median voter better off; indeed, if such manipulation were possible, it would have to be considered as one aspect of the competitive process for political office.

Tax shares and benefit shares are frequently difficult to manipulate. Consider public school financing for the moment. Benefit shares will be determined by the number and ages of children in a family and the location of schools in relation to the family, which are difficult items for political manipulation. Tax shares frequently will be constitutionally given, as, for example, in the property tax. While it is conceptually possible to have a progressive property tax or some other tax base to secure school financing, typically the individual voter's tax share is not easily manipulated. The main occasions when tax shares can be manipulated are income taxes, which are routinely made more or less progressive or which allow deductions and credits to alter tax shares, and specific excise taxes aimed at certain groups. This is no secret: the purpose of income tax progressivity, deductions, and credits, as well as excise taxes, is to shift the burden of taxation from some people to others. Benefit shares are most easily manipulated when programs are initiated to provide specific benefits for special interests, financed out of general revenue. Even in the public school case, where benefit shares are largely fixed, they can be manipulated by adding facilities to some schools, but not to others, or by placing new schools in one neighborhood rather than another. A family with children would receive larger benefits if a new school were located three blocks, rather than three miles, away from the family's house.[27]

The competitive process in a democracy will cause benefit shares and tax shares to be manipulated to enhance the well-being of the median voter. Political candidates who are competing for the median voter's vote can improve their chances by lowering the median voter's tax share or by increasing the share of benefits going to the median voter with the existing tax share. Either strategy will lower the cost per unit of government to the median voter, and as the cost per unit of government declines, the median voter will demand more government output. The manipulation of benefit shares and tax shares therefore causes the equilibrium amount of government spending to rise.

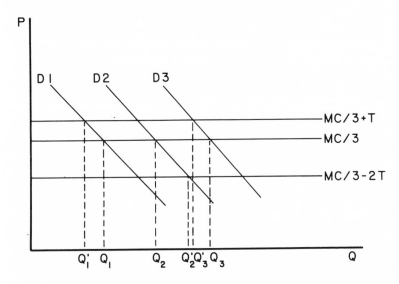

Fig. 3.4   The median voter model with variable tax shares

Consider the following example where tax shares can be proposed as a part of a candidate's platform. Within the context of figure 3.1, there are three voters, D1, D2, and D3, and two candidates running for election on the basis of a platform proposing the amount of the public good to be produced. Assume that candidate L, the low-demand candidate, initially prefers Q_1, while candidate H, the high-demand candidate, prefers Q_3. In the standard median voter model with fixed tax shares, Downsian political competition pulls the platforms of the two candidates together at Q_2, where the median voter's preference is satisfied. Now compare this case with the case in which tax shares can be made a part of the candidate's platforms, so that rather than being forced to accept MC/3 as each voter's tax share, the candidates can propose alterations.

The variable tax shares case is diagramed in figure 3.4. Figure 3.4 shows the same demand curves D1, D2, and D3 as figure 3.1, and the same marginal tax price MC/3 which makes the three voters most prefer Q_1, Q_2, and Q_3, respectively. The

Downsian median voter model requires candidates L and H to move their platforms to Q_2, but if tax shares can be chosen as a plank in the platform, the candidates can each offer tax cuts to the median voter to attempt to win the median vote. In figure 3.4, candidate H raises the general tax rate (to D1 and D3) by T and uses this amount to lower the median voter's tax rate by 2T. By altering tax shares, the candidate would cause the three voters to demand Q_1' Q_2', and Q_3' respectively. The tax cut increases the amount that the median voter most prefers, and so raises the Downsian equilibrium amount from Q_2 to Q_2'. Government output is larger, as in the case of agenda control, but this time government output expands because the median voter prefers more government output. Note that attempts by candidate L to buy the median vote do not work as well as attempts by candidate H. When the median voter's tax price is lowered, the median voter demands more rather than less, so that any candidate's attempt to alter tax shares to win the median vote automatically raises the equilibrium size of government. This conclusion is just a straightforward implication of the economic principle that demand curves slope downward.[28]

A similar phenomenon occurs when benefit shares can be changed as a part of a candidate's platform. In this case, candidates will attempt to win the median vote by increasing the median voter's benefit share, which causes the median voter to receive more benefits for each unit of public output, while reducing the benefits per unit of the other voters.[29] As illustrated in figure 3.5, which again is constructed from the framework of figure 3.1, the median voter's demand curve shifts out, while the demand curves of the other voters shift inward, and again the equilibrium level of government output increases. A comparison of the quantity axes in figures 3.4 and 3.5 shows that in the Q dimension, a change in benefit shares is analytically the same as a change in tax shares. This makes sense, since in each case the median voter's price per unit decreases, while the other voters experience an increase in the price per unit.

The strategy that is followed when politicians alter benefit shares or tax shares makes intuitive sense. In trying to buy the

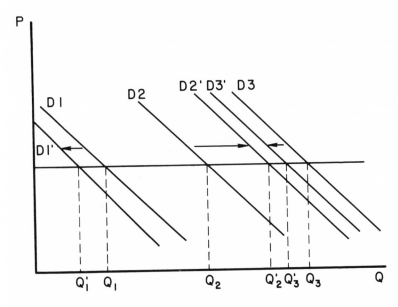

Fig. 3.5   The median voter model with variable benefit shares

median voter's vote, the median voter's quantity demanded rises, and the money to pay for the median vote must come from somewhere. Some of the money comes from the low-demanders who would be against the increase in government and who therefore will not favor the platform anyway. Since the votes of the low-demanders are lost in any case, the politician is not hurt by extracting some payment from them. The high-demanders want an increase in government and receive some surplus from governmental activity. This surplus can be taxed away and given to the median voter. This places the high-demanders closer to the margin and, in a large number setting, increases the size of the median group. Figure 3.6 illustrates this in a Downsian framework with a large number of voters. The solid distribution represents fixed tax and benefit shares. When either or both can vary, the lower tail of the distribution is elongated, the center of the distribution increases as the median goes from M to M', and the upper tail moves closer to the median.

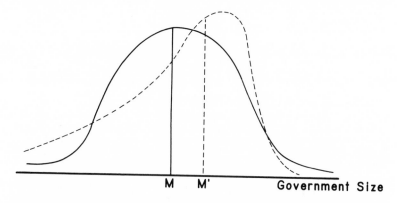

Fig. 3.6   Variable tax or benefit shares with a large number of
voters

The main conclusion of this section is that political competition for the median vote by altering tax or benefit shares
tends to raise the equilibrium size of government because it
lowers the median voter's price per unit of government output.
A more subtle implication of the model, but important nevertheless, is that in a democracy, the voters who care the least
about an issue are the voters that determine its outcome. Political platforms tend to cluster around the median, making the
median voter almost indifferent among them. In the model
developed here, the high-demand candidate has strong sup-
porters among the high-demanders, and can use their resources to try to win the median vote. Likewise, the low-
demanders will be strong opponents that candidate H cannot
hope to convince, so the candidate has no incentive to favor
them. The converse is true of the candidate representing low-
demanders. These voters with intense preferences are unlikely
to be swayed, and so are not important to an election's outcome. It is the median group, which has the least intense preferences and which might vote either way, that is the key to the
election outcome. In a democracy, it is the voters who care the
least about an election's outcome that are the most important in
determining the outcome.

Conclusion

This chapter has examined public choice models of democratic decision making on single-dimensioned issues. Certainly the most significant model of public choice is the median voter model, and the conclusions of that model seem to be descriptive of democratic decision making for the simple types of issues that the model specifically addresses. Specifically, the median voter model seems to be very descriptive of single-dimensioned issues in committee settings where all members have access to the agenda, in referendum settings when the agenda setter is an elected official, and for representative democracies in describing the way in which candidates select their platforms and in describing the nature of the winning platform. Most empirical studies on the median voter model have examined the referendum variant, but casual observation seems to suggest that the model is very descriptive of the way that representatives are elected as well.[30]

The fact that the median voter model is descriptive of many cases of decision making under majority rule by no means implies that it is descriptive of all cases of decision making under majority rule. There are many cases when the median voter model is not at all descriptive—a good example is when only one candidate appears on a ballot for an election. The following chapters will focus on other instances. In particular, when multidimensional issues are involved, the type of logrolling and vote trading that is likely to take place will frequently make the median voter model inappropriate. The fact that the median voter model describes some but not all democratic decisions should be no more surprising than that the neoclassical model of competitive markets describes some but not all industries in an economy. The material that follows is an attempt to develop a model that better describes political decision making in a more complex multidimensional setting.

The agenda control model was described as an alternative to the standard median voter model, but the evidence in general fails to support the agenda control model. This does not mean that the agenda control model is never descriptive, although it appears not to be descriptive when direct tests have been made. The reason is probably that in most cases of public referenda, the agenda setter is an elected official who does not have the incentive for budget maximization that is attributed to the setter in the model. The agenda setter model may be more descriptive of other cases where the agenda setter is a committee not elected by the body that will vote on the agenda. A good example of this is the U.S. Congress, where committees forward bills to the entire body for consideration. The committee members are dependent upon the general public for reelection rather than upon the Congress that will vote on the committee's proposals. This makes a big difference and enters prominently into the models in later chapters. While the agenda control model may not be very descriptive of public referenda, it certainly has a place in describing the decision-making process in representative government. Later chapters will argue that the real descriptive power of the agenda control model is not in single-dimensional direct democracy but is as a part of the complex decision making in multidimensional issues facing representative bodies.

While agenda setters do not usually have an incentive to manipulate the agenda in such a way that the median voter cannot select his most desired outcome, they do have an incentive to manipulate tax and benefit shares so that the median voter's welfare will be enhanced, if institutions allow such manipulation. The model in the chapter illustrated that this has the effect of reducing the median voter's effective price of government, so the median voter demands more. The result is a larger equilibrium size of government. While the median voter's demand increases, other voters experience a decrease in demand, which obscures somewhat the identity of the median group. Because high-demanders of government will face higher tax prices, their most preferred level of government will approach that of the median group. In effect, the strategy is to try to charge Lindahl prices to the median- and high-demanders, although low-demanders are charged much more than their Lindahl prices. The consumer surplus lost by the low-demanders is used to lower the median tax price, to try to attract the median vote. Whereas agenda control can only be practiced by a monopoly agenda setter, the manipulation of benefit and tax shares in this way is a competitive action used to try to win the median voter's vote, and the most successful candidate can expect to win. But again, the result of this competitive practice is to raise the equilibrium size of government.

The median voter model clearly illustrates that in a democracy, it is the voters who care least about the outcome of an election who determine the outcome. Extreme voters who have an intense preference for one outcome or candidate are not the crucial voters; the key voters are those who are almost indifferent between outcomes and so may be swayed by changes in the platforms that are offered. This induces political competition for the median vote, and the models in this chapter have illustrated that political competition for the median vote is the main force that determines outcomes in single-dimensional political issues. Though exceptions undoubtedly exist, the median voter model appears to offer a good description of majority rule politics for single-dimensioned issues.

Contemporary elections can easily be viewed as one-dimensional issues, with candidates arrayed from political left to political right. Public referenda also qualify, meaning that the median voter model can be taken as generally descriptive of the electoral process in a democracy. Candidates and issues subject to public referenda will be determined as described by the median voter model. But while elected representatives may be the median voter's choice, this does not necessarily mean that resources will be allocated as the median voter would most prefer. Public sector resource allocation requires a complex political process, and the one-dimensional median voter model is not nearly so descriptive for multidimensional issues. The remainder of the book is concerned with these multidimensional issues, and it will be argued that the complexities of the political process will frequently prevent the median voter's preference from being chosen in complex settings. In summary, the median voter model is descriptive of many cases of democratic decision making, as this chapter has argued. The remainder of the book considers the more complex issues of the democratic decision-making process, where the simple median voter model is not so descriptive.

4 / Coalitions and Stability in Multidimensional Issues

The median voter model may be descriptive of a significant number of decisions made by majority rule, but it is certainly not descriptive of all majority rule decision-making processes. One of the main limitations of the median voter model when applied to more complex political settings is that the individual voter has no interaction with other voters, so that all voters vote strictly according to their preferences on the single issue being considered. Even in the committee variant of the median voter model, each voter has access to the agenda, and so can interact with other voters in that way, but when issues are voted on, all voters are assumed to vote for their most preferred outcome. When a committee is formed to consider only a single issue, this may be realistic, but for committees that consider more issues, vote trading is a common type of political behavior. Voters may not vote strictly according to their preferences on each issue because they have the opportunity to trade away their votes on issues where they do not have intense preferences in exchange for the votes of others on issues where their preferences are more intense. Logrolling and vote trading are the factors that make multidimensional political issues more complex than single-dimensioned issues.

Multidimensionality can be viewed in two ways with regard to political issues. The first way is to look at any particular issue to see if it has more than one dimension in the perception of the voters. Consider the following two cases: a school bond issue referendum and a U.S. presidential election. The school referendum considers a single-dimensional issue; namely, the number of dollars to be raised to finance education. In contrast, the presidential election encompasses many issues. The size of the total government budget is one issue, and the mix of government spending is another. Should more money be spent on defense, or should more be spent on social programs? The foreign policy of the candidate provides another dimension, and domestic issues such as prison reform and abortion provide additional dimensions.

But while the argument can be made that the bond issue is single-dimensional, while the presidential race is multidimensional, the opposite argument can be made as well. Voters tend to characterize political candidates on a spectrum from left to right, aggregating the complex multidimensional issues into a single left-right dimension in much the same way that a price index aggregates the complex movements of prices into a single number, or a Gini coefficient aggregates the complex characteristics of an income distribution into a single number. Admittedly, the left-right characterization is an oversimplification of many complex issues, but like the Gini coefficient and the price index, it may be a useful characterization for many purposes, and if voters view candidates in this way, then the presidential election assumes the characteristics of a single-dimensioned issue. Returning to the school bond issue, voters may be concerned about whether the money will be used for gymnasium facilities or more laboratories, thus making the bond issue multidimensional in the eyes of the voters. Whether an issue is multidimensional or not in this respect depends upon how voters perceive the issues. Both the bond issue and the presidential election could be perceived as either single-dimensional or multidimensional.

In an important respect, however, both of these issues are single-dimensional regardless of the voters' perceptions. That respect is that the voter has a single choice when the election occurs and, so, cannot trade off some of one dimension for some of another. For example, the electorate may view economic policy and foreign policy as two different dimensions of a presidential election, but on election day, voters must choose a single candidate and cannot choose the economic policy of one and the foreign policy of another. Similarly with the bond issue, voters have the single-dimensional choice of voting for or against the issue; they cannot vote for the portion earmarked for gymnasium facilities and against the laboratory portion. Further analysis is useful. If the issue is broken down into two separate referenda, one a bond issue for gymnasium facilities and the other a bond issue for new laboratories, the issue is still not multidimensional. It has simply become two single-dimensioned issues. The reason why all of these issues have an important characteristic of single dimensionality despite their multidimensional aspects is that ultimately the voter is faced with the task of ranking the alternatives and voting for the most preferred alternative. This ultimate task forces each voter to transform the issue into a single dimension regardless of the issue's complexity.[1]

The school bond issue referendum and the presidential election have the common characteristic of a large number of voters. For present purposes, a large number of voters means a number large enough that voters are not able to trade votes on issues. When the number of voters is small, vote trading is possible, which transforms a series of single-dimensioned issues into a multidimensional issue. In the bond issue example where separate referenda are being held for gymnasium and laboratory facilities, one voter might have a very strong preference in favor of the gymnasium issue and a weak preference opposing the laboratory issue. In a small number setting, the voter could attempt to find another voter with whom to trade votes. The first voter would agree to vote in favor of the laboratory issue in exchange for the other voter's vote on the gymnasium issue. In order to make a profitable exchange, the first voter would have to be sure to trade with someone who would have voted against the gymnasium issue without the exchange, and there would have to be a small enough number of voters that the vote trading could make a difference. When analyzing democratic political processes, an important distinction is a large versus small number of voters. With large numbers, voters cannot trade votes on issues, but with small numbers, coalitions of vote traders are possible.[2]

Note that the issues do not have to be related to have this characteristic of multidimensionality. The only necessity is that votes can be traded. Votes might be traded on the election of a particular candidate in exchange for votes on a spending bill. Even more complex logrolling would be possible, as one person could trade a vote on an issue today for a political IOU to be redeemed in the future. In all of these cases the issues are multidimensional because the outcomes are interrelated.

One important characteristic in vote trading and logrolling is the ability to monitor voting behavior. Effective vote trading is impossible when voting is done by secret ballot, which is one reason in addition to large numbers why vote trading is nearly impossible in general elections. In bodies like the U.S. Congress, votes are a matter of public record, so it is possible to monitor those with whom votes are traded to make sure that the votes are cast as promised. Also note that the secret ballot makes it difficult to buy and sell votes. Individuals can claim to be willing to sell their votes, but with secret ballots the voter cannot offer any evidence that the vote was cast as promised, so that purchasers can have no guarantee that they got what they paid for. When votes are a matter of public record, they can be exchanged much more easily, and the public recording of votes may be more important in facilitating vote trading than the number of voters.

The purpose of this introduction is to distinguish a type of multidimensional issue that is made up of more than one single-dimensioned issue. The outcome of each single-dimensioned issue is determined interactively with the others, so that the outcomes of the issues are interdependent. This can be contrasted with a single-dimensioned issue that may have multiple facets, such as a presidential election. Determining the characteristics of each facet is an interesting problem, but it is outside the scope of the model in this book.[3] The multidimensional issues here can all be broken down into a series of single-dimensioned issues, and the voters will each have an opportunity to vote in each dimension. It is the possibility of logrolling and vote trading that makes the results of the multidimensional model differ from the standard median voter model. Seen in this light, isolating the effects of logrolling and vote trading certainly seems like a worthwhile endeavor.

Toward a Theory of Political Structure

An initial point worth making about public choice models is that the institutional structure is a major determinant of political outcomes. The preferences of voters and representatives are important in determining particular political outcomes, but they are a part of the visible superstructure built upon an important foundation of institutions. Public choice models have sometimes tended to ignore the institutional structure in politics in order to focus on the interactions among individual preferences, and the result has sometimes been the production of theories that are a poor description of the actual political process.[4] As the study of public choice matures, models with more institutional content are being developed, which makes the models more accurate in their descriptions of politics. Sometimes specific political models have been generalized to cases more general than the model originally discussed. For example, there has been a tendency to apply the median voter model to any instance of democratic decision making,[5] even though the cases examined lie well outside the simple one-dimensional framework of the model as then developed. What is called for is a fuller development of the model to include a more realistic institutional structure.

A look at two aspects of economic theory shows how institutional structures can be viewed as important, and how they can be overlooked. The economic theory of a market economy is based upon the institution of voluntary exchange, but the voluntary exchange paradigm has not been subject to much examination by economists. That exchanges will be voluntary is in general just assumed, and mostly not explicitly. Even economic studies that go to great lengths to enumerate their assumptions frequently overlook the most basic assumption that resources are transferred through voluntary exchange. This is not always true,[6] and even when it is true, it is defensible. Scientists must start with some basic assumptions common to their disciplines,[7] and in economics the paradigm of voluntary exchange has served well. Economists can then begin analysis with the voluntary exchange framework without having to demonstrate how the institution came about, or what preserves it. In the fledgling study of public choice, the median voter model has sometimes been used in this way in democratic situations, as was noted earlier. The observation of democratic decision making has sometimes led analysts to conclude that the median voter's preferences are being satisfied without a careful analysis regarding whether this is justified. At this point, the median voter conclusion cannot be taken for granted as a part of the paradigm the way that voluntary exchange is taken for granted in economics. But it must be noted that the institutional characteristic of voluntary exchange is vitally important in economics, yet economists take this institution for granted and do not usually subject it to analysis.

While the institution of voluntary exchange is taken for granted by most economists, other details of the institutional structure are closely scrutinized, which has provided economics with a detailed theory of market structure. The number of firms in the market, the ease of entry and exit, and the nature of products being sold are among the many characteristics that may determine the structure of various markets.[8] In this area of economics, institutions are viewed as being very important. They determine the structure of markets.

Here, there should be a parallel between economics and public choice. Although the median voter model will remain very important in describing democratic decisions, there is no reason to believe that the median voter model is descriptive of all instances of democratic choice any more than pure competition is descriptive of all instances of market exchange. Public choice models that propose some alternative, such as the agenda control model, should be viewed not as alternatives to the median voter model but rather as descriptions of democratic decision making when the institutional characteristics of democracy vary. Sometimes the median voter model may apply, and at other times the agenda control model may apply. An examination of the underlying assumptions should provide some guidance in determining which model applies when.

Looking at the public choice literature, there seems to be more models than there are institutional settings (because sometimes there are many models that attempt to describe the same decision-making process). Frequently, it is unclear how much the results from any particular model can be generalized, and just as frequently it is unclear how one model relates to another. While this is to be expected in a relatively young area of inquiry, it appears that a natural road of development would be to develop a more general theory of political structure in which the institutional structure of the political decision implies the nature of the outcome. This would parallel the economic theory of market structure.

One goal of this book is to try to develop such a theory of political structure. The theory's foundation was sketched in the previous chapter on the median voter. The median voter model, it seems, is very descriptive of political decisions that are being made along a single-dimensioned continuum. Some of the difficulties in making single-dimensioned political decisions were also noted in that chapter. One way to partition models of the political structure is by the number of dimensions over which democratic decisions are made, and the important distinction, it will be argued below, is single-dimensional versus multidimensional. Multidimensional issues offer the opportunity of logrolling and vote trading, which fundamentally alters the nature of political decisions.

At the risk of oversimplification, this analysis of political structure will partition democratic institutions into two groups: one-dimensional decisions and multidimensional decisions. As chapter 3 illustrated, there may be significant differences in single-dimensioned democratic decisions, but it will be argued that these single-dimensioned decisions have more in common with each other than will multidimensional decisions. Just as monopolies may differ, for example, in the amount of price discrimination they can practice, so will multidimensional political decisions differ. What is being presented here, then, is not intended to be the last word on political structure, but one step on the way toward developing a general theory of political structure. Chapter 3 discussed much analysis of single-dimensioned decisions, which seems at least to have some uniformity in its presentation. That is not true of multidimensional political analysis, so one aspect of the analysis to follow is an attempt to simplify and standardize the framework of analysis somewhat.

Dividing political structures into single-dimensional and multidimensional structures provides a basic framework for organization. In developing a multidimensional theory of politics, the multidimensional model will be developed from the single-dimensional model to provide some continuity between the structures. As the complexity of the multidimensional model increases through the book, the assumptions which change the results should be apparent. As multidimensional issues become more complex, it will be seen that distributional activity becomes more important as a governmental activity. The models in the book lead toward this general conclusion, but the ultimate conclusions reached are only a part of the purpose of the models. Another purpose is the development of a theory of political structure similar to the economic theory of market structure, where particular institutional characteristics can be observed to lead toward particular results. Certainly, all political decisions arrived at democratically will not have the same characteristics, either from the standpoint of economic efficiency or from the standpoint of the relationship between voter preferences and democratic outcomes. The purpose of a theory of political structure is to be able to show a relationship between institutions and outcomes.

The next step is to take the basic single-dimensioned model explored in chapter 3 and extend it to two dimensions. The institutional structure under which decisions are made will be an important determinant of the nature of the outcome, but before the institutional structure is examined in great detail, it is useful to explore the nature of the issue space to see how the relationship of individual preferences to each other can affect the outcomes of democratic decisions. Then an institutional structure can be imposed upon the model of individual preferences.

Multidimensional Issue Space

The cyclical majority problem was mentioned in chapter 3. In the three-person, three-alternative case, where individual 1 prefers A to B to C, individual 2 prefers B to C to A, and individual 3 prefers C to A to B, the reader not familiar with cyclical majority problem can verify that a majority will prefer A to B, B to C, and C to A. Thus, the outcome of a majority rule vote to select one of the three alternatives will depend upon the institutional structure and the order in which the alternatives are considered. With no more information than the preferences of the three individuals, there is no way to determine which alternative will be chosen by majority rule. In chapter 3, the specific example of Carter, Ford, and Reagan in a presidential election was used as an illustration, but the alternatives could just as easily have been low, middle, and high levels of spending on schools,[9] or any number of other issues. The point here is that in each case these points can easily be ranked A, B, C on a single-dimensioned continuum. Without restricting the nature of preferences, cycles among alternatives can occur in single-dimensioned issues.

Cycles can also occur in multidimensional issue space. In one dimension, if preferences are such that individuals always prefer points closer to their most preferred alternative to points farther away, then the cycle problem disappears, but this restriction is not sufficient to eliminate cycles in the multidimensional case. This is illustrated in figure 4.1. Three individuals, A, B, and C, have their most preferred levels of X and Y marked on the figure, and for simplicity it is assumed that they prefer points geometrically closer to their most preferred points to points further away, so their indifference curves will be circles. The three individuals must select some level of X and of Y by majority rule. Consider the following scenario. Point 1 is arbitrarily selected as a point in the issue space, and point 2 is selected to run against point 1. The indifference curves for individuals A and B, drawn through point 1, show that point 2 defeats point 1. Similarly, the indifference curves for B and C drawn through point 2 show that point 3 beats point 2. With the points in identical locations in figure 4.2, point 4 beats 3, 5 beats

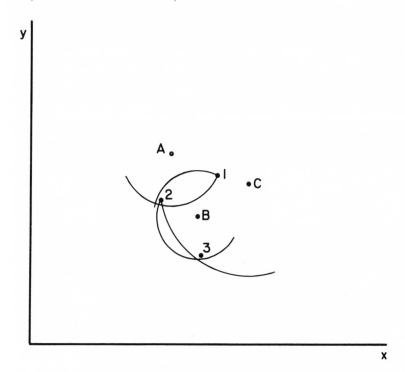

Fig. 4.1   Cycles in multidimensional issue space

4, 6 beats 5, and 7 beats 6. Since point 1 beats 7, those seven points constitute a cycle.

In the particular example chosen for this cycle, the outcomes of successive referenda seem to be farther away from the median voter outcomes, and indeed it would have been possible to select additional points still farther away, up to the point where a majority of the voters would prefer nothing to the level of output proposed. Figure 4.3, drawn in a smaller scale than the other two figures, shows the indifference curves of A, B, and C that pass through the origin. The area inside the heavy line is the area that at least two out of the three voters would prefer to nothing. Assuming that negative amounts of X and Y are not possible, a majority rule process like the one above could end up

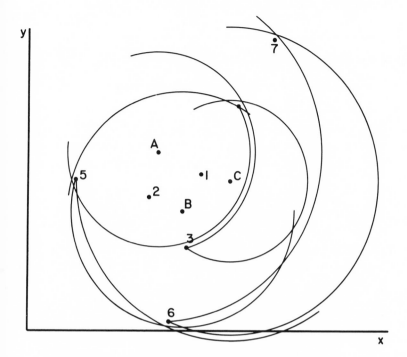

Fig. 4.2   Cycles in multidimensional issue space

selecting any point inside the heavy line. This set of points will be called the feasible majority set, and this terminology will be kept throughout the book. If negative amounts are possible, majority rule decisions could end up at any point in the issue space by strategically choosing the alternatives. In this case, the feasible majority set has no boundary. This example is one case of the general proposition proven by McKelvey that the majority rule process can start at any point and end up at any other point in the issue space by strategically selecting the sequence of alternatives.[10] There is a specific implication here for agenda control. If an individual can control what alternatives are to be considered, and in what order, regardless of the starting point, the individual can manipulate the election to end up at any other

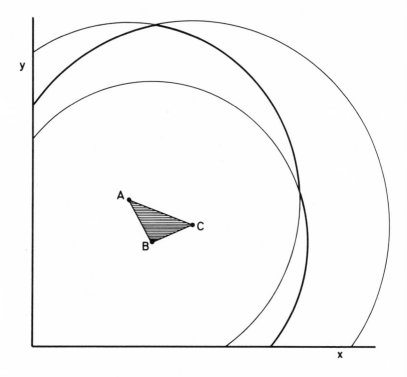

Fig. 4.3   The majority rule issue space

point in the feasible majority set (such as the agenda setter's most preferred point). There is also a general implication. Without specifying the institutional structure, there is no way to know which point in the feasible majority set will be chosen.

Actually, this result will not always be true. Plott has shown that if one voter's maximum point is a point at which all other voters can be divided into pairs whose interests are diametrically opposed, then no other point can defeat that point by majority rule.[11] This condition is satisfied for the five voters in figure 4.4. The line connecting voters A and E and the line connecting voters B and D are contract curves between the two voters,[12] and if all voters can be paired in such a way that

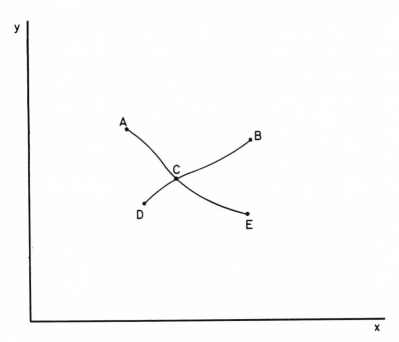

Fig. 4.4   A median voter equilibrium in multidimensional
issue space

their contract curves pass through an individual's most preferred point, like point C in figure 4.4, then no other point can
beat that point. In this case, the relationship of the voters'
preferences to each other produce a median voter solution
analogous to the single-dimensioned case. In figure 4.3, the
circular indifference curves mean that the contract curves will
be straight lines between the individuals' most preferred points.
If point B had been on the line between points A and C, then
point B would have been a median voter equilibrium.

This case has also been examined by Gordon Tullock, who
showed that when there are a large number of voters with circular indifference curves equally spaced in the issue space, there
will be a point like point C in figure 4.4 where voters can be

divided into pairs with diametrically opposed interests.[13] The result is, again, a median voter equilibrium. At this point, the reader should give some thought to the possibility that a voting body could be divided into diametrically opposed pairs. In chapter 3, it was argued that voters may view issues on a left-right spectrum, and this may produce diametrically opposed pairs of voters about the median. In fact, requiring single-peaked preferences in the single-dimensioned case is simply a method of ensuring that there are pairs of diametrically opposed voters, so the conditions for a median voter equilibrium are identical in the single-dimensional and multidimensional cases.

In the real world, small movements in the issue space are not feasible, which means that contract curves would not have to pass exactly through the median voter's most preferred point for a median voter equilibrium to exist; they must only pass within the threshold distance of the median voter. Thus, if in figure 4.5 it was not feasible to propose movements smaller than the radius of the circle, the voter whose most preferred point is at the middle of the circle would be the median voter, because the other voters can be divided into pairs whose contract curves pass through the circle. The reader should consider the possibility that this situation might exist in the real world, especially when issues can be segmented easily into left-right or conservative-liberal molds. In this context, it seems more likely that a median voter solution could exist in elections of representatives rather than in legislatures where distributional issues are more likely to arise.

While this is an interesting question to examine, the answer does not affect the model in this book. The multidimensional model developed in later chapters does not rely on either the existence or nonexistence of a median voter equilibrium. Furthermore, the agenda control model in chapter 3 has already illustrated that just because there is an identifiable median voter there is no guarantee that that voter's most preferred outcome will be chosen by majority rule. Ultimately, given the preferences of voters, it is the specific institutional structure that will determine the majority rule outcome and not the preferences of voters by themselves. This being the case, it

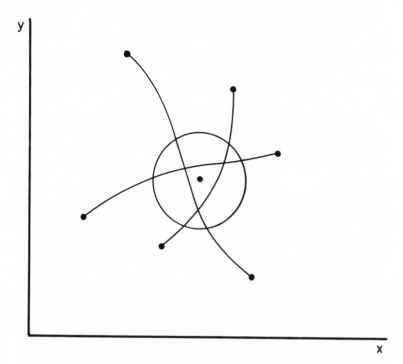

Fig. 4.5   A median voter equilibrium with discrete movements
in issue space

is time to add some institutional content to the majority rule
decision-making process.

Multidimensional Decisions

Thus far, the multidimensional issue space has been examined, and the general conclusion has been that without knowing
something about the institutional structure, any point in the
majority rule issue space could be selected by majority rule. In
the example depicted in figure 4.3, any point inside the heavily
drawn line could be chosen by some majority rule process. The
issue space can be partitioned farther. The lines connecting A,
B, and C in figure 4.3 are the contract curves, and any point

inside the triangle will be Pareto optimal. Outside the Pareto optimal region at least one individual could have his welfare increased without decreasing the welfare of any of the other individuals. Thus, there are economic incentives to make decisions that result in an outcome inside the Pareto optimal region, but once there, any movement must make at least one individual worse off. Outside the Pareto optimal region, there are efficiency gains to be shared; inside the region, movements are distributional.

Several observations are warranted at this point. First, observing that there are incentives for reaching an outcome in the Pareto optimal region does not guarantee that the democratic decision-making process will end up there. Again, it depends on the specific institutional structure. Second, it should be observed that the Pareto optimal region, while smaller than the set of possible outcomes, may still be quite large. If some voters have extreme views, the Pareto optimal region will extend to their most preferred points, and with very extreme voters, the Pareto optimal set might even extend outside the boundaries of the feasible majority set. Third, recall from chapter 3 that an individual's most preferred level of some good will depend on the individual's tax and benefit shares. Thus, manipulation of these variables may alter the relationships among the most preferred points of the voters. This could effectively add another dimension to the issue space and opens the possibility trades. It is this possibility of trading on issues that makes the democratic decisions of small representative bodies fundamentally different from the democratic decisions made directly by the general public, and the differences between these two types of decisions are an important part of this study.

Before moving on to political decisions in a true multidimensional setting, consider the issues facing the voters in figure 4.3 in a single-dimensional context. There are two ways that the decision on the levels of X and Y might be made in a one-dimensional model. One way would be to have the ratio X to Y given before the election, as, for example, the ratio of laboratory to gymnasium expenditures in a school referendum. With the mix given, the issue is only the single-dimensional issue of how much in total expenditures to vote for.[14] Assume that the predetermined mix

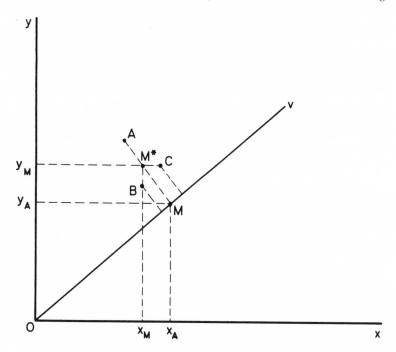

Fig. 4.6   Median voter decisions in two dimensions

of expenditures gives voters the choice of points on vector OV in figure 4.6. In this case, a perpendicular line from the voter's most preferred point to OV will identify the voter's most preferred location on OV. A is the median voter in this example, and if the institutional structure produces the median voter equilibrium, point M will be chosen, and X_A and Y_A will be produced. Note that, as in this case, the outcome need not be in the Pareto optimal region, although if the voters determined the vector OV, they would have an incentive to choose one passing through the Pareto optimal set.

Another way to choose X and Y would be to vote on them sequentially. If the median voter model applies, B is the median voter for X, and C is the median voter for Y. Majority rule elections in this case would produce X_M and Y_M, selecting point M* in the issue space. The outcome of M* is what would normally be thought of as a median voter outcome in two dimensions. The median on each issue is selected.

At last, after much examination of the issue space, the institutional structure has been specified closely enough to find a majority rule equilibrium outcome in two dimensions. However, even here the majority rule decision could have been either M or M*, depending upon which election procedure was used. At this point, there are more questions. If OV is to be determined by majority rule, where will OV be located? This suggests the question of whether M and M* would have to coincide if OV passed through M*. The answer is no. To see this, construct the diagram so that OV passes through M*. Now reduce the amount of Y that C most prefers. This lowers M* but does not move M. As OV is rotated down to the new M*, M traces out an arc, but it would have to trace out a vertical line to remain coincident with M*, so the two will not generally coincide. Thus, if the median preferred mix of X and Y is chosen, followed by the median preferred level, the outcome will in general differ from that of choosing the median X and the median Y. Indeed, different majority rule institutions will produce different outcomes, even within the narrow confines of the traditional median voter model. Institutions are important.

Consider again the sequential case, where first the level of X is chosen and then the level of Y. This situation was just modeled as two one-dimensional decisions, but if logrolling is possible, two of the individuals might agree beforehand on their votes for X and Y in such a way that will benefit both of them. In this case, the levels of X and Y will be determined simultaneously (even though the votes will be taken sequentially), and the decision becomes a true multidimensional decision rather than a sequence of single-dimensioned decisions. At this point, the situation becomes very complex. A and C might form a coalition where A would agree to move X in exchange for C agreeing to move Y, or A might vote with C on X and Y in exchange for votes on future issues. Meanwhile, B will not want to be exploited by the majority coalition and may try some bargaining of his own. The best way to sort out these complexities is to take them one at a time, gradually building a more complex model of the political process. The first step of examining coalition for mation in distributional situations will be undertaken in this chapter.

Coalitions and Stabilitiy in Distributional Games

This section will begin the analysis of political coalitions at the simplest level, with a frequently analyzed three-person distributional game.[15] The government has collected one dollar in taxes, which is to be divided among the three individuals by majority rule. In this example, the level of government spending is fixed at one dollar, and the individual tax shares are also taken as given. Thus, the issue to be decided is purely distributional. This game, while simple, contains a significant amount of descriptive ability for political decisions by representative government. One feature of the game is that tax collections are considered to be exogenously determined; another feature is that the activity of the government is purely distributional.

The subject matter of chapter 5 is redistribution through taxation, and the main conclusion is that in the type of political and economic setting that characterizes Western democracies, the tax system does not have much ability to affect the income distribution. The bulk of the analysis of the tax structure will have to wait until the next chapter, but for now this conclusion can be briefly supported by observing that the main form of taxation is the income tax, and income groups are not organized as special interest groups. There is not a lobby of rich people arguing for less progressive taxes and a lobby of poor people arguing for more progressive taxes.[16] Rather, special interest groups are likely to be organized along occupational or geographic lines. There are constitutional restrictions on the alteration of the tax structure along these lines, so that it is difficult for special tax treatment to be directed to particular occupations or, more so, geographic areas. Representatives represent geographic areas, and because of the difficulties of legislating special tax treatment for one area (e.g., lower federal income taxes in one state than in another), representatives instead try to legislate special interest spending programs to benefit their constituents. Thus, there is good reason to consider the tax structure to be given in order to focus on distributional spending programs.

Government activity in this simple model is also purely distributional. Clearly, the government does things other than distribute benefits to special interests, but later chapters will argue that even the most public interested legislation has significant distributional components that have important effects on the legislative outcomes. In national defense, an example chosen because it is commonly cited as a public good, issues are frequently of a distributional nature, such as in which congressional district facilities will be located, and which firms will be awarded defense contracts. Thus, the production of what appears to be a public good is determined by distributional factors. This argument is extended greatly later in the book; it is introduced now in order to suggest that a model with an exogenously given tax take to be divided among the members of a group by majority rule is a largely realistic description of the political process.

Now consider the case initially described in this section. A legislature made up of three representatives must decide by majority rule how a given amount of tax revenue is to be divided among them. Assume that, as with an actual legislature, the process will be repeated annually. Stated in this way, the problem becomes a simple exercise in game theory. Since two out of three votes are needed for a majority, the first two individuals could form a majority coalition with the outcome (½, ½, 0), where each element represents the fraction of the total going to each of the three representatives. This outcome will not be stable, however, because the third representative could offer the second representative a higher payoff for shifting coalitions, making both representatives better off. That outcome might be (0, ⅔, ⅓). At this point, the first representative could offer the third (⅓, 0, ⅔) in order to regain a place in the majority coalition. This scenario leads to a cyclical majority outcome, and one might imagine the cycle of (⅔, ⅓, 0), (0, ⅔, ⅓), (⅓, 0, ⅔) continuing through time.

The cycle occurs because of the relationships between each representative's distribution and the distribution of the others. In each outcome, one representative receives an above-average distribution, another receives a distribution that is about average, and another receives a below-average distribution. The representative with the below-average distribution always has an incentive to offer the representative with the average distribution a chance to join in a coalition where the average recipient becomes above average in exchange for raising the below-average representative's distribution. By eliminating the above-average recipient from the coalition, there are ample resources available for striking a profitable bargain. Using this mechanism, the example will generalize to any number of representatives. In the ten-state example (7, 7, 6, 6, 6, 6, 6, 6, 4, 4), the last two representatives could offer to replace the first two in the coalition to change the imputation to (0, 0, 8, 8, 8, 8, 8, 8, 5, 5) and improve the welfare of all but the first two representatives. This, in turn, would prompt a coalition of the first two and the last two representatives, but now they would need at least the cooperation of two other members of the majority. A possible outcome would be (5, 5, 4, 4, 3, 3, 9, 9, 8, 8), and the process could continue. Again, the principle is that a coalition between those with average distributions and those with below-average distributions can push the average group above average and increase the well-being of the below-average group by eliminating the existing above-average group from the coalition. While game theory cannot predict the exact distributions that would result in any case, the three-person case is large enough to demonstrate the generality of the principle, since each individual can represent the high, middle, and low groups.

One implied assumption that contributes to the cyclical behavior of the outcomes is that no representative has differential political power that can keep the representative in the position of receiving a high distribution as a member of the winning coalition. A politically powerful representative might consistently be able to do better than average. This may be true when periods are measured in years; however, there are forces working against the ability of one representative to consistently receive above-average distributions. In order to do so, the representative needs the votes of others to remain in the majority and so must have something to offer in return, but individuals receiving low distributions automatically have more to offer. Therefore, recipients of high distributions are automatically in unstable positions, and cyclical behavior is likely. This transitory political wealth can be contrasted with economic wealth, which tends to persist because it is not dependent upon the consent of a majority. The general conclusion is that political power cannot consistently generate above-average distributions in a majority rule system, but this notion is discussed in greater detail in chapter 9.

The model thus far examined will exhibit cycles, but it is not closely enough specified to compute the exact distributions made to each participant. This reflects conditions in the real world where there are few restrictions on potential coalition formation. However, this cyclical behavior which might be expected if viewed in light of work by Arrow or McKelvey, for example, does not seem to be a frequent feature of political life.[17] A persuasive explanation of the observed stability given the possibility of cycles can be given by examining in more detail the preferences of representatives and the nature of the cyclical outcomes.

The inherent instability of the cyclical solution to the problem implies that any representative who receives an above-average distribution in the present period can expect a below-average distribution in the next period, due to the formation of a new coalition that excludes that representative. In the general case, where there are n representatives who will divide total tax revenues TR by majority rule, where R_i is the distribution to the ith representative, and t denotes the time period,[18]

$$\text{If } R_{it} > TR/n, \text{ then } R_{it}+1 < TR/n. \qquad (4.1)$$

This result is implied in the cyclical model developed earlier. This conclusion can actually be taken a step further. Since representatives that receive high distributions now can be expected to be excluded from future majority coalitions, all representatives would expect over time to, on average, receive the average distribution. That is, the expected value of the representative's distribution at any arbitrary future period will be average distribution, which can be written

$$E(R_i) = TR/n. \qquad (4.2)$$

From a mathematical standpoint,

$$\sum_{i=1}^{n} E(R_i) = TR \qquad (4.3)$$

is a tautology, and equation (4.2) automatically follows if over time no representative can expect to do better than average. In this case, both sides of equation (4.3) are divided by n, which yields equation (4.2).

Up to this point, representatives have been assumed to be attempting to maximize the size of the distribution coming their way, but representatives are probably concerned not only with the size of the distribution but also with the continuity of the distribution from one time period to the next. For simple planning purposes if nothing else, recipients would prefer a more constant flow of revenues over time to an erratic flow with the same expected value. Thus, in political bargaining, the representative would prefer a larger distribution and also a steadier flow of disbursements over time. Representing the variance of the R_i distribution over time as $\sigma^2(R_i)$, the representative will attempt to maximize U_i, where

$$U_i = f(E(R_i), \sigma^2(R_i), |_{E(R^i)}). \qquad (4.4)$$

In equation (4.4), a greater value of $E(R_i)$ increases U_i, and a lower value of $\sigma^2(R_i)$ increases U_i.

If TR and n are assumed constant, then from equation (4.2), $E(R_i)$ will also be constant, so the maximizing representative will be concerned only with minimizing $\sigma^2(R_i)$. A representative that shrewdly bargains for a larger-than-average distribution this year is likely to be the victim of a coalition realignment next year that leaves the representative with a smaller than average distribution. Representatives are likely to be able to foresee the cyclical outcome of the distributive game, where a majority coalition exploits a minority, and can bargain to avoid that outcome by including all members in the majority coalition and agreeing to receive TR/n in each period. The all-inclusive coalition does not affect $E(R_i)$, but minimizes $\sigma^2(R_i)$, so the outcome where

$$R_i = TR/n, \; i=1,n \qquad (4.5)$$

dominates the cyclical majority outcome, This explains why political outcomes tend to be stable despite the potential for cycles.[19] The outcomes of political bargains tend to be characterized by universalism and reciprocity;[20] votes are exchanged to reach a bargain which includes something for everybody.

The Minimum Stable Coalition

This solution to the distributive game clearly dominates the cyclical solution that was initially presented. In a stable setting, any participant would have to be cautious about initiating a less than all-inclusive majority coalition, because the participant might not end up in the majority even in the first period; and in any event, the cyclical outcome would provide the same expected payoff, but with higher variance.[21] An additional factor favoring the all-inclusive coalition is that the costs of coalition formation are greatly reduced. Of course, this theory is a game-theoretic solution that attempts to predict individual behavior, and in politics as in other games, sometimes an unexpected strategy works best. However, this model goes a long way toward explaining the apparent stability of political outcomes, as well as the fact that representative democracy seems to provide distributive benefits to the constituents of every representative. This simple model will be expanded greatly in later chapters, but even in this simple form the model appears to have much explanatory power.

The model also provides some insight into the size of coalitions. Riker,[22] in response to Downs,[23] put forth the theory that rather than trying to maximize the size of the majority, politicians instead will seek the minimum winning coalition. The minimum winning coalition would be more profitable because it will allow the gains to be spread over a smaller group. There is an element of truth in both views. A smaller coalition will increase the benefits of members, but the coalition must be large enough to be stable. The motivating factor in the present model is not to maximize the majority or to find the minimum winning coalition but instead to find the minimum stable coalition. In the special case of the game just described, the minimum stable coalition would include every individual, but even though the majority is maximized, this is only an incidental by-product of finding the minimum stable coalition. Slight variations in the institutional structure could alter the size of the minimum stable coalition.

Consider the following variation of the three-person game as an example. The government has a budget constraint of one dollar, and the legislature made up of three representatives, A, B, and C, is to decide by majority rule the level of funding to go to projects A, B, and C. A proposes ⅓ of the money to go to project A, and obtains the vote of B so that the appropriation passes two votes to one. In the same way, B obtains C's vote for project B, and C obtains A's vote. For the first period, the distribution is (⅓, ⅓, ⅓), this time approved by a simple majority rather than unanimously. Next period, C owes A a favor, and so A and C vote for project A. Likewise, A is indebted to B, and B is indebted to C, so repayment again provides the (⅓, ⅓, ⅓) outcome with a simple majority in each case. If this situation could persist, a simple return of favors in each successive period can produce the stable outcome of the unanimous case, but without each representative having to seek out unanimous approval each time. The minimum stable coalition in this instance is two out of three.

As this example illustrates, logrolling in a multidimensional setting can be more complex than a simple trade of votes. In this example, individual B trades his vote to A in the first period not for A's vote but for an unspecified IOU that is not collected until next period. Politicians have an incentive to keep track of these IOUs—and to repay them if they hope to be included in future logrolling activities. Representatives who give up a vote today can wait to ask for repayment until a vote is needed. The situation works much like indirect exchange in the market. Just as barter will frequently be inefficient in economic exchange, so simple vote trades may be in political exchange. More complex logrolling of the type described in this model routinely takes place in politics.

Notice that stability in this model is produced by the fact that no coalition takes so much for itself that it leaves another coalition with a smaller than average distribution. What would be the outcome if A tried to get B's approval for a ½ share? There are two possibilities. B might agree in exchange for the other half, which would set up a cycle, or B might refuse to go along with the idea, seeing that it would destabilize a stable political environment. Economic behavior would predict the second outcome. In markets, individuals bargain in order to maximize joint profits, and the same should be true in politics. All politicians are motivated to sustain the stable political outcome. A single majority passes each bill only because each representative needs only that for passage. Once A has B's vote, C's vote is unnecessary. But it is unlikely that B's vote would be available to vote A a larger than average distribution. It is the sustainability of the ($\frac{1}{3}$, $\frac{1}{3}$, $\frac{1}{3}$) distribution over time that makes the outcome stable.

The government budget constraint is given in this problem, but in a setting closer to the real world, this too would be politically determined. The determination of the government's budget constraint is discussed in later chapters, and in detail in chapter 8. At this point it is sufficient to note that given the government's budget constraint, stability can be produced in political outcomes only when the distribution of benefits among political groups is relatively uniform. To produce this outcome, politicans do not try to maximize the size of their majorities or find the minimum winning coalition; instead, they seek the minimum stable coalition. Stability in turn depends upon the size of the distribution of the coalition awards. In effect, the stable majority outcome described in this section is the same as the unanimous outcome in the section before. The vote could have been unanimous, but was not because once a majority is assured, it does not pay the coalition entrepreneur to seek out more votes. A stable political outcome is produced in a political system that generates minimum stable coalitions.

Conclusion

The median voter model, discussed in chapter 3, appears to be fairly descriptive of democratic decision making when issues are one-dimensional. There may be exceptions, and some of these were discussed, but single-dimensioned issues are different in an important way from multidimensional issues. With multidimensional issues, it is possible for voters to trade votes across issues, which makes the political setting much more complex. Coalition formation is much more complicated, since voters might agree to vote for an issue against their narrow self-interests in exchange for votes on an issue they feel more strongly about. In this type of setting, preferences alone will not determine political outcomes. The institutional structure is a very important factor, and it should be possible to draw general conclusions about the nature of political outcomes from the type of institutional structure that produces them.

All outcomes of market exchange are not the same, and economics has developed a theory of market structure to explain the differences as a result of institutional settings. The same type of theory should be able to explain democratic decisions. Different institutional structures will produce different majority rule outcomes. If this line of analysis can be extended, a theory of political structure could be developed that would parallel the economic theory of market structure. Democratic government will produce different types of resource allocation depending upon the specific institutional structure. The key institutional factor that will be emphasized throughout this book is single-dimensional versus multidimensional issue space. In economics, markets can be characterized as competitive or monopolistic (with many intermediate cases), and in politics, democratic decisions can be characterized as single-dimensional or multidimensional. Public choice theorists have had much to say about democratic decisions in a single-dimensioned issue space, and for most cases the median voter model is very descriptive. The present analysis is trying to emphasize the importance of the distinction between single-dimensional and multidimensional issues and is trying to generate a more general theory of multidimensional democratic decision making.

Without placing any institutional limits on democratic decision making in a multidimensional issue space, democratic decisions could lead to an outcome in any point in the issue space. Thus, given preferences, it is the institutional structure that will determine the democratic outcome. An examination of the issue space can provide a bit more insight without imposing an institutional structure. First, there will be a Pareto optimal set that will be a subset of the issue space. Outside this set, it is possible to make moves that would benefit at least one voter without harming any others. Inside the Pareto optimal set, improvements for one voter can come only at the expense of harming at least one other. Also as a subset of the issue space will be a feasible majority set. If there is no lower bound on issues, then the feasible majority set will include the entire issue space, but if there are lower bounds (for example, negative amounts of goods cannot be produced), then the feasible majority set will be smaller than the issue space. The feasible majority set is simply the set of points that could defeat zero on every issue in a pair-wise majority vote. The Pareto optimal set and the feasible majority set are concepts that will be used in later chapters.

This chapter's introduction to the modeling of multidimensional decisions considered the simple situation where elected representatives had to determine how a fixed amount of government revenues were to be distributed by majority rule. The cyclical outcome was shown to be dominated by an equal distribution to each representative, thus providing a stable allocation of public sector resources. In order to produce this outcome, politicans attempt to construct minimum stable coalitions. Multidimensional political decisions are characterized by universalism and reciprocity. Individuals trade votes on some issues for votes on other issues, and the result is an allocation of public sector resources that provides something for everybody.

This model will be extended throughout the book. In this chapter, the government budget has been taken as given. An important extension will be to drop this restriction to examine how the levels of expenditure on individual programs will be determined. Added together, the individual programs will determine the size of the government budget. This model has also assumed tax rates to be given and has examined how the government spends its revenues. Taxes are also politically given, and chapter 5 is devoted to the examination of taxes. The model developed in this chapter also has been a strictly distributive model, with government activity confined to distributive issues to the exclusion of other issues such as the production of public goods. The model developed throughout the book will argue that this is largely realistic, and that because of the characteristics of multidimensional politics, even the production of public goods can be reduced to distributive issues. The tax structure, which is frequently considered to be a tool for redistribution, is much less important than the character of government expenditures. To explore this idea further, the next chapter is devoted to an examination of the tax structure.

5 / Taxes and Redistribution

The model of democratic government developed in chapter 4 focused on the distributive aspects of government spending. Distributive issues will be important in democratic politics, even in the most idealistic of settings, if for no other reason than that all interested parties will want to make sure that they receive their fair share from the government. Beyond this, government policies are frequently designed specifically in order to redistribute income or wealth, and the rapid expansion of the welfare state in post–World War II democracies certainly is evidence that democratic governments, for one reason or another, have become increasingly interested in engaging in redistribution. The previous chapter has begun the examination of distributive spending policies of government, and that examination will be continued in chapter 6. Meanwhile, this chapter will examine the other side of the governmental redistribution issue: taxes. The tax system has long been viewed as a vehicle for redistribution, and this chapter will critically examine that role.

Redistributive policies, whether they involve taxes or spending, can be placed into two general categories. First, some policies are enacted for the specific purpose of altering the distribution of income, usually with the goal of making the income distribution more equal. Such policies might include progressive taxation, unemployment compensation, and welfare programs. Second, some policies are designed to provide benefits to specific groups of people, and while the goals of these programs are not specifically to alter the distribution of income, they do have the effect of making the recipient groups better off. Examples could be inland waterway programs, the location of military bases, and farm subsidies. It should be noted that the recipients of these special benefits may not all be in the same income group, so these programs may not have a large effect on the overall income distribution, but they do transfer resources from some individuals to others. Of course, there may be an overlap between these two types of policies. The food stamp program, for example, may be designed to raise the well-being of lower-income individuals but may also concentrate benefits in some urban areas, providing concentrated benefits to a well-defined political group. Still, the distinction is useful because in the first case policies are designed to have the general effect of altering the distribution of income, while the second case policies are intended to benefit specific well-defined groups of people.

This distinction is relevant because of the incentives built into the political process. Politicians, like businessmen, must consider their own interests when making decisions, and it is easy to understand why a politician would favor policies that would benefit special interests that could provide the politician with votes or campaign contributions. It is more difficult to understand why politicians would favor redistribution from rich to poor, unless the poor were considered to be an interest group. In this case, though, the rich would also be an interest group that would be harmed by the redistribution. A politican might have many more poor constituents than rich, in which case the straighforward interest group explanation would hold, and in general the distributive model in chapter 4 would seem to have some applicability. More income can be taken from the rich and given to the poor than vice versa, simply because the rich have more money. Income redistribution nominally on equity grounds might be just a manifestation of special interest policies if income classes are viewed as identifiable interest groups. Otherwise, policies designed to alter the distribution of income would be difficult to explain.

At this point, a general observation about distributive politics is in order. Most distributive policies are not tax policies but expenditure policies. True, the tax structure tends to be progressive,[1] but when changes in the government budget are advocated to aid lower-income individuals, a modification of the tax structure is usually not suggested. Instead, new expenditure programs are advocated. Later chapters will analyze the spending programs. This chapter will focus on the tax issue. Two basic avenues will be explored. First, there is a constitutional issue regarding the distribution of the tax burden, which will be discussed briefly. Second, a model of redistribution through taxation will be developed that will argue that the tax structure is not a good vehicle for the redistribution of income. This model explains the relatively heavy reliance on spending programs for redistributive purposes.

The basic line of reasoning in the model is as follows. Individuals who work for a wage bargain for posttax, rather than pretax, income. Therefore, an alteration of the tax structure will cause people to alter their wage demands accordingly. The incidence of taxation will depend upon the relative elasticities of the supply and demand for labor, and it will be argued that suppliers of labor will have a much more elastic response than is traditionally recognized. This is because workers can substitute into marginally more or less demanding jobs with correspondingly different pay scales. This substitution is generally not considered in the so-called optimal tax models that attempt to find a tax structure that optimally redistributes income. Taking this ability of workers into account, changes in the tax structure will mostly be felt by employers rather than employees. The main part of the chapter will develop this model, but first some constitutional issues regarding redistribution by taxation will be considered.

Constitutional Issues

The Constitution of the United States specifically says that taxes "shall be uniform throughout the United States" (art. 1, sec. 8), which may be taken as a constitutional mandate against using the tax structure as a redistributive device, and a constitutional amendment was required in order to initiate the federal income tax. Nevertheless, progressive income taxation is frequently considered to be a redistributional mechanism regardless of the intent of the Constitution. The so-called optimal tax literature in economics has been concerned with designing a tax structure in such a way that the optimal progressivity of the tax structure is found for redistributing income.[2] This literature has not been without its critics,[3] but the basic idea is that progressive taxation should be used to redistribute income to enhance the social welfare.

Progressive income taxation need not be couched in terms of enhancing one person's utility at the expense of another. Viewed within the social contract framework developed in chapter 2, it could easily be justified as an equalizing device unanimously approved behind a veil of ignorance. Not knowing where they might end up in the income distribution, individuals might agree to tax those at the high end of the income distribution in order to redistribute some income to those at the low end.[4] Thus, at a constitutional level, a progressive income tax might be justified independently of interest group politics. The progressive income tax might also be viewed as a collective agreement for charitable activity, where everybody agrees to redistribution if everybody else cooperates. In other words, every individual would be willing to redistribute from rich to poor if all others participate as well. The tax system is the method by which the agreement is enforced.[5]

The concept that links these ideas is that individuals are agreeing to be coerced. One might be suspicious of an argument of this type, especially when the agreement is some type of conceptual agreement, as behind the Rawlsian veil of ignorance, for example. Introspection allows one to see that it would be possible to agree to some arrangement only if others were bound to the agreement as well. However, a society that bases its social policies on the notion that the policies might have been approved behind a veil of ignorance is headed toward tyranny. The idea of agreement behind a veil of ignorance is useful as a tool for understanding why some social rules exist, but it is potentially dangerous as a criterion for developing social policy. In this case, it is useful to see how redistributional goals could include progressive taxation in a constitution for equity reasons.

Progressive taxation might also be justified on efficiency grounds. Over two hundred years ago, Adam Smith observed,

"The subjects of every state ought to contribute towards the support of the government, as nearly as possible, in proportion to their respective abilities; that is, in proportion to the revenue that they respectively enjoy under the protection of the state. The expense of government to the individuals of a great nation, is like the expense of management to the joint tenants of a great estate, who are all obliged to contribute in proportion to their respective interests in the state."[6] Here, Smith combines the notion of ability to pay with the efficiency notion of paying for government services that are rendered. Smith reasons that those who earn more income under the protection of the state should pay in proportion to the income protected—that is, the services they receive. This idea has been developed a step further by Earl Thompson, who argues that those who own wealth in a nation create an externality, since they make the nation more attractive for aggression by other nations.[7] Thompson views the nation's progressive tax structure as a Pigouvian tax to correct this externality. In this way, progressive taxes can be justified on efficiency grounds.

Progressive taxation, then, is not necessarily the result of interest group politics. On equity grounds, upper-income people may agree with progressive taxation because it provides some insurance in the event that they (or their heirs) become poor, or they may agree because of charitable grounds. On efficiency grounds, progressive taxation may be viewed as optimal because it is in effect a user fee which charges a higher price to those who benefit more from the government. For these reasons, progressive taxation might be viewed as a part of a social contract. The argument is not that progressive taxation would be a part of a social contract but that progressive taxation by itself is not evidence of interest group politics at work.

There are many ways that the tax structure could be altered in order to benefit specific interest groups, of which progressivity is only one. The most obvious alteration, given the geographic nature of representation, would be to lower tax rates in a specific geographic region. Other candidates would be to have different tax rates for different occupational groups, for different ages, or for different marital statuses. Some of these methods of differential taxation are used in the United States.

Alteration of tax rates by geographic region is the most obvious alteration given the political structure because elected representatives represent geographic regions. A politician could provide direct benefits to all of his constituents by providing lower tax rates to them, so one needs to explain why representatives will trade an inland waterway project in one state for an irrigation project in another, but it is never suggested that a state receive its political payment in the form of lower taxes.

One possible answer is the constitutional prohibition, but this answer may not be satisfying to those who view many current government actions as outside the bounds of the Constitution. The Constitution in this case might refer to the U.S. Constitution or, more generally, to a social contract, but in either case, the theory from chapter 2 would lead one to expect for the terms of the social contract to erode over time. Another possible answer is that all representatives would see the potential of entering an endless zero-sum game of the type described in the previous chapter if tax shares were to be altered from state to state. The model of the last chapter would predict that rather than enter a game where winners in this period could expect to lose in the next, all participants would agree to equal rates of tax across geographic lines. Following this line of reasoning, taxing and spending would be viewed as two separate games rather than as a part of the same game. Another possible answer is that the benefits from tax cuts are smaller than the benefits from transfers, so that the distributive process relies more on the spending side than on the taxing side of the equation. Of course, there may be an element of truth in each of these explanations. The line of analysis that will be followed here will be to explore the effects of taxation for the purposes of redistribution in order to provide some answers about who might favor it, and for what purposes.

Optimal Taxation

There is an existing body of literature dealing with the role of the tax structure in redistributing income: the "optimal tax" literature. This literature, initiated by an article by Diamond and Mirrless in 1971,[8] follows the general method of trying to use the tax structure to maximize social welfare, as defined by some social welfare function. Typically, the optimal tax policy in this paradigm is a set of lump sum taxes that produces an absolutely equal distribution of income. Since lump-sum taxes are not feasible, some type of income tax is used in order to produce a "second best" solution that maximizes social welfare given the prohibition of lump-sum taxation.[9] The resulting optimal tax system typically does not leave the income distribution absolutely equal because of the disincentive effects of high marginal income tax rates.[10] Due to the disincentive effects, lower marginal tax rates increase the income of upper-income individuals enough so that the enhancement of social welfare more than offsets the negative effects of a less equal income distribution.[11]

The optimal tax literature is subject to criticism on a number of fronts. First, the tax system might be viewed within the fiscal exchange paradigm as the method by which citizens make payments for the government's services, in which case many of the second-best questions about the system are altered because the purpose of taxation is viewed differently.[12] Second, the moral implications of a tax system based on a social welfare function with interpersonal utility comparisons must be closely examined. Whenever the social welfare can be enhanced by making one person's utility increase and another's decrease, the tax system that maximizes social welfare in essence makes the second type of person a slave of the first. For example, if all leisure counts equally in the social welfare function, but some individuals are more productive than others, social welfare will be maximized when the most productive people spend most of their time working to provide goods and services (and leisure time) to the least productive.[13] Tax policies which give some individuals the right to consume the income of others must always be carefully examined on moral grounds. These lines of criticism examine the normative aspects of tax policy, but there are positive issues regarding redistribution through taxation as well.

In particular, the models of optimal taxation generally consider taxation to be purely redistributive, making lump-sum taxes optimal. Note that in the fiscal exchange paradigm, lump-sum taxes are not optimal, since the marginal tax price should equal the marginal cost of the government output.[14] The reason why the optimal tax models must settle for a second-best solution is that when taxes have only a redistributive function, the disincentive effects from taxation induce a welfare cost of taxation as individuals alter their behavior to avoid taxation. The presumably optimal results from the optimal tax paradigm arise by balancing the distributive benefits and the welfare costs of taxation. However, in the very elementary models of taxation used in that literature, there is good reason to believe that the ability of income earners to avoid the burden of taxation is greatly understated (and that as a result the welfare cost of taxation is also understated). In the sections that follow, a model will be developed to explain why taxation is generally unable to perform the redistributive function that is the object of so-called optimal taxation. In 1890, Alfred Marshall observed that "It has now become certain that the problem of distribution is much more difficult than it was thought to be . . . and that no solution of it which claims to be simple can be true."[15] Marshall's observation is as accurate today as it was a century ago, and the idea that the distribution of income can be altered by taxing some and giving the proceeds to others is generally not true.

Income and Work Effort

In optimal tax models, the pretax distribution of income either is exogenously given or is determined by the marginal products of the factors of production under an individual's control. While income distribution theory has been based on the marginal products of factors of production since the time of Ricardo,[16] an important difference between the literature on income distribution and the optimal tax literature is that the income distribution literature has examined the determinants of the marginal products of factors of production, while the optimal tax literature has assumed marginal products to be given and constant.[17] The assumption that the marginal products of the factors of production are given has the effect of overstating the amount of income that can be transferred through the tax structure.

Worker choice in economics is usually modeled in economics by assuming that a worker with a given marginal product faces a trade-off between work and leisure. The worker's marginal product could be changed by circumstances outside of the individual's control, such as changes in the capital/labor ratio, and the worker's compensation for a given amount of work might be affected by tax rates, but in general, given a worker's environment, the only choice that a worker is given in an economic model is how much leisure to give up in exchange for work. This observation is certainly applicable to the optimal tax literature. Workers with a given marginal product choose how many hours to work, and the welfare loss of taxation arises because individuals choose to work less.

In fact, workers almost never face this choice. Jobs that individuals accept frequently specify the hours that an individual is expected to work, so individuals do not in general have the option of varying work hours in exchange for a proportional change in income. Other characteristics of the job will also be specified, and the worker's choice is either to accept one job, with given hours, duties, and expectations of output, or to look for another job with different characteristics. When deciding whether to work more for more pay, the worker's trade-off is not in actuality to work more hours for more pay but whether to take another job that is more demanding but pays more also. A more demanding job, in this sense, is a job that pays more but on net is less agreeable in its other aspects. When examining an individual's employment opportunities, the only way that an individual could receive a higher income would be to take a job that is more disagreeable in its other aspects. Otherwise, the individual would have already taken the job because it both paid more and was more agreeable in its other aspects. In other words, for an individual, higher pay can only come with a more demanding job. Conversely, the only way that an individual can find a job more agreeable in its other aspects is to take one that pays less. A less demanding job comes only with lower pay. Thus, the worker's choice is more accurately portrayed as one between higher pay and a more demanding job rather than the commonly assumed work-leisure trade-off.

The reason why this distinction is important is that in the usual model, worker output is homogeneous, so that one worker's output is a perfect substitute for the output of any other worker. Marginal products may differ among workers, but in the usual model this simply means that different workers have different abilities to produce a homogeneous labor output. When examining the more realistic trade-off that workers face, more demanding jobs will be likely to produce outputs that are qualitatively different from the outputs of less demanding jobs, so the worker will be choosing among jobs that produce complementary outputs rather than substitutes.

Looking at an individual worker, the worker chooses a job that optimizes the trade-off between the wage and the demands of the job. The worker's disposable income will be that wage less the taxes the worker must pay. The worker's tax bill will be a function of the wage, tax rates, and any deductions for which the worker is eligible. Examining the worker's individual choice, the disincentive effects of taxes take on a different characteristic in this description of the problem compared to the usual characterization. In the usual formulation of the problem, the result of higher taxation is that the worker produces less homogeneous labor output, but within the current framework, higher tax rates—holding gross wages equal—cause workers to move from more demanding to less demanding jobs. For example, some coal miners will choose to become residential housing construction workers. This process causes the qualitative characteristics of the output mix to change as workers desire to migrate into different occupations.

The problem with the standard income redistribution models is that they characterize worker choice in far too simple a framework. The next sections use the more complex framework depicted here to describe the results of attempts at using the tax structure to redistribute income.

Redistribution by Geographic Region

Earlier, it was suggested that the most natural way to redistribute income through the political process is by geographic region. This is because representatives are elected to represent geographic areas, so they enhance their chances of reelection by providing benefits to the constituents of their geographic area. With regard to the tax structure, this would imply that representatives have an incentive to seek special interest tax cuts aimed at their constituents, much as they have the incentive to seek special interest benefits in expenditure programs that are targeted specifically to their constituents. A number of constitutional reasons were suggested to explain why representatives may not seek special interest tax cuts even though they seek special interest spending programs. While these reasons may have much explanatory power, they will be set aside for the time being to examine within a simple framework the results that could be expected from charging differential tax rates in different areas. The assumption throughout is made that changes in tax rates do not imply different levels of government service. Of course some individuals could desire higher taxes if a higher level of government services were implied.

Consider the very simple example where there are many states composing a nation, competitive labor markets in each state, and where it is costless to move from one state to another. The states have the same federal income tax rates and are identical in all other respects as well. From this initial situation, a representative from one state is able to lower federal income tax rates in that state relative to all other states. Initially, this will provide more disposable income to those residents of the low-tax state, discouraging people from moving to other states and encouraging residents of other states to migrate to the low state. The resulting increase in the supply of labor in the low-tax state would reduce wages in that state, and labor would continue its migration until the after-tax wages were the same in all states. After all, it is the after-tax income that workers value, rather than pretax income, and in this simple example, it is apparent that labor migration will equal the after-tax wage roles.

While it is true that labor migration is not costless, this should not impede the eventual result of after-tax wage equalization in a country as mobile as the United States. Such equalization may not occur because of climatological or other differences, of course, but such differences would be included in a broader definition of income. Also note that the result would not apply to higher or lower state taxes when revenues are spent in the state. Some people prefer more (or less) public services, which would be a factor similar to climate in determining location in the real world. One caveat is in order: the low-tax state would benefit from a lower excess burden of taxation, and so for this reason would enjoy real benefits from lower tax rates. However, the reduction in tax rates would be shifted to factors like land that could not migrate to the lower-tax state.

Consider another similar example. This time, two adjoining states are identical in every way, and both have proportional income taxes used to finance public expenditures. Now, with no change in one state, the other state replaces its proportional income tax with a progressive tax designed to raise the same amount of revenue. Before any labor migration, the disposable income of high-income people in the proportional tax state will be higher than the disposable income of high-income people in the progressive tax state, with the converse being true for low-income people. This change in disposable income will cause the migration of high-income people from the progressive tax state and low-income people to the progressive tax state. The migration will continue until the disposable incomes of the two states are the same, which returns the labor market to equilibrium.

In both of the models analyzed in this section, an individual performing the same job in either state would receive the same after-tax income. The reason is that labor is perfectly mobile as the example is constructed, and so has a perfectly elastic supply in both states. The standard tax shifting model applies here, and the entire burden of the tax is shifted to factors that are not mobile across state lines. As was earlier mentioned, the degree of labor mobility in the United States probably makes this model a reasonable description of reality, so that differential tax rates across states would not have the ability to redistribute much income. If politicians have an intuitive feel for this conclusion, they would prefer direct transfers to individuals rather than changes in tax rates, if transfers are easier to directly appropriate than tax changes. Arguments about why this may be the case will be given at the end of the chapter.

A real effect of differential tax rates that will remain in a state is the excess burden of higher, or more progressive, taxes in a state. If little migration is needed to equalize wage rates, then the excess burden of higher or more progressive taxes will be small, but in any case workers, who are mobile, will have to be compensated for the excess burden as well, so that ultimately the burden of taxation is paid by immobile factors of production.

The conclusion of this section is that it does not benefit a state very much to have a differentially lower tax rate. Workers care about their after-tax wages rather than before-tax wages, so any reduction in tax rates in one area, with no changes in government services, will cause workers to migrate into the area so that wage rates will be equalized. The same would be true for other factors: their rates of return would either be equalized by inward migration, or, in the case of fixed factors, price changes would equalize rates of return. While it is true that fixed factors would realize an immediate capital gain from lower tax rates, the owners of fixed factors apparently do not have the political power to persuade politicians to produce geographic tax benefits rather than geographic expenditure programs that can be more generally shared. In any event, the main point of this section is that tax rates that differ among geographic regions do little if anything to redistribute incomes. This may go a long way toward explaining why representatives do little to attempt to lower taxes for their constituents.

Progressive Federal Taxation

Geographic mobility across the national boundaries is not nearly as great as across state boundaries, so the argument of the last section at first does not appear to generalize to the progressive federal income tax. Making federal income taxes more progressive is not likely to induce much migration to other nations. However, the argument is more general than it first appears. The argument that changes in the tax structure would be met by offsetting changes in the pretax wage structure, leaving the disposable incomes of individuals unchanged, was the result of assumptions that caused labor supply for particular jobs to be infinitely elastic. This would be the case if, as in the last section, jobs that were close substitutes existed, so that laborers could take those jobs. Note that the aggregate labor supply in the examples could have been perfectly inelastic, and yet the supply of labor for specific occupations can be very elastic as laborers shift from one job within the labor force. Economists should have little problem with this conceptualization; others might want to consider the demand for food as an analogy. The demand for food is likely to be very inelastic. Huge changes in the price for food would probably have little effect on the total amount of food demanded. However, for any individual food item, an increase in its price would reduce the amount demanded as people switch to other types of food. Likewise, a general income tax increase may have little effect on aggregate labor supply, but a tax increase on some types of labor relative to others will induce substitution into the lower-taxed occupations. This was what induced labor migration in the last section.

Now consider the effects of increasing the progressivity of the income tax. Assume that there is a continuous array of job opportunities for each individual, so that the individual has the opportunity to take a less demanding job for lower pay or a more demanding job for more pay. In this case, migration will occur, as in the model in the last section, but instead of the migration occurring across geographic boundaries, it will occur across job types, as higher-income people move into less demanding jobs and lower-income people move into more demanding jobs. Seen in this light, the supply of labor for any given occupation will be perfectly elastic, as every worker has the ability to shift to a marginally different job for a marginally different wage. The demand for labor will not be perfectly elastic, however, because, as noted above, labor does not produce a homogeneous output. The labor output of some workers is complementary with others, meaning that a mix of different types of labor is needed to produce output. The well-known tax shifting result applies here, and the entire burden of a change in the income tax structure will be shifted away from workers.[18] It is not possible to use tax policy to alter the distribution of disposable incomes among occupations.[19] A change in the tax structure will cause people to move from more highly taxed occupations to less highly taxed occupations until the net reduction in disposable income will be only that attributable to the deadweight loss of labor migration from more productive to less productive jobs. The potential for individuals to migrate into less demanding occupations implies that a more progressive tax structure has a minimal ability to redistribute income.

The major difference between this model and other models that evaluate the effect of taxes on the distribution of income is that this model allows for a wider and more realistic array of job opportunities for labor. Workers in different jobs produce complementary, rather than substitutable, output, and workers have a wide array of possible jobs that they could accept. This leads to the result that an alteration of the tax structure will not alter the after-tax income of any occupation, because workers will be compensated by offsetting changes in pretax income. The nominal distribution of income will show fewer high-income people and more low-income people when taxes become more progressive, as a result of workers migrating into lower-income occupations, and when deadweight losses are significant, all occupations will receive lower incomes as a result of the deadweight loss. There is no reason to expect that an increase in progressivity would have any effect on the variance of the distribution of income, even though it will lower the output of the economy as a result of the deadweight loss of the tax.

A straightforward implication of this conclusion is that an increase in tax deductions to a particular employment group (e.g., business lunches) will not affect the disposable income of that group. The effect on the tax bill would be favorable, but the increase in income would entice others into those occupations until the gross wage of the occupation due to the additional workers just offsets the lower tax burden. Once again, though, a deadweight loss would arise if resources had to be invested to take advantage of the deductions.

The conclusion that changes in the tax structure will not affect the disposable incomes of individuals will be generally true, but there are some nontrivial exceptions. Deductions that do not apply equally to specific occupational groups would have the ability to affect the disposable incomes of the affected individuals so that, for example, under current tax laws individuals with more children will have higher disposable incomes than those with fewer children, all other things held equal, and individuals with high medical expenses will have higher incomes than those with equally large automobile repair bills. Within the context of this model, direct transfers to individuals might be viewed in the same way as deductions. If they accrue to specific employment groups, lower salaries would leave the disposable incomes of the recipients unchanged. However, general transfers that are not associated with specific occupations will increase the disposable incomes of the recipients.

There is another important exception to the conclusion that the tax structure will not alter the disposable incomes of individuals in specific occupations. A person who does not have the possibility of shifting to other similar lines of work would be earning economic rents in an occupation, and these rents could be taxed away. An increase in the progressivity of tax rates could cause an increase in the person's tax bill, but no offsetting increase in wages would be necessary to keep the person in the same job. Thus, an increase in the progressivity of taxes could have the ability to flatten the distribution of income by taxing away rents.

These rents generally could be expected to be accruing to some form of human or nonhuman capital. An unanticipated increase in the progressivity of tax rates could tax away any of the returns that an individual might receive from investment in accruing some specialized talents, abilities, or knowledge valuable only to a certain firm. Such a change in the tax structure would also cause a capital loss to the holder of income-producing real capital or land. Thus, in the short run, rents accruing to job-specific human and nonhuman capital could be taxed away. In the long run, even this could not be taxed away, because individuals would reduce their investment in human and nonhuman capital in response to changes in tax rates. It follows that if there is uncertainty regarding the future tax structure, individuals will be reluctant to invest in job-specific capital that could be taxed away, since the key to being able to shift taxes initially placed on an individual is the ability to move to alternate occupations. Thus, while rents can be taxed away in the short run, the long-run conclusion still holds that the tax system cannot redistribute income, and that in the long run only the deadweight loss remains.

The general conclusion of this line of reasoning is that it is not possible to alter the distribution of income using the tax structure. The income demanded by workers is after-tax income, and any changes in the general tax structure will be offset by changes in before tax wage rates, leaving after tax wages unaffected. There are some exceptions to this; rents could be temporarily taxed away, and tax breaks essentially unrelated to the occupation of the taxpayer could have an effect. One would expect, therefore, to see political lobbying for specific tax loopholes rather than for general changes in the tax structure, and this appears to be the case. The earlier part of this chapter gave several reasons why politicians tend to produce expenditure benefits, rather than tax cuts, for their constituents. The argument in this section is another reason: changes in the tax structure will ultimately have a negligible effect on the income distribution.

Empirical Evidence

The theory just developed arrives at some conclusions quite different from much of the typical income distribution literature in economics, largely because of the way in which worker choice has been modeled. The modeling procedure seems to be more realistic, lending some credibility to the theoretical results, but the question arises as to how the theory compares with reality. In summary, real-world evidence seems to be consistent with the theory, but a truly thorough examination would require another book. Along these lines, it is worthwhile noting that Reynolds and Smolensky have written a book on the subject,[20] and their evidence does support the model in this chapter. Their evidence is more persuasive because they do not develop a theoretical framework as is done above, and so do not have an interest in supporting a particular theory.[21] They simply examine the income distribution to see how it has changed.

Reynolds and Smolensky examine prefisc and postfisc distributions of income in 1950, 1961, and 1970 and conclude that although the government redistributes a great deal of income, this has not tended to alter the postfisc distribution of income over the twenty years they examine. Prefisc income is income before taxes and government spending, and the years they examined showed a significant increase in tax progressivity. While one might expect a more equal postfisc distribution of income, they do not find it. Reynolds and Smolensky note (p. 77), "Our empirical analysis has shown that inclusion of all government

TABLE 5.1 THE PERCENTAGE OF TOTAL INCOME RECEIVED BY EACH
QUINTILE OF FAMILIES IN THE U.S.

Year	Lowest Fifth	Second Fifth	Middle Fifth	Fourth Fifth	Highest Fifth
1950	4.5	12.0	17.4	23.4	42.7
1960	4.8	12.2	17.8	24.0	41.3
1970	5.4	12.2	17.6	23.8	40.9
1980	5.1	11.6	17.5	24.3	41.6

Source: Bureau of the Census, *Current Population Reports*

spending and taxation in household incomes significantly reduces effective income differences among income classes in
each year but that dispersion in these post-fisc income distributions has not changed significantly between 1950 and 1970."
Reynolds and Smolensky refer to this finding as a puzzle, but a
possible explanation is the model presented in this chapter. As
a result of changes in the tax structure, pretax incomes have
adjusted so that, postfisc, the distribution of income remains
stable.[22]

While this evidence is not conclusive proof by itself, it supports the model in this chapter. As was earlier mentioned, a
thorough examination of the material in this chapter would fill
another book, but it is worthwhile to look at some of the statistics
regarding the actual distribution of income in the United States
before moving on. Table 5.1 shows the distribution of income by
quintiles in the United States for four years. Each entry in the
table shows the percentage of total income going to families in a
given quintile in a given year. For example, in 1950, the lowest
fifth of families received 4.5 percent of total income in that year,
while the highest fifth received 42.7 percent. Income here includes not only earned income but income from all sources, so
that, for example, transfers are included in the figures. The first
characteristic that strikes one when examining the data is that
the percentage of income going to each quintile appears remark-
ably stable. This is somewhat remarkable due to the large increase in government transfers that occurred during the period,
if for no other reason. Table 5.2 lists average transfer payments

TABLE 5.2   INCOME FROM PUBLIC ASSISTANCE AND WELFARE
PAYMENTS: SELECTED INCOME GROUPS, 1980

Income Class ($)	Public Payments ($)	Percent
Under 2,500	1,432	57
2,500–4,999	2,937	78
5,000–7,499	3,631	58
7,500–9,999	3,412	39
10,000–12,499	3,514	31
12,500–14,999	2,821	21

Source: Bureau of the Census, *Current Population Reports*

to families in various income classes for 1980. The percentage column shows transfers as a percent of the middle income of the category (e.g., $3,750 for the $2,500–$4,999 category), except for the $2,500 category, where $1,432 is 57 percent of $2,500. What table 5.2 shows is that public assistance and welfare payments compose a major portion of the income of low-income families.

Table 5.2 implies that a substantial portion of the income of the lower groups comes from transfers, but these transfers have done nothing perceptible to increase the percentage of income going to the lowest group of families by income. In fact, from 1970 to 1980, the percentages of income going to the lowest and second fifths have fallen by about 5 percent. At the other end of the scale, the percent of income going to the two highest fifths increased, although this may have been offset by changes in the tax structure. Table 5.3 shows evidence that more directly supports the type of theory discussed earlier in this chapter. Progressive taxes have been used increasingly in an attempt to engineer redistributive policies, but table 5.3 shows that with similar median incomes, the percentage of families with incomes under $5,000 increased from 1970 to 1980, and the percentage of families with incomes over $50,000 increased as well. These changes are consistent with the theory of this chapter. The adjustment may be continuing, because in 1981, despite a decline in the median income to below the 1970 level, the percentage of

TABLE 5.3 PERCENT OF FAMILIES WITH HIGH AND LOW INCOMES,
1981 DOLLARS

	Under $5,000	Over $50,000	Median Income
1970	5.2	7.5	$23,111
1980	5.6	8.9	$23,204
1981	5.8	9.1	$22,388

Source: *Statistical Abstract of the United States*

families with incomes above $50,000 continued to increase. Apparently, the tax structure has not been successful at equalizing the income distribution.

In Henry Hazlitt's book *Economics in One Lesson*,[23] the one lesson is to look for the secondary effects of policy changes. Attempting to alter the distribution of income by altering the progressivity of the tax structure appears to be a case where that lesson forcefully applies. The evidence examined here is consistent with the earlier theory which illustrated that changes in the tax structure will be met by offsetting changes in gross incomes, so that the structure will be an ineffective tool for income redistribution. Certainly, more evidence on the subject would be welcome, but there is good reason to suspect that the tax structure is an ineffective redistributive device.

Conclusion

The theoretical model developed in this chapter suggests that the tax structure will not be an effective tool for redistribution. This is the case when looking at progressivity as a method of redistribution from rich to poor, and it is also the case when looking at the more politically obvious possibility of redistribution to an area by lowering its tax rate. The reason is that the incomes that individuals demand are after-tax incomes, so any change in the tax structure will be met with an offsetting change in wages. Changes in the tax structure will ultimately affect only fixed factors of production. This may go a long way toward explaining why the political process typically uses spending programs rather than tax cuts as a method of distribution. The spending programs tend to be more effective redistributive vehicles. This theory would go on to predict that when special tax cuts are granted, they will be granted with the fixed factors of production in mind. Typically, fixed factors will be represented by relatively small numbers of wealthy voters, but when large numbers of voters have a stake in a fixed factor of production, it may be politically expedient to grant the fixed factor a tax cut rather than a spending program. This may explain the existence of enterprise zones in urban areas as the rare exception to the general rule that geographic tax cuts are not granted. The residents of a city all may feel that they have a stake in the city as a fixed factor. Enterprise zones also illustrate that tax cuts to particular geographic areas are possible in the present political system.

It is worth noting at this point another factor that may prevent taxes from being used as a distributive tool: interest groups are not generally organized by income class, so that there is no special interest group that specifically lobbies to benefit rich or poor people. Wealthy individuals will generally do better by lobbying for special benefits aimed at the industry at which they make their living rather than using political capital to lobby for tax cuts that will be shared by all high-income earners. There are more organizations that more directly represent low-income individuals as a class, but here tax cuts cannot produce large benefits because low-income people do not have large tax bills. Once again, lobbying for special interest spending programs shows more potential than lobbying for tax cuts.

One should also note that tax write-offs and other favorable tax treatment ultimately benefit high-income earners, because they are in high tax brackets. For example, favorable tax treatment for farms may be intended to help low-income farmers, but these tax breaks are worth more to the wealthy, who will tend to buy farms for their tax benefits. A tax break is worth twice as much to someone in the 50 percent tax bracket than it is to someone in the 25 percent tax bracket, for example; so anything receiving favorable tax treatment will be worth more to a person in a higher tax bracket. However, since higher-income individuals generally do not organize politically along income lines, political capital is more likely to be spent to acquire special benefits to particular industries rather than income classes.

Since spending programs are more easily targeted, special interest spending is more likely to be sought than tax cuts.

Another factor which may play a major role in making increased spending more feasible than tax cuts in the political system is that the government itself may act as an interest group.[24] Tax cuts constrain government spending, whereas additional spending programs expand the public sector. When the threat is made to reduce some public sector service, the providers of that service, whose jobs will be at stake, can be expected to campaign against the reduction, but an expansion of the public sector will benefit those who work in that area of the public sector in addition to the direct recipients of the benefits. Thus, when the interest group activities of the government itself is considered, there is another reason to expect that spending increases will dominate tax cuts as distributional tools.

This chapter has given a number of reasons why, in general, taxes are not used as a redistributive device, ranging from constitutional and contractarian reasons to reasons regarding their effectiveness. The fact is that changes in the tax structure are relatively infrequent when compared to changes in government benefit programs, and this fact begs for an explanation, especially since tax cuts provide a dollar in direct benefits for each dollar cut, whereas the same is not likely to be true for spending programs. That is, it probably costs more than a dollar to provide a dollar's worth of utility through most spending programs. Of course, one way to increase the efficiency of spending programs in this sense is to hand out more cash and less in-kind benefits, and politicians seem to have discovered this as the government tends to be more redistributive. Nevertheless, it is interesting to note that redistribution tends to take place via spending programs rather than through tax cuts.

In chapter 4, distributive government was modeled as essentially two separate processes. First, taxes were collected and placed into a general fund, and then representatives decided how the money in the general fund was to be distributed. This chapter has provided some justification for separating the taxing and spending decisions, since taxation will play a relatively minor role in redistribution. Taxes are merely the source of revenue from which distributive programs are funded. Chapter

6 will continue the development of the model along these lines. The model will be expanded so that a representative body will determine the level of funding going to various special interest programs, but following the suggestion of this chapter, taxation will be involved in the distributive model only to the extent that the total cost of all government programs will equal the aggregate tax bill.

6 / Distributive Government

The preceding chapters have built a framework within which governmental activity can be analyzed. The role of this chapter is to extend that framework and to develop a simple model of distributive government. The model will be developed using economic theory and will be explained in economic terms. This is not meant to imply that the model only applies to strictly economic activities of government but, rather, that governmental activities can in general be analyzed in economic terms. Representative bodies typically make their decisions by majority rule, and in representative bodies, vote trading and logrolling are commonly used methods of generating enough votes to produce a majority. These exchanges are economic activity and can be beneficially analyzed using economic methods. This chapter will use economic methods to develop a model of distributive government and to argue that governmental activity in general can be viewed as purely distributive.

Analysts of government have characterized governmental activities in many ways, ranging from wealth or power maximization to the provision of public goods and services. At one level, the analyst can examine what the government ought to do and can come up with a list that may range from the protection of individual rights to producing those public goods and services that are desirable, but that will not be produced in the private sector because of incentive problems. However, if incentive problems exist in the private sector, they surely exist in the public sector as well, and any realistic appraisal of what the government should do must first start with an appraisal of the structure of governmental decision making to see what the government can do. Because of the organization and incentive structure of representative government, the incentive structure is biased against the production of output that is in the general public interest—and toward special interest legislation. This is due to the very nature of majority rule.

The basic argument is as follows. Legislators must pass legislation that benefits their constituents in order to be reelected. In general, special interest legislation will benefit the legislator's constituents more than public interest legislation, because the benefits of special interest legislation can be concentrated on the legislator's constituents. Thus, all legislators will work toward providing special interest legislation to their constituents, and any benefits to the general public would occur only as an accidental by-product of special interest legislation. In order to get this legislation passed, since it is aimed at benefiting a special interest, each legislator will have to trade votes with other legislators to form a majority. As discussed in chapter 4, the cycle problem will be avoided by providing something for everybody, thus producing a government that caters to a group of special interests rather than to the general public interest. In the process, a package of legislation is produced that is much larger than would be optimal, and has an undesirable mix as well.

This characterization suggests the possibility of gains from trade, and indeed the possibility exists. There is a problem in realizing the possibility, however, because each individual legislator is in a prisoners' dilemma-type situation. The legislator's choice is either to remain in the majority coalition and to continue to produce special benefits for the special interests that can aid reelection or to leave the majority coalition and to lose the special interest legislation. Each legislator is better off in than out of the coalition, even though there are allocations that are Pareto superior to the coalition's. This prisoners' dilemma will be examined in detail in this chapter, after a brief review of the theoretical framework in which it takes place.

Chapter 2 provides the basic foundation for this framework, because it illustrates that a society could voluntarily choose democratic political institutions. This is significant because the implication is that if some of the aspects of democracy lead to nonoptimal results, this does not imply that the citizens of a democracy are being taken advantage of by institutions forced upon them. It is easily conceivable that a tyrannical government could impose a government on people that is not in the best interest of the governed, but the model developed here demonstrates that a governmental arrangement freely chosen by its citizens can still lead to nonoptimal resource allocation. The purpose of the material developed in chapter 2 is to distinguish democratic government from a set of political institutions forced upon the governed.

Chapters 3 and 4 examined the median voter model in some detail. In an attempt to develop a model of political structure, majority rule decision making was divided into two basic categories: single-dimensional issues and multidimensional issues. In single-dimensioned issues, the median voter's preference will tend to be selected by majority rule. When issues are multidimensional, however, the problem of cycles will threaten to destabilize the political process. Some type of institutional constraint can eliminate the cyclical behavior, and the constraint of universalism, which realistically is a part of the political process, serves the purpose. Rather than being formally imposed on the decision-making structure, universalism is an informal agreement that the democratic government will divide its benefits among all members. This way, instead of having unstable majorities that exploit minorities, political decisions tend to be stable overtime. Universalism provides each member of the coalition with the same average expected benefits over time and minimizes the variance of the benefits as well. Chapter 5 suggested that political benefits will tend to be disbursed as spending programs rather than tax cuts, so up to this point representative democracy has been characterized as a group of elected representatives who decide how the taxes that the government has collected should be distributed among various spending programs. Universalism is the guiding principle in making the determination.

This chapter will extend this model of government by arguing that the incentive structure faced by elected representatives makes representative democracy essentially a distributive government. The general argument was presented at the beginning of the chapter. The argument will be examined in more detail, first by comparing some basic public choice models within a unified framework.

Some Basic Public Choice Models

The generality of majority rule models is sometimes obscured by the fact that different writers have presented information on individual preferences in different formats. For example, the cyclical majority is typically illustrated using the rank order of individual preferences, while the median voter model is illustrated with preferences along a single-dimensioned continuum. It would aid clarity if the models were presented in a unified framework. With this in mind, this section will develop a complete three-dimensional preference map for three individuals to use as a unifying device. The purpose is to try to illustrate the general applicability of different models and to enable the reader to visualize a general system of preferences underlying many different majority rule models. Later in the chapter the model will be expanded to more than three dimensions, but the three-dimensional model will still be a useful tool for visualizing the model.

The model ultimately is intended to depict the majority rule decisions of a representative body in a representative democracy. The preferences of representatives A, B, and C for governmentally produced goods X, Y, and Z are represented in the three-dimensional picture in figure 6.1. The points A, B, and C show the most preferred levels of output for those individuals for the three goods X, Y, Z. Each unit of a good is assumed to cost $1, so that the quantity axes also measure the number of dollars spent on each program. Thus, for example, representative A would most prefer to see $3 spent on X, $2 spent on Y, and $1 spent on Z. The representatives are assumed to have

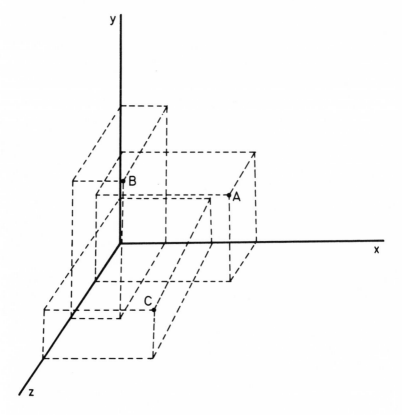

Fig. 6.1   A three-dimensional preference map

spherical indifference curves around their most preferred points, so that when mapped in three-space, preferences are single peaked. An additional assumption will be that individuals rank-order the goods in the same order as the number of dollars they want to spend on each program.

Many existing majority rule models can be analyzed as subsets of this general framework. For example, a rank-ordering of the individual preferences in figure 6.1 is shown in table 6.1. Inspection of table 6.1 reveals that these preferences would produce a cyclical majority in a series of pairwise majority rule elections, where X would beat Y, Z would beat X, and Y would beat

TABLE 6.1   RANK-ORDERING
OF INDIVIDUAL PREFERENCES

A	B	C
X	Y	Z
Y	Z	X
Z	X	Y

Z. This is the cyclical majority exactly as depicted by Arrow.[1] If only a single issue were to be considered—how much to spend on good Z, for example—the preferences could be mapped into a single dimension as in figure 6.2, and the median voter model of political competition could be used to determine that representative B's most preferred level of Z would be produced under majority rule, as argued by Bowen, Black, and Downs.[2] The model in two dimensions is shown in figure 6.3, which is equivalent to the model analyzed extensively in chapter 4, and depicted in figures 4.1, 4.2, and 4.3. Thus, the general pattern of preferences illustrated in figure 6.1 can be used as a framework for analyzing many different majority rule models, ranging from the cyclical majority to the median voter model.

This observation in itself emphasizes that figure 6.1 represents only individual preferences and does not contain an institutional structure that will produce a majority rule outcome. Given the preferences in figure 6.1, the simple statement that an outcome will be chosen by majority rule is not sufficient to deduce what the majority will agree upon. More information is needed about the institutional structure. If one of the three programs will be chosen in pairwise competition by majority rule, then a cyclical majority will occur, in which case more information is needed to know at what point the cycle will stop, and which program will be chosen. If any point in the issue space can be paired against any other in pairwise competition, then any point in the issue space is a possible outcome.[3] If each program is to be considered individually, then the median voter model may apply, but even here, the possibility of agenda control may produce an outcome larger than the median voter's preference,[4] or the possibility of logrolling may cause the three individual issues

Fig. 6.2   Preferences from figure 6.1 mapped into one
dimension

to be viewed as a single multidimensional issue by the voters.[5]
The point is that the knowledge of preferences above is not
sufficient to deduce the outcome under majority rule decision
making. Much more about the particular majority rule institutions needs to be specified.

Here, one might pause to reflect on the fact that in market
exchange, where individuals make trades only when they believe
exchanges to further their own self-interests, a simple institutional specification is enough to provide powerful insights. In
majority rule politics, a more complete specification is required
because on all except unanimously agreed-upon issues a majority selects an outcome not in the best interest of the minority.[6] In
this light, the study of democratic institutions might be viewed as
the study of the extent to which the majority can exploit the
minority, and whether the minority has any power to participate
in producing an outcome it likes any better than the majority's
most preferred outcome. Even in the relatively benign median
voter model, only the median voter gets his most preferred outcome, but the institutional structure in that model is such that
the individuals on both sides of the median determine the identity of the median voter, so all voters have an impact on the final
outcome. In market exchange, and with a political rule of unanimity, much less needs to be said about the institutional structure in order to identify characteristics of the outcome, when
contrasted to majority rule.

Even with preferences carefully specified, as in figure 6.1,
the majority rule outcome requires a carefully specified institutional structure as well. One possible specification would be a
simple extension of the median voter model to three dimensions. Consider the case where each good is considered sequentially, arriving at the median voter's preference each time. Figure 6.2 clearly shows that B's most preferred level of Z would be

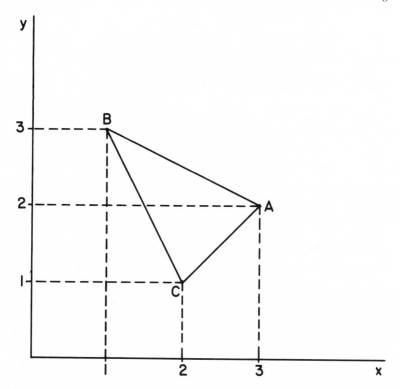

Fig. 6.3   Preferences from figure 6.1 mapped into two
dimensions

produced, and from figure 6.1, C's most preferred output of X
and A's most preferred output of Y would be produced as well.
The X and Y dimensions can be more clearly seen in the two-dimensional representation in X-Y space of figure 6.3. This median voter outcome is probably very descriptive of the way in
which the levels of output would be determined in a large number setting of direct democracy, where issues could remain truly
independent of one another.

As discussed at the beginning of chapter 4, independence
here does not refer to whether the goods are complements or
substitutes so that the order in which the goods are voted on

could matter.[7] Independence here refers to issues that are decided sequentially, one at a time, rather than simultaneously. Even though issues may be determined sequentially in time, the outcomes could be simultaneously determined if logrolling and vote trading could occur within issues. In general referendum voting, three things tend to preserve the sequential nature of voting that are not present in the majority rule decisions made by elected representatives. First, referenda typically occur infrequently, making one referendum independent of others. Second, large numbers of individuals vote on each issue, making transactions costs very high for potential vote trading. Third, and most important, secret ballots are used, making a vote trade impossible to enforce because traders cannot offer proof that they voted as promised in a trade. None of these three conditions is satisfied regarding the majority rule decisions of representative bodies, so that when the voters are elected representatives, the issues will tend to have the characteristics of a multidimensional political issue, even if the issues are to be considered sequentially in time. Thus, the majority rule decisions of representative bodies will have the characteristics of multidimensional issues, since the possibility of logrolling and vote trading means that issues will in practice be simultaneously determined.

One way to model the multidimensional decision is to extend the simple median voter model to three dimensions. The optima of representatives A, B, and C can be connected by contract-curves, which will be straight lines when the indifference curves are spherical. This would form a triangular plane in figure 6.1, drawn explicitly in two dimensions in figure 6.3. Outside this triangle, it is possible to make Pareto superior moves to a point on the plane, but all points on the plane are Pareto optima. This is the Pareto optimal set described in chapter 4. As the number of voters increases, the size of the Pareto optimal set also is likely to increase (if more extreme voters are included), but at any rate, the Pareto optimal set encompasses every voter's optimum. One way to find a determinate solution, as illustrated in figures 4.4 and 4.5, is to conjecture that each voter except the median will have another with diametrically opposed preferences in the issue space, which yields a multidimensional median voter equilibrium as described in chapter 4. This solution satisfies the test of logical consistency, but other majority rule institutional structures are possible as well and, as will be argued below, are more descriptive of the institutions of decision making by representative democracies.

Representatives and Special Interests

One of the characteristics designed into most representative governments is special interest influence on legislation. Special interests are a part of representative government by design because each representative represents a certain subset of the population—usually a geographic subset—so the representative must cater to that subset of the population in order to be reelected. Note that this would not have to be the case if representatives were all elected at large, but the usual case in representative governments is to have representatives represent geographic areas, which automatically makes the population in the geographic area an interest group to which the representative must deliver benefits in order to be elected. Of course, special interest groups do not have to be defined by geographic boundaries, but geographic representation naturally defines one set of interest groups along these lines.

A fundamental motivating force behind elected representatives is the desire to be reelected, and the representative's political activity in general can be analyzed as activity designed to maximize the probability of reelection, much as firms are analyzed in microeconomic theory as being profit maximizers. As is the case with profit maximization in firms, it is not necessarily the case that each representative sets a goal of vote maximization;[8] instead, the constraints facing the representative require her to act as if she is maximizing the probability of reelection, or else a challenger could run against her and, by acting like a vote maximizer, defeat the existing representative. In short, a representative who does not act like a vote maximizer can be defeated by one who does. This does not say anything about the character of elected representatives; it is an observation about the incentive structure they face. Even the most altruistic and public-spirited representative must be reelected to continue in public service. To be reelected, the representative must act in order to maximize the probability of being reelected, or else a challenger who will act that way can defeat the incumbent. In the competition for elected office, surviving representatives will be those that act like vote maximizers.

One might object at this point that a representative really only needs a majority of the votes, and so, once a majority is captured, has no incentive to collect additional votes.[9] While narrowly true, this objection is not relevant to elections in which there is only one winner, because an incumbent must consider not only present competition but potential future competitors that could unseat a complacent candidate with large past majorities.[10] Thus, for practical purposes, attempting to maintain a majority is identical to vote maximization for candidates to elective office.

The next step in the anaylsis is to determine what type of political behavior will maximize the votes of a representative. Representatives seeking reelection must vote as their constituents prefer, so in reality the preference functions of the representatives, as depicted in figure 6.1, would be the perceived preferences of the representatives' constituents. For example, representative A may live in a state that has navigable inland waterways, and project X might be funding for navigable waterway improvements and maintenance. A will be a higher demander of X, not necessarily because the representative has a personal preference for the spending program, but because the representative's constituents have a preference for the program. This may seem obvious, but it is not too obvious for mention, since a special interest theory of legislation follows directly from the observation. Representatives, in order to be reelected, will favor those programs that benefit the individuals who can deliver votes for the representative. Interest groups may deliver votes in a variety of ways, from offering campaign contributions to reporting directly to the group membership about the beneficial activities of the representative, but the group most obviously able to deliver votes will be the voters who live in the representative's district.

At this point, some mention should be made about the information used by voters and by politicians in making political decisions.[11] Voters in general do not have an incentive to become informed about political issues. They know that however they vote, their one vote does not have a perceptible impact on the outcome of an election, so voters will be rationally ignorant about most political issues. For some issues, however, a particular group of voters may have a special interest in the outcome of the legislation, such as the navigable waterway legislation mentioned earlier. Most voters will be rationally ignorant about the legislation, while a special interest group that will be directly elected by the legislation will have a large incentive to be informed, and to lobby their representative for the outcome that would benefit the group. Thus, representatives will tend to hear only from special interest groups regarding legislation, and the silent majority probably will be ignorant about the pros, cons, and costs of the legislation, and likely will also be unaware of the existence of the legislation. As a result, the political lobbying industry tends to be dominated by special interest groups, with nobody representing the general public interest.

The political structure depicted by this type of analysis includes elected representatives who are attempting to create legislation that maximizes their chances of reelection, special interest groups that lobby the representatives on behalf of their interests, and a general public that is largely uninformed about the political process. Individuals who are in special interest groups will be well informed about their special interest issues but will tend to be uninformed regarding the special interests of other interest groups. In order to build on the model in figure 6.1, consider the simple example where X, Y, and Z are government programs that provide benefits to the constituents of representatives A, B, and C, such that the optima of the constituents are at points A, B, and C, and the indifference contours of the constituents are spheres around those points. The representatives then prefer those points only because their constituents prefer them; in this view, the motivation of representatives is only to maximize the chance of reelection, so representatives A, B, and C prefer program mixes A, B, and C because producing benefits for their constituents enhances their chances for reelection.

This view is subtly different from directly attributing preferences for public spending to elected representatives. The representatives prefer only to keep their jobs and, so, try to satisfy their constituents in order to be reelected. It is only to that extent that representatives have preferences regarding the level of public sector programs in this model.

Special interest groups try to favorably influence legislation that will benefit their interest. Special interest groups will in general try to influence legislation on only one issue in order to concentrate their lobbying power. For example, an interest group representing the constituents from district A has preferences on goods X, Y, and Z but will concentrate its lobbying efforts on good X, which it prefers most. While it could lobby for less of good Z, this may dilute the interest group's influence. Furthermore, the lower taxes because less Z is produced will be a benefit shared among the whole population and, so, will be less valuable to the interest group than producing more X, which benefits the group the most. For example, lobbyists for inland waterway shippers will tend to lobby exclusively for more money spent on locks, dams, and waterway maintenance on navigable waterways. While it is true that the group could benefit from a reduction in federal spending on irrigation projects in the west, this benefit would be small compared to the relatively large benefit of more waterway spending, so the interest group concentrates its lobbying on the one issue that will benefit it the most. Casual observation suggests that this hypothesis is in line with the facts. Most lobbying groups focus on a narrow range of issues.

Consider the simple case where there are three special interest groups, one lobbying for the interest of each of the constituent groups A, B, and C. The groups will tend to be single interest groups, so that in the model in figure 6.1, interest group A will lobby representative A to have the government produce three units of X, interest group B will lobby representative B to have the government produce three units of Y, and group C likewise will lobby representative C for three units of Z. The representatives will try to produce what their constituents want on the issues for which their constituents are well informed, so representative A will present a bill for three units of X, B for three units of Y, and C for three units of Z.

Now the question arises as to what level of output of the three goods will be produced by the legislature that must decide by majority rule. It was shown in chapter 4 that in a multidimensional issue space, no point dominates all others, and that by selecting the appropriate agenda, one could start at any point in the issue space and end at any other. The answer to this type of problem in chapter 4 hinged on the observation that cyclical majorities are not in the interests of any of the participants when compared to a stable outcome. This may explain why political outcomes are observed to be stable despite the potential for cycles. The outcome here will be a bit more complex than in chapter 4, however, because in chapter 4, the model considered a division of a fixed amount among the representatives. Now, the amount must be determined in addition to the way in which the amount will be divided.

There is one point of natural agreement that obviously presents itself—a Schelling point.[12] Since the three representatives all present bills for the three units of the goods, and since all representatives need another vote in order to pass their bills, an obvious point of agreement would be to pass all three bills as they stand, and produce three units of each good. None of the alternatives looks as good from a purely political standpoint. One alternative would be for two of the three to form a majority coalition which excludes the third. This outcome would produce cycles over time and was the subject of detailed analysis in chapter 4. An all inclusive coalition would dominate the cyclical majority. Another alternative would be to produce some other amounts of the goods rather than the three units of each as originally proposed. Once again, this would begin a cycle in the issue space, and it was illustrated that after incurring the bargaining costs of finding another outcome there is no outcome that will dominate all others. Thus, the alternative to three units of each good is a bargaining process with an uncertain outcome. There is no reason for the representatives to choose the uncertain outcome over the Schelling point of three units of each good.

This is especially true when the institutional structure of the political bargain is examined. The interest groups in the model (and in reality, more generally) are single interest groups. In order to maximize its effectiveness, each group lobbied only for its most preferred level of the good it most desired and ignored the other goods. In reality, interest groups are likely to behave this way not only because they want to maximize their effectiveness on their single issue but also because they are likely to be largely ignorant of other issues. Thus, in this model, each interest group asks only for three units of its most preferred good, and if the Schelling point coalition is selected, all groups get what they ask for. From a representative's standpoint, there is hardly a better way to ensure reelection than to give people what they ask for, so each representative ought to be happy with the unanimous coalition that allows all representatives to give their constituents what they ask for. Considering the institutional structure, the majority rule outcome in the legislature will be to produce three units of each good, and in this simple model, that outcome will be unanimously approved.

It is obvious by looking at figure 6.1, and even more obvious by looking at two dimensions in figure 6.3, that this outcome is not Pareto optimal. Thus, it would be possible for the representatives to agree to produce less of each good and in the process make all of their constituents better off. For the argument just presented to be descriptive of reality, there must be some reason why the agreement to make the Pareto superior move does not take place. In economic terms, the general reason is that transactions costs will be too high. Transactions costs do not necessarily have to be too high, of course,[13] but neoclassical economics traditionally has ignored transactions costs, and there is a tendency for economists to apply the Coase theorem[14] to everything and develop models which exploit all gains from trade. This methodology has led to some great insights, to be sure, but everything in the world is not optimal, and there are also insights to be gained from looking for the transactions costs that prevent Pareto optimal outcomes in some instances.[15] Admittedly, a political entrepreneur could possible develop a bargain that would benefit everybody, but there are also some reasons why such a bargain is unlikely to be made.

The first place to look is at the incentives facing the representatives. The representatives interact with special interests who lobby for programs in exchange for political support. In this model, the representatives deliver the requested programs and, so, can expect the political support in return. Since the motivation of the representative is to get reelected, this outcome, even though it is not Pareto optimal, is optimal within the narrow self-interest of the representative. Consider the alternative where the representatives agree to a Pareto optimal allocation that produces less of the special interest goods than the interests desire. The constituents will be better off, but the representatives may suffer for two reasons. First, the special interest group will be disappointed that the representative did not provide the benefits it wanted, which will lower the interest group's support of the representative. Second, each representative will have to share the credit for the benefits of lower taxes and enhanced welfare with all other representatives. Representatives can generate more political support by catering to special interests rather than promoting the general public interest.

Next, look at the incentive facing interest groups and constituents. To be effective, interest groups must focus on a narrow range of issues, and both interest groups and constituents are likely to be relatively uninformed about the issues that concern other interest groups. Barge operators in Alabama want federal money for waterway maintenance and improvements, but will be relatively uninformed about tobacco allotments benefiting farmers in North Carolina or dairy price supports for Wisconsin dairy farmers. Furthermore, special interests have a diluted incentive to become informed about the interests of others because the tax cut from a reduction in the special benefits of others would have to be shared with the rest of the nation. The benefit to Alabama waterway operators from a reduction in dairy price supports would be so small that the waterway lobbyists have little incentive to concern themselves with the dairy issue and, so, are able to concentrate all of their efforts on the waterway issue. In fact, lobbyists even compare themselves with other special interests, arguing that because other special interests receive some benefits, the government should also favor the lobbyist's group.[16] Combine this with the fact that the direct benefits to contituents are easy to see when compared to the costs of individual programs going to the constituents of other representatives, and the outcome where each interest group gets what it asks for looks very plausible.

The next step is to examine in more detail the options facing the representatives. The argument has already been made that representatives have little incentive to opt for a Pareto optimal allocation rather than the allocation where all interest groups receive their requested benefits. In addition, representatives have few options available even if they do wish to drop out of the majority coalition in favor of a more efficient allocation. Only two of the three representatives are necessary for a majority, so if one representative desired a more efficient allocation, the others could continue to produce a high level of benefits for their constituents without the uncooperative representative. The three-representative model does not illustrate this point as well as a model with more representatives because with three representatives the transactions costs involved in striking a bargain are relatively low. Thus, the next section will expand the analysis to include more representatives.

Before representatives are added, consider the point in the three-person model. A representative can be a member of the majority coalition and provide the requested three units of the good to his constituents while having the constituents pay their share for three units of other goods to the other interest groups. The alternative of dropping out of the coalition would mean that the representative's constituents would still have to pay for the three units going to the other two groups, since the other two representatives still constitute a majority, but they would not get three units for the good they most prefer. Clearly, each representative has an incentive to remain in the majority coalition.

The next section illustrates this point with more representatives. Chapter 7 will extend the model even further. There, interest groups will be allowed to have insatiable demands, there will be more than one interest group per representative, and interest groups will be allowed to lobby more than one representative. At this point, however, a more simple model will provide a clearer illustration of the problems involved in escaping from the outcome that caters to special interest groups, even though the outcome results in inefficiently large special interest expenditures.

The Majority Coalition

Consider now the case where there are n representatives, each catering to a special interest group. Each group lobbies its representative, requesting an expenditure of $D. Associated with each expenditure is a welfare loss of $W, which includes the excess burden of taxation, and administrative and bureaucratic cost associated with making the expenditure. The general principle has been established that representatives, interest groups, and constituents will concern themselves with the goods that provide the most concentrated benefits, with other goods being largely irrelevant. For example, the outcome in the three-representative case did not depend upon the constituent's preferences for goods other than the good for which they lobbied. This being true, the analysis can proceed under the assumption that $D spent at the request of one interest group will provide benefits only to that group. Given these initial conditions, the analysis will proceed along much the same lines as in the previous section.

To begin the process, each representative presents to the representative body a proposal to spend $D on the special interest good desired by the representative's constituents. Once again, the Schelling point agreement would be for all representatives to form a coalition and approve every program as proposed. The reasoning from the previous section carries over here. This outcome allows all representatives to meet the desires of their special interests, enhancing the representatives' chances for reelection. Constituents and special interests will be satisfied on the issues for which they are well informed, even though they may realize that they would be better off if less was spent on programs for which they are poorly informed. Still, constituents will be more likely to give credit for the benefits provided by the representative than to blame the representative for the high taxes that are mostly the result of everyone else's programs.

A look at the situation facing the individual representative

TABLE 6.2   THE CHOICES FACING AN INDIVIDUAL REPRESENTATIVE

	Not Participate	Participate
Not Participate	0	$-\dfrac{n-1}{n}(\$D+\$W)$
Participate	$\$D-(\$D+\$W)/n$	$-\$W$

reveals why. The majority coalition encompasses all members of the legislature, and in a democracy, the coalition will still have a majority if an individual member drops out. Thus, the individual member's choice is either to remain a member and receive the benefits accruing to the majority in a majority rule system or to drop out of the coalition and continue paying taxes to benefit the majority while not receiving benefits as a member of the minority. In effect, by remaining in the coalition, the representative has the ability to be the agenda setter for the output that most benefits the representative's constituents.[17] The best option is clearly to remain in the majority coalition.

When considering whether to participate in requesting special interests benefits from the legislature, the individual representative has two options: to participate or to not participate. All other representatives face the same options, and the result is a variant of the prisoners' dilemma game. If nobody else requests special interest benefits from the legislature, the individual representative can also choose not to request the benefits, in which case the sum of costs and benefits equals zero, which is entered in the upper left cell of the prisoners' dilemma matrix in table 6.2. However, the payoff to the representative's constituents from receiving a special interest benefit when no other representatives request one is the benefit, $D, minus the representatives' constituents' share of the taxes and welfare cost, or

($D+$W)/n. This is entered in the lower left cell of the matrix. Except in cases where the welfare cost associated with the expenditure is nearly n times greater than the expenditure, the individual representative's constituents will benefit from the expenditure. Thus, when no other representatives participate in seeking special interest benefits, the individual representative has an incentive to seek them.

Since this analysis applies to all representatives, it follows that all representatives have an incentive to seek special interest benefits. Once again, the individual representative could choose to participate or not participate, and the payoffs to the constituents are shown in the right columns of the matrix. The top column shows the payoff if the representative does not participate, eliminating the benefit and the taxes to finance it. The bottom element shows the payoff to one representative's constituents when the benefits and costs of n programs are included. The benefit of the constituents' special interest program will be $D, and the cost of each of the n programs to the constituents in one district will be ($D+$W)/n. Multiplying the cost by the n programs that are funded makes the cost to each district n($D+$W)/n, making the net benefit $D− ($D+$W) = −$W. Once again, the payoff is greater for the representative to join the coalition and obtain the special benefits for his constituents rather than to not participate in the majority coalition. The conclusion is that whether or not other representatives attempt to seek special interest benefits for their constituents, the individual representative will always provide more benefits to his constituents by seeking special interest legislation.

Note the prisoners' dilemma nature of the outcome. The representative's constituents always fare better when the representative seeks special interest legislation to benefit the constituents, yet when all representatives form a coalition to provide the special interest legislation, the payoff is less then if no representatives sought the special interest legislation. Even though the process on the whole is detrimental to the welfare of the representative's constituents, the constituents cannot find fault with their representative for participating. If an individual representative chose not to participate, the constituents of that representative would be worse off. Thus, the constituents are correct in crediting their representative for the special interest benefits that come their way, but not blaming the representative for their taxes. The majority coalition would still produce the bulk of the taxes without the individual representative's participation, since no one representative's vote is essential for producing the majority. The majority coalition encompasses every representative, and unanimously approves an output that is larger than would be optimal.

While it is true that there is a potential bargain that could be struck to avoid the prisoners' dilemma outcome, nobody has an incentive to strike such a bargain, as discussed in the previous section. The results here amplify the last section's conclusions, because it is clear that the prisoners' dilemma nature of the majority coalition allows the individual representative to escape blame for the aggregate outcome and yet take credit for the benefits provided to constituents.[18]

A Digression on Unanimity

The outcome described here is the result of coalition that includes every representative, so that if the package to provide all goods was presented at one time for the legislature to accept or reject, it would be approved unanimously. Most bills before a legislature are not approved unanimously, but that is because all issues are not voted on at once. In order to obtain a majority, representatives will have to trade their votes away on some issues in order to collect votes on others. Once a majority is assured, a representative has no incentive to trade away more votes. The outcome will be the same, and all programs will be funded; however, the bills wil not pass unanimously. The all-inclusive coalition will still be tacitly lurking in the background, because if the principle of universalism were not observed, some representatives who received less-than-equal shares would be in a position to form a coalition dominating those receiving more than equal shares. Universalism and reciprocity assure the highest expected value of an outcome because cyclical behavior is eliminated from politics, as discussed in chapter 4. A less-than-unanimous outcome does not preclude the all-inclusive coalition, concealed in the background, from providing the necessary votes for every representative's programs.

In the example given here, unanimous approval results from all issues being voted on as a single package. Every representative has the option of joining the majority coalition or not, and every representative benefits from being a member as opposed to not being a member, as shown in the matrix in the previous section. Thus, an outcome that is not Pareto optimal is unanimously approved. Looked at from this standpoint, this model provides an interesting contrast with market exchange and its political analog, the rule of unanimity. Market exchange and the rule of unanimity are efficient institutions that produce Pareto superior moves[19] because everybody who is party to the exchange agrees that it is beneficial. At first glance, this would also seem to apply to unanimous approval within a majority rule system, but the analysis just completed illustrates why this is not the case. A unanimity rule is not the same as unanimous approval under majority rule. The former always results in a Pareto superior move; the latter may not.

The reason is that under unanimity rule, every individual has veto power. If a proposed change is not in the best interest of even one person, then that person may vote against the change and block its implementation. In contrast, under majority rule, a simple majority may initiate a change that is not in the best interest of the minority. The minority then either must bear the costs imposed by the majority or, if possible, join the majority coalition in order to share in some of the gains. Thus, unanimous approval in a majority rule system only signifies that all voters view themselves as better off being a member of the majority coalition rather than being a member of the minority. This is much different from signifying that the proposed change is an improvement over the status quo.

This observation builds upon an insight made by James Buchanan decades ago that majority rule decisions generate externalities.[20] Externalities exist when one person or group imposes costs (or benefits) on another without the other's consent. In the market, the observation of an externality has often prompted observers to call for government action to correct the externality. Yet, under majority rule, a majority imposes its will upon a minority, making the minority worse off as a result of the decision. Since the majority imposes costs on the minority without the consent of the minority, this is an obvious case of an externality, so the call for government action may only replace one externality with another. The present analysis shows that this observation can even extend to unanimously approved decisions in a majority rule system. Under unanimity rule, approval indicates that the voters are better off with the change than without it; unanimous consent under majority rule merely signifies that all voters are better off in the majority coalition than in the potentially exploitable minority. This does not necessarily mean that the voters are better off having the issue passed rather than defeated.

Distributive Government

The model being developed here depicts a government that essentially engages in distributive activities to the exclusion of all others. The reason is that the incentive structure in a representative democracy rewards the distributive activities of representatives. Constituents and interest groups have an incentive to pursue special interest benefits through the political process, but do not have an incentive to become well informed about issues outside their special interests or to be concerned about the general public interest. As a result, representatives will be beseiged by requests for special interest legislation. Meanwhile, nobody lobbies for—or becomes informed about—general public interest legislation.

Legislators have an incentive to pass legislation that will ensure their reelection. Even the most altruistic representative must be reelected in order to continue in public service, and the representative who does not act in order to maximize the chances of reelection is vulnerable to being challenged by a candidate who will pursue the vote-maximizing strategy. This means that representatives have an incentive to give constituents and special interests what they request. Since they request special interest legislation, representatives can get the legislation passed only by trading votes for special interest legislation of others. The result is the approval of a package of special interest programs that leave all voters worse off than if none of the package had been approved.

From the individual representative's standpoint, approval of the package is the optimal reelection strategy. Voters will credit the representative for the special benefits that come their way, but they cannot fault the representative for the excessive taxation (or borrowing) that finances the special interest programs of others. In a majority rule system, the representative's alternative is either to join the majority coalition and receive the special benefits or not to join and pay taxes for the special interest programs of others without receiving a share of the benefits. There is a prisoners' dilemma situation set up by the fact that with a large stable majority coalition, no one representative's vote is necessary to maintain the coalition. Thus, the incentive structure is set up such that no Pareto superior move will be made, even though one is possible. Government spending will be larger than optimal.

There is another characteristic of this model of government that is equally significant but perhaps not as obvious. At the same time that too many special interest programs are being passed, no representative has an incentive to pursue programs that are in the general public interest. Programs that are in the general public interest are like public goods to the representatives. The benefits of such programs are diffused over all representatives' districts, so the benefits to the constituents of any one representative will be only a small fraction of the total benefits of the program. Since a representative receives votes only from the residents of their districts, they have an incentive to produce special interest legislation that will provide concentrated benefits to their voters, rather than public interest legislation that will provide diluted benefits to every representative's constituents. Public interest legislation may be passed, but only as an accidental by-product of the special benefits that are provided to the constituents of some representatives.

Perhaps the best example of this is in the area of national defense. There are general public interest benefits to national defense, but when defense issues are considered, they are debated largely in terms of the special interests served. Representatives will favor one weapons system over another because it will be produced in their district, and military bases open and close more as the result of special interest politics than national security. When dividing the military budget, the army, navy, and air force also act as special interests, each trying to increase its share of the budget and proposing new programs and systems to do so. Cooperation among the services is almost nonexistent as they compete among themselves for programs.[21] For example, the air force has proposed that air force aircraft be used to patrol and defend the sea lanes, while the navy rebuts that the present and requested navy programs are superior. Neither service suggests a cooperative approach.[22] If military spending is an example of special interest politics, then it is not difficult to extend the analysis to the host of the government programs that so obviously benefit special interests.

One issue, then, is the level of government spending, but another important issue is the mix. This analysis argues that the government spends too much on special interest programs, but also that the mix of government spending is biased toward special interests and away from the general public interest. Representative democracy is essentially a distributive government, where legislation in the public interest is passed only as an accidental by-product of special interest legislation. Special interest legislation may be easier to pass if it provides some spillover benefits to the constituents of other representatives, and this issue will be discussed more extensively in chapter 9. However, political markets tend to undervalue these spillover benefits because of the special interest nature of political lobbying.

In conclusion, government activity will tend to be characterized by special interest legislation rather than legislation in the general public interest. Representatives have an incentive to form coalitions to approve of their special interest programs, and this produces the approval of a package of special interest programs that is larger than optimal. Although a Pareto superior move eliminating the special interest legislation would be possible, nobody has an incentive to initiate such a move. The result is a distributive government whose activities are aimed at benefiting special interests rather than acting in the general public interest.

7 / Interest Groups and Distributional Activity

The general argument has been made that governmental activity is essentially distributional, meaning that the government caters to the desires of concentrated special interests rather than pursuing the general public interest. The framework within which the argument has been developed thus far has been quite simple, giving it the virtue of making the forces driving the model readily apparent but also leaving the drawback that the model has some unrealistic characteristics. The purpose of this chapter is to extend the model to allow it to include some more realistic elements. In particular, this chapter will increase the number of interest groups from one per representative to a potentially unlimited number; the interest groups will not have to be geographically oriented; each interest group will be able to lobby more than one representative; and interest groups will be allowed to have insatiable demands for expenditure on their interests instead of the finite optima in the model in chapter 5. These extensions will make the model more realistic and will provide more insight into the operation of the government's distributional activity.

Although the model will be developed and refined, its basic structure will not be changed. The general conclusions will remain unchanged as well, so that the government will still be depicted as spending more than is Pareto optimal on distributional activities while neglecting activities that would serve the general public interest. A brief review of the factors leading to these conclusions will provide a good introduction to the extensions. First, the principle of universalism was established as the method by which the democratic legislature avoids cycles. Given the possibility of endless cycles and the conclusion that for a given expected payoff all will be better off with the minimum variance in the payoff, the maximizing strategy is to provide an equal payoff for everybody. If the distribution given to some exceeds that given to others, then those who receive smaller-than-average distributions will be in a position to form a majority coalition to take the above-average distributions from those who currently receive them and distribute them to the majority coalition members. As described in chapter 4, this creates a new group with below-average distributions, which will produce a new majority coalition. This process can then iterate endlessly. The potential for cycles occurs in a democracy because a majority can impose its will upon a majority, which, in essence creates an externality.[1]

If a unanimous decision rule were required, no individual or group could impose costs on any other, but when majority rule is used, the majority has the ability to impose costs on a minority by making decisions against the best interest of the minority. This puts the minority in a position where they can bargain to form a new majority coalition, as described above. Thus, dissatisfied minorities pose a threat to the majority, but at the same time, minorities want to be a part of the majority. The solution is to have a universal majority coalition, where everybody is a member, and where all members receive roughly equal distributions. This outcome does not logically have to follow from the initial conditions. There are other mechanisms that could generate stability, such as a minimum majority coalition in which no members defect or, of course, endless cycles. While there does not appear to be an unique outcome to this game-theoretical problem, the solution suggested here seems plausible and also appears to be descriptive of contemporary politics. The outcome of universalism provides stability in politics and provides equal distributions to all participants.

Another feature of the model is that distributional activity will take place through spending programs rather than tax cuts.

Tax cuts are likely to be ineffective as distributional tools, as argued in chapter 5. Furthermore, government agencies themselves may act as interest groups that desire more spending, so that spending increases are politically more expedient than tax cuts. Having argued that distributional activity will take place through spending programs, and that all representatives will receive equal distributions, the question arises about the size of the distributions. In chapter 6, each representative was most interested in one program, and the representative was in effect allowed to be the agenda setter for that program. When the agenda setter concept was examined in chapter 3, evidence seemed to go against the agenda setter model in a single-dimensioned setting. However, in the multidimensional setting in chapter 6, the agenda setter model seems more reasonable because representatives exchange the right to set the agenda for various issues so that each representative can be the agenda setter for the issue most important to the representative's constituents.

This type of political activity can take place in a representative democracy because of the prisoners' dilemma nature of the position that each individual representative is in. The representative can either participate in the distributional game, which means paying taxes for everyone's distribution and also receiving a distribution, or can choose not to participate, which means paying taxes for everyone else's distribution but not receiving anything. The individually rational thing for each representative to do is to participate. The resulting government has more special interest programs than is optimal but ignores programs that would be in the general public interest. This material will be carried over from earlier chapters, and the present chapter will attempt to add more realistic details to the model. The first issue that will be discussed, which was touched upon briefly in chapter 6, is the voting for individual issues. Within the framework of the model, the question is: If there is an all-inclusive majority coalition, why do all issues not receive unanimous approval?

Majority Coalitions in Representative Bodies

All representatives would like to pass special interest legislation for their constituents, but by themselves, none of these issues could receive a majority of the votes. They all depend on each other for passage. That is, if the issues were to appear as single-dimensioned issues, one at a time, for the legislature's approval, each issue would receive only one vote—that of its sponsor. In a multidimensional setting, the sponsor attracts more votes for the issue by trading his vote on other issues for the votes of others on his issue. Trades can take place in a number of ways. The simplest way is for two representatives to trade votes on each of their issues. More complex logrolling could occur if a representative agreed to vote for another's program today in exchange for an IOU. Another method might be to put together a bill that would encompass a number of special interest programs. The point is that logrolling and vote trading can occur in a number of complex ways, but the simple result is that representatives have traded votes on some programs for votes on others.

One way that the universal coalition could pass its legislation would be for all members to simultaneously present their programs for passage, putting together a bill including all programs, which would receive unanimous approval. This method of logrolling would be cumbersome and complex, however, because it requires all members to present their legislative demands simultaneously, analogous to barter in an economic system. Barter is very cumbersome because all representatives may not have legislative desires at the same time, just like the shoemaker may not have a demand for bread at the same time that the baker desires shoes. In a complex economy, the solution is indirect exchange, where the shoemaker trades shoes for money and can demand bread or another good later. The money keeps track of how much the shoemaker is owed. An economy encompasses millions of individuals. A representative body in politics encompasses relatively few by comparison, and a record of political IOUs can be (and is) kept without the need of a written record. Votes are still traded across issues and through time.

In the absence of a single legislative item encompassing the special interests of everyone, items are introduced one at a time, and votes are traded so that the effect is the same as if all traders arrive at the market simultaneously and barter for special interest legislation. The unanimous coalition is an analog to political trades much as the market in Walrasian general equilibrium theory is an analog to a competitive economy. This is likely to be more clear to an economist who will be familiar with a model where the auctioneer calls out prices and then everyone simultaneously barters once the equilibrium price vector is found. In politics, all representatives do not arrive at the chamber to barter for special interest programs and then trade when the equilibrium political package is found. But in both cases, the effect is the same.

A reflection on the actual process reveals why unanimous approval for bills is neither needed nor obtained. A representative who is trading for votes needs only a simple majority for passage. Once a simple majority is obtained, there is no point in accumulating additional votes that are not needed. Outside of the simple transactions cost, the representative will not want to spend IOUs needlessly. Of course, a representative may vote for another's program without much lobbying in order to use the vote for a bargaining chip later, in effect saying, "I voted for your program then; I want your vote now." The vote will be worth less if it was not really needed, so representatives have an incentive to save their votes for cases in which they are strongly requested. This gets into issues of political strategy that are somewhat far afield from the argument here. The point is that approval of legislation will not be unanimous because unanimous approval is costly to the bill's sponsor, and because unanimous approval is not necessary under majority rule. However, the end political result is as if all special interest legislation had been simultaneously considered and unanimously approved.

The idea here should not be foreign to economists because there are so many analogies in economic theory. Walrasian general equilibrium was already mentioned. In addition, the neoclassical theory of the firm assumes that firms equate marginal cost and marginal revenue to maximize profits. Firms may not realize what they are doing or the implications of their actions, but the forces of competition will weed out those firms that do not act as if they maximize profits.[2] Likewise, the political system of representative democracy produces an outcome as if all representatives presented their special interest legislation to the entire legislature to be simultaneously and unanimously approved. In fact, the actual mechanism by which this occurs results in majority rule approval that will be less than unanimous.

The Demand and Supply of Interest Group Legislation

In earlier chapters, it was assumed that interest groups had finite demands for special interest legislation. This assumption may be true when legislation produces public goods that generate benefits for the general public, and that are paid for by taxes levied on the consumers of the goods. In this case, given the price of a public good, taxpayers are likely to demand a finite amount. When legislation produces special interest benefits, however, taxpayers are likely to have insatiable demands, because taxpayers as a group are paying for what amounts to a transfer to a small group. The small group will have an infinite appetite for taxing the general public in order to pay the proceeds to the small group. Accordingly, the previously employed assumption will now be replaced with the assumption that interest groups always want additional special interest legislation.

Appended directly onto the model in chapter 6, this assumption would lead to an infinitely large government, as the agenda setter for each interest group proposed infinitely large distributions to each group. In fact, the government cannot grow infinitely large because it faces some budget constraint. The budget constraint may simply be the fiscal capacity of the nation; the government cannot expand because it cannot raise any more revenue. Alternatively, the government may be constrained because a majority of the representatives will not approve higher spending. This is the notion of the feasible majority set that was introduced in chapter 4. But whatever the reason, government expenditures cannot expand endlessly. Chapter 8, titled "The Government Budget Constraint," discusses the factors that constrain government spending in detail. At this point, it can simply be observed that the government does have a budget constraint.

With insatiable demands for special interest distributions, the government will spend up to its budget constraint. Applying the principle of universalism, this means that each representative will get an equal share of the budget to hand out to the interest group that lobbies the representative. Without considering the origin of the budget constraint, the distributional model looks like the model in chapter 4 from which the principle of universalism was deduced.

The political process that includes both a government budget constraint and the principle of universalism essentially gives each representative a budget constraint, allowing the representative to allocate a certain amount of government money toward the satisfaction of the demands of the representative's special interest group. A consideration to be taken up shortly is that there are many interest groups competing for the representative's favors. Another consideration that will be discussed first is that interest groups may want money at times, but also they desire regulations that will not require any government spending, and that at times (e.g., protective tariffs), may even raise revenue for the government. The theories of regulation put forward by Posner and Stigler provide an easy vehicle for including regulation in the model.[3] In this view, groups and individuals desire regulation to further their own interests. Regulation may be sought for a host of reasons, among them: to limit foreign competition in an industry, to limit domestic competition by licensing or other means, to organize an industry into an effective cartel (as, for example, the effects of the Interstate Commerce Commission), to limit entry into certain professions (which has the effect of raising the incomes of those in the profession), to preserve the environment by antipollution laws and the designation of public parks and forests. These regulatory efforts all have a common element. They provide benefits to those who seek the regulations, but at the expense of others.

This statement does not pass judgment about the desirability of the regulations. Environmental groups who lobby for tighter pollution controls are seeking benefits for themselves at the expense of the polluters. Doctors, lawyers, and accountants, who seek legal restrictions on who may work in those occupations, receive more income because of the restrictions, but customers pay higher prices as a result. Trucking regulations, tarriffs, and quotas provide income to those in the industry, at the expense of the industry's customers. On net, the regulations may or may not be socially beneficial. That is irrelevant here. The point is that the regulations provide income to those who lobby in favor of them, but at the expense of some other group.

This view of regulation fits directly into the model of distributive government developed here. The regulation provides a distributive benefit to a special interest group. The special interest group could receive a cash payment and be made just as well off, but the regulation has the same effect as a cash payment. The special interest group may prefer the regulation to cash, among other reasons, because it may view the regulation as more long-lasting, since a budgetary allocation does not need to be made every year. At any rate, the regulation provides benefits to the special interest group just as a cash or in-kind transfer.

On the other side of the transaction, the effect is much the same as a budgetary allocation as well. The regulatory benefits are paid for by costs imposed on another group that typically will be less concentrated and less well organized. Consumers are good candidates. Regulations that benefit firms or an industry will raise prices to consumers, so that the regulation is in effect a tax on consumers for the benefit of the industry. Environmental regulations raise the costs of firms and ultimately the prices paid by consumers—for the benefit of the lobbying organization (and perhaps, others). In all of these cases, an organized and concentrated special interest group lobbies for benefits to itself, with the costs being paid by a less well organized and more diffused group. These costs are, in effect, the taxation that pays for the benefits of the regulation. Thus, while the model here has been developed in terms of taxes being collected in order to provide distributions to special interest groups, the model is really more general. In-kind benefits obviously can be substituted for cash, and regulation can be substituted as well. The model will continue to be framed in terms of distributions made to special interests, but in light of the foregoing, distributions can take many forms, including regulatory benefits.

The Formation of Interest Groups

The formation of interest groups has been depicted in a very simple manner up to this point. Representatives, wishing to be reelected, attempt to respond to the desires of the voters in their districts. While voters in general are not very well informed, voters tend to see the benefits of government spending in their district to a greater extent than they see the costs of government spending in other districts. Special interest groups form to lobby their representatives for more spending in their districts, and in this simple conception, the special interest group lobbies for special interest programs that benefit the representatives' constituents. Interest groups are aligned geographically so that whatever benefits the interest group also benefits the representative's constituents.

This simplistic view of interest group formation is not wholly unrealistic. Interest groups do tend to be organized along geographic boundaries, and the legislation that they lobby for does tend to benefit the constituents of the representatives that the interest groups lobby. Good examples are Alabama barge operators, North Carolina tobacco farmers, and Wisconsin dairy farmers. In each case, there is a special interest group organized roughly along state lines that has a lobbying organization in Washington. Also in each case, the lobbying organization has found the support of its state representatives who are able to provide special interest legislation that benefits the group. Surely the theory developed here is very descriptive of these types of situations.

The theory is not exactly descriptive, though, because for one thing, the special interest groups mentioned do not represent the entire population of the states mentioned, but only a particular subset of the population. There is a simple explanation for this. There are costs involved in organizing an interest group, and the larger the group, the higher the organizational costs. In addition, and perhaps more significantly, the larger the interest group, the smaller the fraction of the distribution will be that will go to each individual member. Thus, interest groups have a reason to limit their numbers in order to maximize the benefits to each individual member. On the other side of the market, the representative will want the interest group to be as large as possible, in order to try to cater to as many voters as possible. This gives the interest group organizer a good reason to associate the well-being of the interest group with the well-being of the representative's entire set of constituents. Consumers throughout Alabama benefit from barge subsidies owing to lower prices (especially of gasoline, electricity, and other widely consumed goods). Lower shipping costs of agricultural and industrial products create jobs for the state. Thus, every member of the representative's district benefits from the barge subsidies. The same is said of other programs in other areas. In this way, the geographic interest group claims to represent the entire region, even though some specific individuals gain more.[4]

The politics of geographic interest groups makes much sense in this framework. A small, well-organized group claims that benefits given to the group will filter down to the rest of the representative's constituents. By arranging for the distribution, the bulk of the benefits go to the special interest group, which provides political support to the representative. In addition to the votes of the interest group members, the interest group also has an incentive to campaign on behalf of the representative to win the votes of others, in order to perpetuate the favorable distribution. This support can be either in the form of direct campaigning, or campaign contributions, or both.

This same logic also applies to interest groups that are not organized along geographical lines. The interest group can offer the votes of its members within the representative's area and can also offer campaign contributions, direct campaign support, and so on. The nongeographic interest group's members will be more widely dispersed, implying a disadvantage for two reasons. First, all of the interest group's members will not be able to vote for the representative, and second, the benefits of the special interest group will not be concentrated within the representative's district. Thus, it follows that nongeographic interest groups must rely more on providing general campaign assistance—the best example being campaign contributions—rather than relying on advertising how the representative's assistance to the interest group has benefited the representative's constituents.

When looking at the balance of geographic versus nongeographic interest groups, the first factor to notice is that, all other things equal, a representative would rather provide benefits to a geographic interest group in the representative's district than to a nongeographic interest group. Geographic interest groups provide concentrated benefits to the representative's constituents, in addition to the campaign support and financing that can be offered by nongeographic interest groups. Why would a representative ever choose to provide benefits to a nongeographic interest group, then? The most obvious answer is that the nongeographic interest group may be in a position to provide more campaign financing or other campaign support. As campaign financing becomes more important relative to direct local support, one would expect the ratio of nongeographic to geographic interest groups to increase.

Campaign financing must be paid in exchange for something, and as government grows, there is more that special interest groups can pay for. Interest groups in essence bid for government support through lobbying activities and campaign contributions, and larger government spending means that campaign contributions will increase, both absolutely, and relative to direct geographic representation, in importance for the interest group. Growing government means more reliance on direct payments for special interest benefits, which means that as government grows, nongeographic interest groups will tend to increase in importance relative to geographic interest groups. Each representative, then, will receive requests from a number of special interest groups organized along geographic and nongeographic lines.[5] The representative must then decide which interest groups to support, and to what extent.

The Representative's Options

At this point, enough has been said about the political environment of the representative to describe the options facing the typical representative, and how the representative chooses among the options. The principle of universalism places the representative, along with all other representatives, in a type of majority coalition, whereby a majority of the representative body agrees to provide the representative with discretion over a share of the government's budget. The principle of universalism implies that all representatives will share about equally in determining the budgetary allocation. The share does not come automatically, of course. It is the result of the logrolling and vote-trading process that is a part of politics, but the equilibrium outcome of this process, as earlier described, is the roughly equal division of the budget.

Given the method of division, the representative's share will then be a function of the total budget. Here, that will be taken as given. Chapter 8, titled "The Government Budget Constraint," will discuss how the total is determined. The individual representative then is faced with the choice of how to allocate the governmental funds at the representative's discretion. Again, not that the representative is not simply given the funds; they must be obtained through the logrolling process. However, the process in essence allows each representative to allocate some government revenue to special interests of the representative's choosing.

The representative, who needs political support to be re-elected, will choose to allocate the total amount among interest groups in such a way as to maximize the probability of the representative's reelection. Specifically to whom the money will be allocated is beyond the scope of this study, but the general principles of the allocation are clear. The representative has many interest groups from which to choose, and the representative will allocate the funds among groups such that the last dollar spent on each group will buy the same amount of political support. The maximization of political support for the representative is analogous to utility maximization subject to a budget constraint in the economic theory of consumer behavior.

It certainly is possible for the representative to have goals other than the maximization of political support, and the representative with a healthy margin of political support may choose to spend excess federal dollars to further these goals. It may even be that some of these goals could be in the general public interest. But the politician must always keep in mind that potential political challengers are likely to arise at the next election who will promise to satisfy neglected interest groups, and this potential competition has the effect of forcing each representative to allocate the government's resources in a manner that maximizes the representative's political support.[6] The representative will adjust at the margin like the utility maximizer in the economic theory of consumer behavior. An interest group that appears to offer the potential for greater political support will receive additional funds at the expense of funds to the least supportive groups.

The Government as an Interest Group

The title of this section conveys the general flavor of its argument. The government can and does act as an interest group.[7] Every government program has government employees who oversee and administer the program. These employees, who earn their incomes through the program, provide a built-in interest group with good reasons to want to see the program continued and expanded. The government employees obviously have the self-serving motives of wanting to maintain their jobs, but it is also true that people will tend to seek employment in stimulating environments doing work that they consider to be meaningful. The implication is that those who work with a program will be those most inclined to view the program as worthwhile, strengthening the interest group nature of those employed by government programs. An added factor to consider is that those employed in government programs will be the government's experts on the subject.

Because the government acts as an interest group, the mere act of establishing a new government program (or expanding an existing one) increases the political support for the program. This is likely to work in favor of the representatives who are responsible for the program, because government employees vote and participate in politics in other ways. Thus the representative gains the support of the original interest group plus the additional government employees who become a part of the program. This same procedure works in reverse, as well. Reducing or eliminating a program will be opposed by the government employees who work in the program as well as by the interest group that provided the original support. It is easy to see why government programs are easier to block before they are established than to terminate once they are in place. The mere act of establishing a program increases its political support.

Fiscal Exchange

The picture of government painted by the analysis of government in this book is essentially distributional. The government is engaged in systematically collecting money from the public at large and then parceling it back in the form of expenditures made at the request of special interest groups. Viewed in this way, government is much different from the ideal conception of government held by some, but is the natural extension of the ideal government as viewed by others. For those holding a fiscal exchange model of government as an ideal, this conception of government violates the basic principles.[8] In the fiscal exchange model, the government collects taxes in exchange for services rendered. Thus, there should be a correspondence between the services provided and the taxes paid. The role of government in this view is to overcome the externality and public goods problems inherent in some goods. It is apparent that if the fiscal exchange model were consistently applied, the distributional activity described here would never take place.

The motivating factor causing interest groups to seek distributions from the government is that the benefit goes to the interest group, but the cost is shared by all. If the government agreed to provide services only in exchange for tax payments by the beneficiaries, governmental activity would be very different. For example, it is unlikely that barge operators would be willing to pay the cost of maintaining navigable waterways on any but the most highly used waterways that are being maintained today. If navigable waterway maintenance was a fiscal exchange instead of a subsidy, many existing navigable waterways would not be maintained. In fairness to waterway operators, most waterways could probably be maintained at a fraction of their current cost if left to market forces, making the actual outcomes less certain than the elimination of current waterways that are not cost-effective. This same defense cannot be made for many other programs.

The farm subsidies that have been previously mentioned are a prime example. Farm subsidies always must cost more to the taxpayer than they give to the farmer because of the administrative costs. Such programs could not be carried on in the fiscal exchange model, because farmers would consistently be paying more into the program than they were receiving.[9] The same is true of all programs that redistribute cash. The recipients would never agree to pay the full cost of the benefits they receive.

A policy implication suggests itself at this point. The fiscal exchange model could be applied to determine who should pay the taxes to finance particular programs. This may sound a bit unworkable, but there are methods that could be used to move toward the fiscal exchange model. One of the best is a movement toward fiscal federalism, moving government programs from the federal level to the state level. Alabama claims that the waterway program benefits the state. North Carolina claims that the tobacco allotment program benefits the state. Wisconsin claims that the dairy subsidy program benefits the state. If this is so, then the state should be willing to pay the taxes to continue the program, so these (and other) programs can be returned to the state level. Of course, it is unlikely that the states would be willing to finance any of these programs on their own. They currently benefit the states because the individual state receives a concentrated benefit that is paid for by the nation as a whole. A significant amount of the inefficiency discussed here could be eliminated by transferring programs from higher to lower levels of government.

Allocation and Distribution

The fiscal exchange model of government may appear desirable to some, but it by no means qualifies as the universal model of ideal government. In his classic treatise on public finance, Richard Musgrave explicitly divides government into allocative and distributive functions.[10] In this view, a part of the role of the government is to redistribute income from some to others. The recipients obviously are not expected to pay for the benefits they receive. The logical extension of Musgrave's characterization is the optimal taxation literature that was discussed at some length in chapter 5. At that time, the analysis suggested that economic mobility would serve to defeat attempts to implement the so-called optimal tax schemes. Independent of that model, the distributive nature of politics will undermine attempts at optimal redistribution of any kind.

Models of optimal redistribution, beginning with the Musgrave variety, including the optimal tax literature, and even the Pareto optimal redistribution suggested by Hochman and Rogers, start by viewing the income distribution from afar and suggesting improvements that could be made based on their various criteria. From here, there is a role for the distributive branch of government. The distributive branch of government may start out with benign intentions, but its essence is that some individuals or groups are entitled to receive concentrated benefits from the government, paid for by the taxpayers at large. The individuals and groups that receive these entitlements will be determined by the representatives elected to run the government.

Once the distributive branch of the government is explicitly recognized as legitimate and the fiscal exchange paradigm is left behind, it is a small step to move toward the model of distributive government developed here. The distributive branch allows some groups to receive distributions paid for by the taxpayers in general, and elected representatives determine who gets what. Advocates of a distributive branch have a view of how redistribution should take place, but to see how it actually will take place, one needs to examine the incentives involved in distributive government. Not even all advocates share the same distributional objectives, after all, so the ideal distribution cannot serve as a model in any case. But by examining the incentives faced by decision makers, it is possible to get some insight into the way that redistribution actually will occur.

The answer can be found in the model of this book. A representative body that decides who receives distributions from the government will act as described in the model. The result will be far from the ideal redistribution viewed by most advocates of redistribution, but it will be the result of individuals responding to the political incentive structure inherent in representative democracy. This model of distributive government follows logically from the establishment of the principle of the distributive branch. When the fiscal exchange model is abandoned, distributive government is the result.

The establishment of the principle of redistribution through government not only adds distributive programs to the allocative ones but weakens the allocative branch as well. The growth of redistribution through government builds a network of special interest groups that compete for government funding independent of the somewhat artificial distinction between allocative and distributive. The possibility of distribution through interest group politics means that interest groups have an incentive to try to win a share of the allocative dollars as well. Furthermore, representatives have an incentive to use these allocative dollars to cater to interest group desires and attempt to increase their political support. As a result, the growth of distributive government erodes the allocative aspects of government. The entire government tends to be distributive. As noted in chapter 6, representatives do not have an incentive to pass legislation in the general public interest, because the benefits will be diluted throughout the nation. Rather, they have the incentive to use government dollars to produce concentrated benefits to special interests, in exchange for political support.

The government does provide goods that are in the general public interest, but today that is a minority of the federal government budget and is itself largely an accidental by-product of legislation catering to special interests. National defense provides a good example because it is a public good often thought of as being produced in the public interest. Yet even here much defense spending and legislation tend to be determined by special interests rather than by what is in the general public interest. The government itself acts as an interest group, as earlier noted, and this tends to perpetuate and strengthen defense programs. The Department of Defense, after all, is a large employer. Furthermore, each service is a strong interest group in itself, and the interservice rivalries that occur in procurement missions, and so forth, are well known.[11] As a result, defense policy is often made as a compromise to the special interests in the pentagon rather than in the general public interest.

Interest groups extend outside the Pentagon as well, and the choices of opening and closing military bases, of awarding procurement contracts, and the like, are often made as a result of special interest politics. A notable, although by no means unique, example occurred in the fall of 1982 when the air force was deciding on a large military transport. The contenders were a modified Boeing 747 and the Lockheed C5-B. While such a decision would seem in the traditional analysis to be one concerning a public good, all accounts of the debate showed that lobbyists from Georgia, where the C5-B would be built, were competing for federal money with lobbyists from Washington State, home of Boeing. What idealistically should have been a debate about the public interest was instead a battle of special interests for federal dollars. This is all the more remarkable because the news accounts at the time saw nothing out of the ordinary in the process. The role of special interest politics in all political decisions is simply taken for granted in Washington.

Government activity, then, is indeed distributive, and the growth of the distributive branch of government has virtually eliminated the allocative branch as it is ideally described. Representatives have the incentive to pursue distributive policies, and if legislation happens to be in the public interest, it is only as an accidental by-product of special interest activities. This is not the result of any premeditated acts of evil people who are trying to get something for nothing. Rather, it is inherent in the incentive structure of a representative democracy. Representatives, in order to keep their jobs, must act to maximize their chances of reelection. Since the general public is rationally unaware of most political activitiy, this means catering to those who have a special interest in becoming informed about specific issues. The result is the distributive government described here.

A Theory of Political Structure

The close of this chapter is an appropriate place to attempt to describe this model as a part of a theory of political structure, similar to the theory of market structure in economics. The parallel has been mentioned before. The basic theory of market structure sees two polar cases: competition and monopoly. Each case has implications regarding resource allocation, pricing, efficiency, and so on. There are a number of intermediate cases such as monopolistic competition and oligopoly that have some insights to contribute, but they draw upon the attributes of the polar cases of competition and monopoly. Likewise, in the theory of political structure, there are the polar cases of single-dimensional competition and multidimensional competition.

The median voter model, as described by Bowen, Black, Downs, and others, illustrates the operation of single-dimensional political competition. Although the conclusion is reached in a number of different ways, all of these models conclude that the preferences of the median voter will determine the outcome of a majority rule election. More specifically, the outcome will be the outcome most preferred by the median voter. The median voter model is a powerful simplifying device, because it shows that the market demand curve, which aggregates the preferences of all voters, is the median voter's demand curve. Chapter 2 showed that while this outcome may not produce a Samuelsonian optimum, it may be close and, at any rate, has a number of agreeable properties and is analytically easy to work with. In a single-dimensioned setting, there may be problems that could inhibit the occurrence of the median voter result, but empirical evidence suggests its applicability. In a theory of political structure, the median voter model in the single-dimensioned case is analogous to perfect competition in the theory of market structure.

At the other extreme is the model of multidimensional political competition developed here. In the multidimensional model, individuals can have the same preferences and make decisions by the same rules as in the single-dimensioned model, and yet the results are very different. In the most basic model, endless cycles will occur, but reasonable institutional constraints cause the voters with the highest demands to choose the outcome in each dimension in the multidimensional model. Thus, the outcome will be the preference of the high-demander rather than the median, although this result may be modified by a budget constraint that will be the subject of the next chapter. The theory has room for additional development, certainly, and there may be some intermediate cases that can lend some insight, but this model does have the potential to develop into a theory of political structure that parallels the economic theory of market structure.

The multidimensional theory shows a government budget allocated among representatives according to the principle of universalism, with representatives then allocating their shares to special interest groups. The question to be examined in the next chapter is how the government's budget constraint is determined.

8 / The Government Budget Constraint

In a democracy, the government's budget can be constrained in two basic ways. First, there could be a limit to the level of expenditures that can be approved by a majority. This notion was introduced in chapter 4 and called the feasible majority set. Basically, a majority will not approve of expenditure levels outside the feasible majority set, so it acts as a constraint on government expenditures. The second constraint, which applies to any type of government, is the fiscal capacity of the nation. Regardless of political institutions, every nation will have some maximum amount that could possibly be raised for government expenditures. This notion has been popularized lately in the Laffer curve, which illustrates that there is a limit to how much revenue can be raised by tax increases. The plan of this chapter is to examine both of these concepts in a general way and then to look at more specific cases of constrained government budgets. The investigation will begin with the concept of the feasible majority set.

The Feasible Majority Set

The feasible majority set delineates the boundaries beyond which the majority would prefer to have no government expenditures at all rather than to increase government spending further. This notion of the feasible majority set was explored in chapter 4. The boundary of the feasible majority set, then, is similar to the notion of the all-or-nothing demand curve, since it shows the level of government spending at which the majority would be indifferent between that amount and nothing.

When considering a public sector that produces many heterogeneous goods, the actual dollar amount of the boundary of the feasible majority set will depend upon the institutional setting. This is because the mix of goods will make a difference in the level of spending that can be approved. A look back at figure 4.3 in chapter 4 shows this to be the case. In figure 4.3, the shaded triangle ABC is the Pareto optimal region, and the boundary of the feasible majority set is the heavy line composed of three arcs. Beyond this boundary, a majority of the voters would prefer no government output to the amounts in that region. It is apparent from figure 4.3 that the boundary of the feasible majority set is not a constant dollar amount. Constant dollar amounts will be given by negatively sloped straight lines in the figure, and since the units of each good were specified as costing equal amounts, the lines would have slopes of -1. A line with the slope -1 could be drawn through the figure to intersect the boundary twice, clearly showing that some points on the boundary of the feasible majority set represent larger dollar amounts of spending than others.

This implies that, given the ratio of one good to another, different ratios will result in different levels of government spending at the boundary of the feasible majority set. Buchanan has illustrated that if two public sector goods that are sold separately are combined and sold in fixed proportions, the total amount spent on the two goods will in general not remain constant.[1] Given the voters' most preferred proportions, if the ratio is altered to include more of the good with the more elastic demand, total outlays will increase. The converse will be true if the ratio is altered to include more of the good that has the less elastic demand.

This concept generalizes to all-or-nothing sales as well. If two public sector goods are to be produced in isolation, where the decision-making process for one is independent of the decision-making process of the other, each will have a boundary for its feasible majority set. If the goods are then combined in rigid proportions, the dollar value of the boundary of the combined goods will be greater if the proportions are altered to include a greater ratio of the elastic good to the inelastic one.

An example may clarify this point. Consider a two-good case where one individual is the median voter for both goods. Both goods have a cost to the median voter of $10 per unit. The median voter's demand function for good 1 is $Q_1 = 16 - P_1$, and for good 2 is $Q_2 = 16 - 4/5P_2$. Under these conditions, the reader can verify that the boundary of the feasible majority set is $Q_1 = 12$ and $Q_2 = 16$. Beyond these amounts, the median voter would prefer no output to the quantity offered. If n voters each paid $10 per unit for the goods, the boundary of the feasible majority set would be $280n.

Now assume that the decision-making processes for the two goods are combined, and that the goods can be purchased only in a predetermined ratio. If the ratio happens to be 12/16, which was chosen before, the feasible majority set would still be bounded by $280n total spending. But assume that it is determined beforehand that one unit of good 1 must be purchased with every unit of good 2. In this case, the two goods are combined to produce one composite good. For example, the levels of police and fire protection are determined simultaneously in a given ratio, rather than being independently chosen. In the numerical example, good 1 has the most elastic demand, and its proportion is increased. Adding the two demand curves gives $Q = 16 - 4/9P$, with a price of $20 for one unit of each good. The new boundary for the feasible majority set is $Q = 14.2$, which is a dollar amount of $284n. The boundary of the feasible majority set has increased.

Upon reflection, this makes intuitive sense. In essence, the price of the less elastic good has been raised to subsidize the more elastic good. The quantity demanded of the less elastic good falls by less than the increase for the more elastic good. The reverse would occur if the proportion of the less elastic good were increased.

While the details of the analysis are of interest on their own, the interesting finding in the context of the larger model is that the dollar boundary of the feasible majority set will depend upon the ratios of the goods that the government produces. In the two-dimensional case in figure 4.3, a constant ratio of Y to X would be given by a vector through the origin. Any straight line through the origin would give a constant ratio, but given the nature of the boundary of the feasible majority set, most ratios will not maximize the government's budget.

The boundary of the feasible majority set acts as a constraint on the government's budget because a majority will prefer zero expenditures to points outside the set. Since different points on the boundary have different dollar values, a simple budget-maximizing government will want to pick the point on the feasible majority set that represents the largest dollar outlay. A simple geometric construction can locate this point on figure 4.3. For clarity, the boundary of the feasible majority set in figure 4.3 is reproduced as FF in figure 8.1. Since the unit costs of X and Y are equal, equal dollar outlays are shown by lines with the slope -1, and line AA, tangent to FF, is the line with slope -1 farthest from the origin. Therefore, point B is the point that maximizes the government's budget subject to the constraint of the feasible majority set.

One of the conclusions frequently used in earlier chapters is that representative democracies will adhere to the principle of universalism as a stability-producing device. In two dimensions, this principle would provide equal amounts of X and Y, placing the outcome on a 45-degree line from the origin. OU is such a line, so the principle of universalism implies an outcome at point V, as opposed to the budget-maximizing point B. The outcome of the model in this book is one that adheres to the principle of universalism, placing the outcome on OU in figure 8.1. When the budget is maximized subject to the constraint of the feasible majority set, the outcome is not necessarily the largest outlay in the feasible majority set.

In this model, government expenditures are determined by elected representatives who benefit from higher expenditures. One might ask, therefore, why is it not possible to trade Y for X and move to point B. The reason is that the representative responsible for producing X for an interest group cannot satisfy

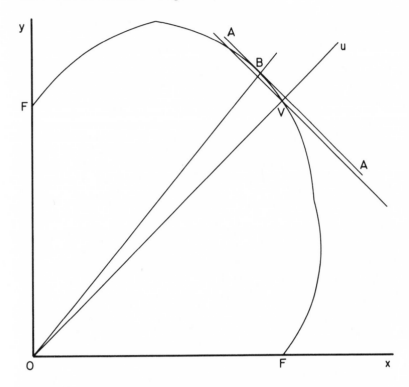

Fig. 8.1   The government budget constraint

the interest group with Y instead. The boundary of the feasible majority set is well beyond the Pareto optimal region, so there are not Pareto superior moves to be made by further increasing the budget. Line OU represents outcomes that accord with the principle of universalism, and FF is the boundary of the outcomes that would be preferred to no government spending. If this boundary constrains the government, then altering the mix of government spending could alter the level as well.

The possibility should also be noted that the agenda setter for a particular good may desire less than the budget-maximizing amount of the good. In a limited model, this may be a possibility. Looking back at figure 4.3, for example, if C were the agenda setter for X, and A the agenda setter for Y, these proposed amounts would be inside the boundary of the feasible majority set. The reader can see by looking at the arcs in figure 4.3 that if A and C were moved closer to their axes, the boundary of the feasible majority set would shift so that the agenda setters' proposals would be closer to the boundary. This implies that the greater the special interest orientation of the goods being produced, the more likely it will be that the government budget will be constrained by the boundary of the feasible majority set. In a more complex world, however, money not allocated to X or Y could be spent on other goods, as discussed in chapter 7.

So far, the discussion in this section has been rather analytic, focusing on geometric and algebraic properties of economic models. These conclusions will be discussed on a less formal level before closing the section. A basic conclusion from earlier chapters is that the government spends more than is Pareto optimal when government resources are allocated by representative democracy. Stability is provided by universalism, which is the outcome on line OU in figure 8.1. Since more spending will provide more votes, there seemingly is no limit to the level of government spending in this model. Thus, earlier chapters assumed a government budget constraint which has not been analyzed until now. Analytically, the principle of universalism and the implications derived from the prisoners' dilemma model in chapter 6 imply an outcome as far from the origin on OU as possible. The government's budget constraint limits the distance on OU.

This section has discussed the feasible majority set as a constraint. Analytically, the constraint arises because there is some point beyond which representatives would vote for no government rather than the logrolling coalition's proposed level. When a majority would vote against the coalition's level, the proposal is outside the feasible majority set. Stepping outside of the geometry, it appears that this model has some correspondence to the real world. The majority coalition can expand special interest programs beyond the Pareto optimal level because, according to the model in chapter 6, voters credit their representatives for the special interest programs that benefit them, but they do not blame their representatives for the taxes that are paid to finance everyone else's programs. The voters reason that the majority coalition could still fund their special interest programs without the vote of any one particular representative. Thus, voters reason that the bulk of the taxes will continue no matter what their representative does, but the special interest programs that benefit the voters are the result of the representative's actions.

While voters recognize the prisoners' dilemma nature of the representative's choice set, they also recognize that the excessive special interest spending of the government is due to the collective choices of the body of representatives, of which their representative is a part. Beyond some point, voters are willing to fault their representative for choosing the lower right cell of the prisoners' dilemma matrix, even while recognizing the incentive structure. Understanding this incentive structure, they find fault with the representative who selects the self-interested optimum rather than the option that is in the public interest.

That this is possible should not surprise anyone who has attempted to explain these types of concepts to others. For example, when the typical person is given the argument that it is not rational to vote because one vote has a very low probability of affecting the outcome of an election, the most frequent response is "But if everybody felt that way . . . ," and this response is not limited to people who have not studied the problem in detail. Douglas Hofstadter, who is an expert in artificial intelligence, examined the basic prisoners' dilemma problem at some length and concluded that when playing the game with other intelligent people who understand the game, the optimal individual strategy is to pick the social optimum rather than the private optimum.[2] Hofstadter drew this conclusion in the case where the game was to be played only once; if the game is to be played over and over, as in politics, the conclusion would be even stronger.

The point here is that even when the nature of the choices facing a representative is well understood, some people will still prefer the representative to choose the social optimum rather than the private optimum. The larger and more inefficient the government becomes, the more likely it is that voters will prefer representatives who do not cooperate with the inefficiency-producing majority coalition. The rational individual voter, after all, can vote against the logrolling representative as a protest, knowing that one vote will not perceptibly affect the representative's chances of reelection. When many voters protest, the representative will be unseated. This puts a limit to how large the government can grow and defines the boundary of the feasible majority set. Representatives will vote for additional government spending and remain in the majority coalition until the point where the loss in votes attributable to big government is larger than the gain from special interest spending.

This is an intuitive explanation for the geometric model that places bounds on the feasible majority set. It seems to have some relevance to politics in the 1980s, as voters at the polls have elected representatives who object to the special interest distributional programs that bloat the government's budget. But although the boundary of the feasible majority set may have been reached, there is no reason to believe that it will shift. A final question will provide a transition to the next section. One might wonder why, if a coalition of representatives can agree to distribute $X to the special interests of each representative, that they cannot also agree to $2X, $3X, or any $nX distribution. Why should constituents who agree to distributions of $X not agree to $nX? One explanation is that the excess burden of each distribution of $X is larger than the distribution before it. This leads to the topic of fiscal constraints on government spending.

Fiscal Constraints

The constraint of the feasible majority set is one that operates within the political structure. Fiscal considerations may affect the feasible majority set, but fiscal constraints may also be so binding that the feasible majority set offers no constraint. This section first will examine the nature of fiscal factors affecting the government budget and then will explicitly examine these factors as a constraint on the budget.

The revenue-raising process of the government has been taken for granted up to this point. The government has merely had to vote for more spending, and the revenues would be col-

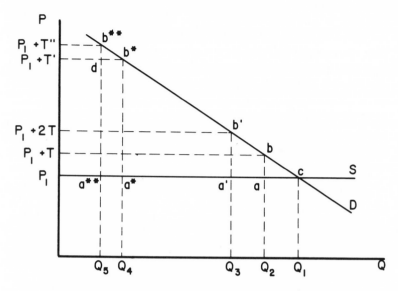

Fig. 8.2   The excess burden of taxation

lected to pay for the spending. This revenue collection involves an excess burden of taxation, so the section will begin by examining a few basic principles regarding the excess burden of taxation. These principles of taxation are not new to this analysis and, so, can be quickly explained with the aid of figure 8.2. Figure 8.2 is a supply and demand diagram for a typical market. The horizontal supply curve means that the market exhibits constant returns to scale and is used to make the diagram more clear. The reader can verify that these same principles will be true when the supply curve is upward sloping.

The first principle is that as the tax rate is raised by equal increments, the additional increment added to tax revenue declines, but the increment added to excess burden increases. Consider the market with no tax on the good, thus yielding price P_1 and quantity Q_1. Now a tax of T per unit is placed on the good. The price of the good, including the tax, increases to $P_1 + T$, reducing the quantity exchanged to Q_2. The tax revenue will be equal to the tax per unit times the number of units, or TQ_2. This equals the area of rectangle $(P_2 + T)P_1ab$. The excess burden, or welfare loss, of taxation equals the gains from trade not captured by buyers and sellers because of the tax, and equal the area of triangle abc.

Now consider a doubling of the tax rate to 2T. Since the quantity exchanged falls from Q_2 to Q_3, the total tax revenue of $2TQ_3$ is less than twice the old tax revenue of TQ_2. It will be generally true that the ratio of the higher tax rate to the lower tax rate will be greater than the ratio of the higher tax revenues to the lower tax revenues, because the higher tax rate causes people to substitute out of the taxed activity. An examination of the excess burden shows the opposite to be true. The new excess burden measured by triangle a'b'c is more than twice as large as abc, even though the tax rate has only doubled. The exercise could be continued to show that for equal increments added to the tax rate, the increment added to the excess burden becomes larger.[3]

This provides an appealing explanation for why voters might support a representative who participates in a distributive coalition that distributes $X, but would object to the representative's behavior when the coalition distributes $nX, for n above some critical value. As the value of $nX grows, the excess burden associated with the distribution grows more than proportionally.

With the linear demand curve depicted in figure 8.2, equal increments added to the tax rate will cause equal increments to be subtracted from the quantity exchanged. Since the price (including the tax) is rising and the quantity is falling this means that equal increments added to the tax rate will cause the percentage increase in the tax rate to be smaller at each increment and the percentage decrease in the quantity to be larger at each increment. Economists generally believe that demand becomes more elastic at higher prices, and this principle illustrated for linear demand curves holds for any demand curve that is more elastic the higher the price. For equal increments added to the tax rate, the percentage increase in the tax decreases, and the percentage decrease in the quantity exchanged increases. At some point, the percentage increase in the tax will be less than the percentage decrease in the quantity, which means that an increase in the tax rate, T, will cause a decrease in tax revenues, TQ.

This can clearly be seen at tax rate T' in figure 8.2. An increase in the tax rate from T' to T''' causes tax revenues to change from $T'Q_4$ to $T''Q_5$. The loss in tax revenues from the lower quantity, rectangle a**a*b*d, is clearly greater than the gain $(P_1 + T')(P_1 + T'')$b**d which is attributable to the higher rate. Beyond some point, an increase in tax rates will cause tax revenues to fall.

This idea has been popularized as the Laffer curve, and it has been suggested by some that the U.S. economy is at a point where a decrease in tax rates could cause tax revenues to increase.[4] This may or may not be the case, but two observations are warranted at this point. First, since tax rates could rise to the point where higher rates could not raise more revenue, there is some maximum amount of tax revenue that could be raised. Thus, the Laffer curve could act as a fiscal constraint on government spending. If this is the case, then the government cannot spend more because the government cannot raise any more revenue. This type of constraint on government spending will henceforth be called a fiscal constraint.

The second observation is that different tax bases can be taxed at different rates, so that some tax bases may be fiscally constrained from raising more revenue, while others may not. With property taxes, sales taxes, excise taxes, income taxes, import duties, and the like, it is unlikely that each tax base is at the same point on its own Laffer curve. One of the suggestions regarding the progressive income tax has been that for the highest brackets, a lower rate would raise more revenue, even though this would not be the case for lower brackets. The point here is that a government that becomes fiscally constrained on one tax base may have to seek increases in alternate tax bases to continue the government's growth. It may be, for example, that at one time the government's budget constraint was the feasible majority set, but over time the feasible majority set has shifted outward. At some point, the feasible majority set might meet a fiscal constraint for some tax base, at which time the mix of taxes might be altered by a government interested in more spending.

The basic points made in this section can be summarized as follows. First, increasing tax rates result in more-than-proportional increases in the excess burden of taxation. This provides a transition from the previous section, because it explains why voters may not object to having their representative engage in some distributive logrolling but may object to this activity beyond some critical level. Second, higher tax rates result in a less-than-proportional increase in revenue raised. Beyond some point, the percentage increase in tax rates will be less than the percentage decrease in the taxed activity, meaning that higher tax rates will cause lower tax revenues. This acts as a fiscal constraint on government spending, since there is a maximum amount of revenue that the government can raise. Finally, some tax bases may have reached this point of fiscal constraint while others may not. Thus, a government that is running into fiscal constraints on some tax bases may alter the tax structure to try to exploit unconstrained sources of revenue.

Combining the discussion in the previous two sections, the government faces two constraints to its level of spending. One constraint is the feasible majority set, which sets the limits on the amount of spending that a majority will approve. The other is a fiscal constraint which limits the amount of revenue that can be taxed out of an economy. In a mathematical sense, only one of these constraints will be binding, although the level of government spending may be close to both constraints. In this case, both constraints will be relevant even though only one may be binding. Previous chapters have argued that the representatives in a representative government have an incentive to increase government spending. This can be accomplished by increasing the boundaries of the government's budget constraint. The remainder of the chapter will be devoted to examining some aspects of the government's budgetry process to see how they relate to the govenment's budget constraint.

Federalism

One factor that may have a bearing on the boundary of the feasible majority set is the level of government at which goods and services are provided. One aspect of this factor has already been discussed. The distributive model of government developed in earlier chapters arose because voters credit their representatives for the special interest programs that benefit them at the expense of the general taxpayer but do not blame their representatives for the taxes that pay for the special interest programs of others. One way to counteract this effect is to provide public sector goods and services at the smallest level of government possible. This concentrates the cost on the smallest group of taxpayers possible and thus provides more concentrated costs to accompany the concentrated benefits. Special interest legislation provides concentrated federal benefits to Wisconsin dairy farmers and North Carolina tobacco farmers, but it is unlikely that if the federal programs were moved to the state level that the states would continue the programs. The costs would be too concentrated. Thus, federalism, by providing for the costs of government to be more closely matched to the beneficiaries, can reduce the boundary of the feasible majority set.

Another factor which enables a federal system to constrain governmental expenditures is the prospect of intergovernmental competition.[5] Intergovernmental competition constrains government spending in several ways. The most widely recognized is the phenomenon known as "voting with your feet." When there are many local governments in an area, an individual can choose the local government that provides the most satisfactory mix of taxes and government goods and services. In a mobile society, this factor is likely to be especially effective. There are limits to the level of efficiency that can be generated by mobility, but this should not detract the observer from appreciating the possibility of efficiency gains.[6]

While mobility may be important, another factor in intergovernmental competition that has not been sufficiently appreciated by economists is simply the ability of taxpayer-voters to observe other similar governments which can be compared to their own. If a neighboring school district provides better education at a lower cost, voters will be ready to replace their school board, for example. Mobility is not required for this type of intergovernmental competition; all that is necessary is comparable units of government and competition for public office. This type of competition works best where mobility is an option, as in competing local communities. It also works, but less well, at the state level. At the state level, there are enough differences between states to make simple comparisons more difficult. The comparisons become almost impossible at the national level.

As a result, representatives at higher levels of government have a greater ability to produce spending programs that are inefficiently large. At lower levels, comparisons are more easily made with similar governments, requiring representatives who compete for office to produce a government that compares favorably with surrounding governments. A better-than-average government is more likely to have its representatives reelected than a worse than average government. Viewed from the standpoint of a revenue-maximizing government, it is preferable to produce public sector output at the highest level possible.

The revenue-maximizing government is overly simple in this case because there is a conflict involved among the levels of government. An activity moved from a lower level to a higher level may be favored by those at the higher level, but those at lower levels of government will lose revenue as a result of the loss of programs that have moved to a higher level. One possible solution for this problem would be to have the higher level of government collect the taxes and then transfer the tax revenue to the lower level of government. At the same time, the higher level of government can impose standards on the lower level, or require matching funds, or both. This leaves governmental officials at all levels of government better off.

The individuals at higher levels of government benefit because they gain control over revenues that were formerly controlled at lower levels. The individuals at lower levels of government benefit because the marginal cost to the local taxpayers of additional local programs will decrease. To receive funding from the higher level, regulations may require that certain standards be met. In addition, since funding will come at least partially from the higher level of government, local voters have an incentive to have their representatives produce the programs that will get them a share of the state or federal money. Furthermore, the role of standards to qualify for money from higher governments makes the local governments more homogeneous, which reduces intergovernmental competition. In effect, programs like revenue sharing are a method of cartelizing lower governments to eliminate intergovernmental competition.[7]

Revenue sharing cartelizes lower governments by standardizing their outputs. The more homogeneous governments are, the less competition will exist among them. This reduction in competition alone should give governments more of an ability to grow. The marginal cost of programs with matching funds is also lower, further encouraging expansion. When this is combined with the fact that revenues are collected at higher levels of government, there are many reasons why voters would favor more spending, and why government could have the capability to produce more spending even if the increases did not constitute a Pareto superior move. Aggregating programs at higher levels of government is a method of pushing out the boundary of the feasible majority set. It, in effect, cartelizes lower levels of government and produces an environment where a majority will agree to larger expenditures than if spending were more disaggregated. Revenue sharing, federally mandated standards, and the like, are methods of expanding the feasible majority set of the government. This suggests that at least in some areas government spending is constrained by the feasible majority set.

Budgeting Procedures

The government's budgeting procedures can have a significant effect on the size of the feasible majority set. The previous section on federalism provides an indication of this with regard to the benefit principle of taxation. According to the benefit principle, tax payments are rendered in exchange for governmental goods and services. Fiscal federalism would move government programs to lower levels of government, which would make the programs adhere more to the benefit principle and reduce the size of the feasible majority set. Special interests will readily let others pay for inefficient programs that provide some benefits to the special interests, but they will not be willing to pay for the inefficient programs themselves, since the cost will exceed the value of the programs. Thus, Wicksell suggested that the fund raising for government programs be voted on at the same time as the program as a method of directly comparing the costs and benefits.[8]

Programs with cost/benefit ratios of greater than 1 certainly have a lower chance of approval if the taxation must be approved simultaneously with the spending. There is no guarantee in majority rule that a majority would not exploit a minority to pass inefficient programs, but the reciprocity principle would suggest that a stable exploitative majority would not exist, and voters would have a clear opportunity of seeing their representatives vote for issues against the voters' interests. The ideal situation would be to consider programs one at a time, with the taxes to pay for the programs included in the proposal. A problem with this scheme arises even if proposals may be lumped together and considered as a set. Then, a unanimous coalition could arise supporting a set of proposals that contained something for everybody. As in the model earlier in the book, each representative could be sheltered by the fact that if the individual representative did not participate, the representatives' constituents would still pay taxes for everyone else's programs but would not get special interest programs of their own.[9]

This relates directly to a procedure that is sometimes used in logrolling. A bill with broad general support will sometimes have appended to it a proposal obviously catering to some special interest group. This tactic is useful when the president favors the bill, and so he will not veto it even though he may object to the special interest proposal. As a matter of policy, allowing the president the power for item veto would allow the special interest proposal to be vetoed while the rest of the bill is made law. This makes sense particularly because the president is elected by the nation as a whole and, so, has more of an incentive to consider the general public interest.

Writers in public finance tend to emphasize the difference between public finance and personal finance, but the adhering to some principles of sound personal finance would constrain the size of government spending to keep programs from getting out of hand. One such idea would be to approve spending programs only for a certain number of dollars rather than making them open-ended. For example, a food stamp program that grants aid to anyone who meets certain criteria has the potential for spending much more than the program estimate. This is especially true as the program ages and its general provisions do not change. Congress tends to simply approve funds to continue the existing program. This observation avoids the difficult question of how a representative body can be constrained from approving funds in this manner, however.

One possibility would be to change the budgeting process altogether. Presently, Congress passes spending bills, and the sum of all of the spending bills ends up being the government budget. Each program may look desirable on its own, but the sum looks undesirably large. Most individuals can see the problems with this type of budgeting, because most individuals find that there are many worthwhile things they could spend their money on, and that when all of these worthwhile things are added up, the cost is greater than the individual's income. The individual must choose among the many possible worthwhile expenditures, but this is something the government never does. Even when almost everyone in government searches for ways to limit government spending, it is easy to point to multitudes of special interest programs that are obviously not cost-effective yet cannot be reduced because of the political environment in which they are generated.

By drawing a parallel to personal finance, the reader can see that the argument does not turn on the programs being inefficient, however. It could merely be a case where each program looks acceptable in isolation, but the sum of all programs looks too large. In this case, personal finance can suggest a solution as well. An individual has a budget and then divides it into smaller portions, allocating some for housing, some for food, some for transportation, and so forth. The government could budget in the same way, by first approving an aggregate level of spending and then allocating portions of the total to various programs. By approving the total level of spending first, there is a greater likelihood that the aggregate size of the budget will be closer to optimal.

Under such a system, if Congress wanted to spend more money, it would have to go through the process of approving an increase in the existing budget level. This way, an explicit decision would have to be made to spend more money. What about programs with unexpectedly large expenditures? This is a problem that households must deal with also, but the government's solution would be easier than the household's. The government could merely vote itself more money. Such a change would be likely to act as a constraint. Presently, Congress anguishes over voting to increase the debt ceiling, and this is merely a decision to pay for programs that have already been authorized. Congress might find it more difficult to explicitly approve a larger aggregate budget than it does to approve a few more special interest programs.

A possible way to reduce the size of the feasible majority set would be to change the budgeting procedure to require Congress to approve an aggregate spending level first and then to allocate portions of the total to spending programs. An increase in aggregate spending would require a new vote to explicitly increase government spending. As it is now, individual programs are approved which result in some spending level, and the level can be increased relatively painlessly just by passing another program. This idea may sound attractive, but it is unlikely to ever be enacted. The reason is that Congress would have to approve of the change, and Congress would be most unlikely to vote to constrain itself that way.

Borrowing

The issues discussed in the past few sections have been regarding the boundary of the feasible majority set as a budget constraint. The government may also face fiscal constraints, and there is some evidence that the government has been pushing back these fiscal constraints in the past few decades. One of the most obvious ways is through borrowing. By way of a general introduction, governments use a variety of tax bases to raise revenues. Centuries ago, import duties were common, and they still are in less developed nations.[10] Income taxes, sales taxes, property taxes, and excise taxes provide examples of the many other tax bases that are used. By using more tax bases, the government can raise more revenue with a lower excess burden than if fewer tax bases are used. This expands the amount of revenue that the government can raise before being fiscally constrained.

As a simple example, imagine a government that decides to raise all of its revenue through a tax on motor gasoline. Before the tax rate got very high, people would substitute into propane, solar power, electricity, walking, and other alternatives, so the government would soon become fiscally constrained. In order to capture some revenue lost because of the substitutions, the government might also begin taxing propane, electricity, and other energy sources. Broadening the tax base increases the amount of revenue that can be raised.

An income tax is a broadly based tax because individuals can avoid it only by substituting into leisure. The desirability to the government of an income tax from this standpoint is somewhat offset by the difficulties of monitoring and collecting the tax. These cuts make an income tax difficult to collect in less developed economies. A major factor in the high rates of income taxation in the United States is withholding. Taxes are monitored and collected by employers and certainly income tax collections would be far below their existing levels without withholding. Income tax rates may also be constrained by the feasible majority set, and progressive tax rates appear to be a way to avoid this constraint. A majority is willing to approve of higher tax rates for a minority of wealthy taxpayers, expanding the tax base, but by special interest legislation, wealthy taxpayers have been able to find ways to avoid tax payments. This is somewhat far afield from the topic at hand; the discussion is trying to illustrate the principle that expanding the tax base can increase the maximum amount of tax revenues that can be collected before the government becomes fiscally constrained.

Government borrowing has been the most notable source of new revenues for the government in recent decades. Before the 1930s, the government ran deficits during wars, but generally ran surpluses in peacetime to try to repay the public debt. Precedent was set for deficit spending during emergencies, and although the Great Depression was not a war, the severity of the depression allowed deficit financing to be viewed as acceptable as a temporary measure to try to restore economic health. Economic health finally returned only during World War II, and then during a time of deficit spending. The 1950s saw a return to the fiscal responsibility of balanced budgets.

During the 1930s and 1940s, borrowing had provided a method for the government to spend more than otherwise would have been possible. In other words, without deficit spending the government would have been fiscally constrained to a lower level of spending than actually occurred. The use of government borrowing can expand the government's budget constraint, but the problem with borrowing is that voters, in drawing an analogy between personal finance and public finance, see borrowing as fiscally irresponsible except in times of emergency. Buchanan and Wagner[11] have persuasively argued that the acceptance of Keyne's ideas in his *General Theory*[12] provided an intellectual foundation for the continuing running of budget deficits, and that this intellectual foundation provided politicans with an avenue for expanding the size of the government's budget beyond its then existing fiscal constraints by making a new tax base available. One might debate who actually pays the taxes,[13] but the addition of borrowing to the government's tax base expands the ability of the government to collect revenue.[14]

Taxation by Regulation

The observation that the government increases its tax bases in order to expand the amount of revenue it can raise before it becomes fiscally constrained is interesting in general, but there is no need to enumerate every case. Borrowing is notable because of its recent prominent use, which is coincident with a period of growing government. Another notable instance is taxation by regulation, and while regulation is not ordinarily viewed as a method of broadening the tax base, it can certainly serve that function.

Regulation as a form of taxation has been explicitly recognized only recently,[15] but the theory is quite straightforward. Regulations have the effect of producing benefits for some people while imposing costs on others. Someone must benefit, or nobody would have the incentive to see that regulations are established. Costs must be imposed on someone, or the effects of the regulation could have been achieved by voluntary exchange. The costs of regulation have the same effect as taxation on the bearer of the costs, and the benefits of the regulation are effectively a benefit paid to the recipient from the government, so that regulation is equivalent to taxation. Regulation might be preferred to taxation if benefits of the same value can be achieved more cheaply by regulation than taxation. Alternatively, regulation may be viewed as another tax base that can be exploited to push out the boundary of the government's budget constraint.

Unlike deficit financing, the use of regulation to further the aims of special interest groups through the political process is not a recent development. While government spending has grown rapidly in the twentieth century, there is evidence that special interests have always used the regulatory powers of government to their advantage.[16] Nevertheless, this regulation must be viewed as a part of the tax base, and if the government runs into fiscal constraints on other margins, regulation may be substituted for taxation with much the same effects.

Conclusions and Recommendations

At this point, it is possible to make some recommendations to increase the efficiency of public sector resource allocation. The recommendations at this point involve ways in which the government's budget constraint can be shifted inward to try to contain special interest programs fostered by representative government, so they rest heavily on the conclusions of earlier chapters. Those who believe that government spending is excessive will seek ways to control it. Those who believe otherwise will want to relax the government's budget constraint.[17] Also, the recommendations here only involve the level of government spending. The program mix of spending, which also is inefficient, will be dealt with later.

The basic theory of the book is that representatives enhance their opportunities of reelection by passing special interest legislation. They must trade votes in order to get the legislation passed. Logrolling to pass special interest legislation continues until government spending is constrained by the government budget constraint. This constraint may take two forms. First, there is the boundary of the feasible majority set, and second, there is fiscal constraint that limits the amount of revenue that the government can raise. Recommendations that limit the amount of government spending are recommendations to tighten one of these two constraints.

Direct budgetary limitations, such as Proposition 13 in California, readily come to mind as a method of fiscal constraint. The government is prevented by law from raising more than the prescribed level. A requirement for a balanced budget would also fall under the same category. Deficit spending in effect enlarges the tax base, so a mandated balanced budget could constrain government spending. These recommendations have the drawback that they may curb spending on efficient programs as well as inefficient ones.

Another possibility would be to require the Congress to approve a level of government spending that could not be exceeded without the majority approval of Congress. Congress would have the option of taking money from some programs to finance others, but an increase in the aggregate level of spending would require an explicit vote. This way, the government could not exceed its budget simply by voting for another special interest program or two. Since Congress seems to find it so objectionable to vote to raise the debt ceiling for spending already authorized, they might also find it difficult to get a majority to explicitly approve of a larger budget. This proposal argues that, as in responsible personal finance, the aggregate budget is determined first and then is allocated to various spending priorities to stay within the budget, rather than determining how much it would be desirable to spend in each category and then summing to discover the total budget. This proposal shares with the earlier ones the possible defect that representative government might shift spending from more efficient areas to less efficient areas in order to pursue interest group politics and still remain within the constraint.

Another proposal which has much to offer is to decentralize government taxing and spending as much as possible. Increased fiscal federalism would have several advantages. First, it would enable the benefit principle of taxation to be more nearly applied. Those who would benefit from government spending would also be those who would pay the taxes. With taxes and benefits more closely correlated, those who receive special interest benefits would pay a larger share of the taxes. In addition, taxpayers who are not in the recipient special interest group would be taxed more for each program as a result of the more concentrated nature of the taxes. This would result in a more clearly identifiable group bearing the costs as well as a clearly identifiable group receiving the benefits. Increased federalism would also increase the scope of intergovernmental competition. People would be more able to "vote with their feet," and residents in one jurisdiction would have others nearby for comparison with their own government. Officials in better-than-average governments would have a better chance of reelection than those in worse-than-average governments. Where possible, the movement of programs to a lower level of government is a good idea.

Another recommendation with much merit is to allow the president item veto on bills from Congress. This would allow the president to veto items on bills without vetoing the whole bill. Since the president is elected by the nation at large, he is less susceptible to the influence of special interests. Allowing an item veto would allow the veto of pork-barrel legislation while leaving the rest of a bill intact.

The final recommendation, which is perhaps the best, can be traced back to Wicksell. This recommendation is to require explicit provisions for the source of revenue to be incorporated into each spending bill. This way, it is perfectly clear at the time the bill is passed who will be paying the cost, so representatives will always be required to pass a taxing bill at the same time a spending bill is passed. In addition, in order for a program to go over its original budget, another spending bill would have to be explicitly passed. In order for such a change to be meaningful, a tax source would have to be specified clearly so that all taxes would become earmarked taxes. A good example would be to earmark the gasoline tax for highway maintenance. More could not be spent on highways unless Congress explicitly raised the tax or allocated another source. There would be no general fund financing because there would be no general revenues. The tax base and the funds use would not have to be related (although there are other arguments for making them so). For example, Congress could increase highway funding by earmarking 5 percent of the corporate income tax to highways as well.

It would also be possible to limit a program's spending to the earmarked tax revenues or a dollar limit, whichever is less. This could provide some temporary revenues for other programs. What if earmarked revenues were less than anticipated?

Then Congress would have to explicitly consider the opportunity cost of additional funding to pass a spending bill. These are details, though, that can be refined at a later time. The main point is that by requiring every spending bill to specify its source of revenue, taxes and spending will be explicitly considered together, giving those who will pay the taxes more of a chance to defend their interests.

The representative government modeled in this book is one that caters to special interests, passing special interest legislation to enhance the probability of being reelected. Special interest legislation will be passed as long as the representative government does not exceed its budget constraint, so one way to control the government is to further constrain its budget. The suggestions made here could constrain the government's budget further, but some suggestions are better than others. A simple limitation of the budget, while it may on net be beneficial, does not address the root of the problem. A more satisfactory solution would alter the incentive structure of the public sector to limit the incentives for special interest legislation, so the recommendations like linking taxation and spending programs and increasing the degree of federalism look attractive. They would be likely to produce a more efficient mix of government spending in addition to limiting its level.

9 / Cycles, Stability, and Economic Efficiency

The theory developed in earlier chapters argues that special interest group politics in a representative government causes spending on special interest programs to be inefficiently large. Meanwhile, legislators do not have the incentive to pursue programs that are in the general public interest. The government will be inefficiently large because it will spend until it reaches its budget constraint, and the budget constraint is beyond the Pareto optimal government size. In addition to the inefficient size of government, the composition of government spending is also inefficient. This theory seems to be descriptive of the actual workings of representative democracies; and in addition, it should be emphasized that the inefficient results of governmental activity occur as a result of each individual behaving in a way that is privately optimal. The result is not socially optimal because of the incentive structure inherent in the public sector. Some people are given the right to decide how other people's money will be spent. Furthermore, the representative body is not directly allowed to appropriate governmental funds but must spend the funds for programs to benefit other people. Needless to say, representatives will choose to benefit people who can offer reciprocal benefits. Add to this the fact that voters in general do not have an incentive to become informed about government activity in general, but that special interests do have an incentive to become informed about their particular programs, and it would seem that the only possible outcome would be inefficiency.

There is an argument on the other side that must be considered, and that cannot be completely refuted on theoretical grounds. If the government really is inefficient, then there would be a possible reallocation of resources that could make some people better off without making anyone worse off. Inefficiency implies this to be so, and if it is so, then the incentive exists for someone to propose a more efficient reallocation that will harm nobody but benefit some. The entrepreneur that proposes such a reallocation will then be in a position to capture some of the gains from increased efficiency. The more inefficient the government is, the larger the potential gains will be, meaning that the political entrepreneur will have a larger incentive to produce efficiency the greater the inefficiency is. Some might object that the theory of inefficient government is implausible on these grounds, because it means that political entrepreneurs are failing to see and take advantage of possible opportunities for gain.[1]

This argument against inefficiency in government will probably find more sympathy among economic theorists than anyone else. The typical citizen sees inefficiency in government daily and can cite instance after instance. The economic theorist, on the other hand, argues that given transactions and information costs, things that appear inefficient at first actually may be efficient when all costs are considered. Economics since Adam Smith's day has had a great tradition in explaining how individuals are guided as if by an invisible hand to use their self-interest to allocate resources efficiently. The formula for the invisible hand has been enhanced over the centuries, and the Coase theorem,[2] which is perhaps its strongest variant, is a powerful elixir. Economists have had much success with the argument that where the incentive exists, all gains from trade will be exploited. If they are not, then transactions costs must be too high.

This argument can be taken at two levels. At one level, it is axiomatically true. If nobody has done anything to elminate an observed instance of inefficiency, then either it is not worth anyone's while (transaction costs are too high), or the inefficiency may not be clearly perceived or understood by those who are in a position to profit from its elimination (information costs are too high). Either way, when all costs are considered, the world is optimal as it now exists. Taking this critique at the axiomatic level, everything in the world is always optimal. Applied to government, this axiomatic approach to the Coase theorem argues that government activity is optimal as it currently exists, because if it were not, somebody would have acted on the incentive to change it.

This axiomatic approach may be trivially true, but it seems especially inappropriate when applied to government. A government, after all, is not a group of autonomous individuals interacting as in a market. A government is not, to use a favorite phrase of Hayek's, the result of human action but not of human design.[3] A government is the result of human design. Thus, it seems appropriate to analyze the institutions designed by humans to see if some design features cause high transactions costs and high information costs. Understanding how inefficient institutions can arise and perpetuate themselves in itself lowers information costs. If the sources of inefficiency can be better understood, then the designers of institutions will be in a better position to eliminate them.

This discussion is not meant to detract from the power of the argument that where inefficiencies exist, someone has an incentive to eliminate them. One problem may be that large numbers of people must organize to increase efficiency,[4] but governments are organizations of large numbers of people. The model in this book appears to be descriptive of the actual operation of a representative democracy, but there are incentives to overcome inefficient allocations of resources. It is the institutional structure of government—the result of human design—that causes the inefficiency, but that does not rule out the possibility that political entrepreneurs may discover a way to distribute the gains from efficiency in such a way to make an efficient change possible.

An important problem that is a transaction cost inhibiting

efficiency is the problem of distributing the gains from increased efficiency. An efficient change will provide gains so that it would be possible to improve the welfare of some people while harming nobody. If everyone is going to agree to a change, then not only must it be possible to benefit some without harming anyone, it must also be done.[5] Otherwise, those who would be harmed will object to the change, and may be able to block it. For example, price supports to dairy farmers are inefficient, so it should be possible to eliminate the supports, pay the farmers the value of what the supports would have been worth to them, and have money left over. If this is to be done, the dairy farmers could be paid immediately for the present value of the future stream of benefits they would have received, or they could be paid some each year once the price supports were abolished. The first solution is likely to meet with resistance from taxpayers who would object to large lump-sum payments going to people just because they are dairy farmers. Furthermore, taxpayers would have good reason to believe that once the payments were made, dairly farmers would again try to use their political influence to receive additional special interest benefits. But if dairy farmers were to be paid a small amount each year, the dairy farmers might worry that such an obvious welfare program to dairy farmers would be halted. Furthermore, there must be some way to identify those who qualify for the payment. One easy way to monitor is to pay in proportion to the amount of dairy products produced. This is what the price support does, and it is inefficient because it causes too many resources to be devoted to dairy farming in order to qualify for the program.

The problem, in short, is this. The elimination of inefficient programs will create gainers and losers, but the losers will be those who had the political power to have the program established in the first place. Thus, in order to get political approval for the elimination of the program, the losers must be compensated. However, it is difficult to come up with a credible compensation scheme that, first, cannot be reneged on and, second, guarantees that the interest group will not again exploit the political process for more special interest benefits once the compensation has been paid. Although there may be potential efficiency gains, sometimes the difficulty of compensating losers in a political environment will prevent the efficiency gains from arising.

Much has been said about the inefficiency of government, yet the model developed here discusses only one particular type of inefficiency. It will be useful at this point to discuss governmental inefficiency in general in order to clarify the relationship of this study with others regarding the effiency of government.

The Anatomy of Government Failure

An important article in the public finance literature in the late 1950s was Francis Bator's "The Anatomy of Market Failure." In that article, Bator enumerated reasons why the market might fail to produce results as efficient as a frictionless perfectly competitive economy. At the time, economists tended to draw the policy implication that if the market could not perfectly produce this state that was theoretically ideal, then there is a role for the government to intervene to try to push the economy toward that ideal. One of the contributions of the public choice literature that has been published since Bator's classic article has been to show that the government may also fail to produce this ideal. Some of the reasons why will be discussed here.[6] The details of the reasons for government failure will be familiar to economists and public choice theorists, so they are discussed very superficially in this section. The purpose for this discussion is not elaboration but, rather, the organization of the general principles.

One reason for government inefficiency that has been extensively analyzed by public finance theorists is the excess burden of taxation. The excess burden of taxation arises because when a tax is placed on some activity, it discourages that activity. This distortion in relative prices means that government activity causes the economy to move away from the theoretical ideal of perfect competition. It should be noted that if market prices are distorted, for example, by an externality, then a corrective tax will produce an excess benefit.

A second reason for government inefficiency is that the

managerial incentives in a government bureaucracy cause the bureaucrat to benefit from budget maximization rather than profit maximization as in the private sector.[7] Bureaucrats acting as budget maximizers are able to increase their budgets beyond the optimal size, resulting in excessive government spending. Niskanen's insightful analysis of bureaucracy coined the term process efficiency, which means that the government produces its output at the lowest possible resource cost given its output. Niskanen assumed that the government would be process efficient as long as government output has any value at the margin, in order to focus on the incentive structure that leads to budget maximization rather than profit maximization and to the inefficiencies that result from budget-maximizing activity.

A third reason for government inefficiency is, to retain Niskanen's terminology, process inefficiency. Again, the incentive structure of the government is the cause, but this time it relates to the fact that nobody who is producing the output has a property right in profits from production, so nobody has an incentive to see that output is produced at minimum cost.[8] As a result, government will spend more to produce the same output than would a similar firm in the private sector. Numerous studies by economists have supported this claim.[9] A common public perception of government activity is that the government is inefficient, and it seems that the public perceives process inefficiency much more readily than the other types listed.

A fourth reason for government inefficiency is what has recently been called rent seeking.[10] The government has the power to produce economic rents for individuals. Some examples include placing tariffs or quotas on goods that compete with the goods that the individual produces, or granting an individual or group the right to complete monopoly power in a market. The rents to be earned are valuable; therefore, individuals will invest resources to earn those rents. The tariff or monopoly may be inefficient in itself, but the great insight of the rent-seeking literature is that resources are used by individuals who try to capture those rents, and that often the resource expenditure to try to capture the rents can far exceed the excess burden associated with the rent-generating activity.

From the individual's point of view, it may be productive to invest in trying to capture rents, but from a social standpoint, the expenditure of resources produces nothing new, and so is socially wasteful. Again, the government is inefficient.

The inefficiency that results from special interest politics in a representative government, which is the main theme of this book, is yet another type of inefficiency. This taxonomy is presented at this point to illustrate that the inefficiency described here is a small part of the reason why government could produce inefficiently, and to further illustrate that the model in the book does not explain why government is inefficient. It explains only one aspect of that inefficiency dealing with decision making by representative democracy. This discussion should help to clarify how the present work is related to other work in the general area of democratic decision making. Needless to say, much more can be—and has been—said about each of these other types of government failure.

Most people agree with the statement that other people will not spend your money as carefully as you will. The general idea certainly applies to government, where your money is collected as taxes and then spent by other people. Most people can cite instances of governmental inefficiency, but a general taxonomy helps to clearly identify the sources of inefficiency. There is little hope of improving efficiency if the sources of inefficiency are not understood.

Stability-Producing Mechanisms

This chapter, thus, far, has tried to make two main points. First, the type of inefficiency that arises in this book's model is only one of many possible sources of inefficiency in government. Second, the inefficiency is a result of the individual incentives produced by the institutional structure of representative democracy. However, the inefficient outcome leaves open the possibility of a Pareto superior move, and the potential gains from trade provide an incentive for such a trade. Thus, the question arises concerning why these potential gains from trade are left unclaimed.

There is a natural tendency for economists to seek the optimal outcome for any exchange. Indeed, profit maximization and utility maximization are accepted descriptions of economic behavior, even though they describe the result of the behavior and not the behavior itself.[11] This maximizing behavior leads to stable equilibriums in the private sector of the economy. Even if the many assumptions of the models are met,[12] it is still useful to realize that at the simplest level, there is a basic instability with regard to market exchange.[13] Consider the elementary example where A has a banana and B has an apple, but A prefers apples to bananas, and B prefers bananas to apples. The optimal outcome results when A and B trade. However, notice that a potential cycle can occur. Compared to the trade, A would prefer that both the apple and the banana go to A. Likewise, B would prefer that both go to B. Thus, for both participants in the exchange, there is another outcome that is preferred to the exchange. However, B would not voluntarily agree to unilaterally transfer the apple to A; thus, without B's consent, no trade will occur and A will keep the banana, while B keeps the apple. From the situation where no trade occurs, both individuals would prefer an exchange. Thus, the cycle is complete.

This cycle can be illustrated in figure 9.1[14] In that figure, A stands for apple and B stands for banana. The letters to the left of the bar show individual A's fruit portfolio, and B's is shown to the right. Thus, B|A indicates that A owns the banana and B owns the apple, while |AB means A owns nothing while B has both fruit. The initial situation, B|A, is shown at the bottom of the figure, and the arrow shows that a trade-producing A|B dominates B|A because both individuals prefer the other's fruit. However, A, who must agree to the trade, would prefer AB|, while B, in the same situation, would prefer |AB. However, neither would voluntarily agree to the unilateral transfer, meaning that B|A dominates AB| and |AB. This illustrates the potential cycle, despite the usual economist's assertion that in this case A|B—the exchange—is the stable equilibrium solution. At this point, it is important to understand why an economist can make this assertion.

First, observe that A|B is not the only possible stable solution.

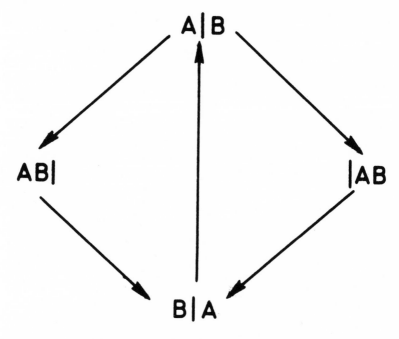

Fig. 9.1   Cycles in a market exchange

If A is more powerful than B, A may be able to force B to a unilateral transfer. This brings to mind insitutions like slavery and taxation, but in a two-person setting, it is not hard to imagine the more powerful threatening harm to the less powerful unless a unilateral transfer is periodically made. Thus, |AB and AB| can be possible stable equilibria. Likewise, some potentially profitable trades may not occur because of possible problems with enforcing the terms. B would agree to tender an apple today for an orange tomorrow only if B had some assurance that A actually would return tomorrow with the orange. Also, if the quality of a good cannot be known at the time of exchange, an individual might pay more to trade with an established vendor with brand name capital and might pass up a trade with an unknown for the samegood at a lower price. Thus, the outcome B|A, where no trade takes place, is also a possible stable equilibrium.

What ground, then, does an economist have for claiming that

the profitable market exchange is a stable equilibrium? It is a series of assumptions implied in the model of competitive markets. The first (which certainly does not apply to the public sector) is that all transfers of resources are voluntary. This prevents the unilateral transfers (|AB and AB|) which share with the exchange the characteristic of being Pareto optimal. In addition, trades take place because there is an enforcement mechanism that forces one individual to tender the goods once the other individual has done so. While contracts are sometimes used as an enforcement mechanism, the usual device is simultaneous exchange. B gives A the apple at the same time that A gives B the banana.

The point here is that there is an instability inherent in market exchange that is overcome by the institutional structure of market economies. This institutional structure is often taken for granted by economists, but throughout history it has not existed in many places where the desire for self-sufficiency has caused individuals to pass up possible gains from trade, where unilateral transfers have been forced, and so forth. There is also an instability inherent in democratic decisions, and this instability is also overcome by the institutional structure of democracy. In market exchange, stability-producing mechanisms tend to produce Pareto superior trades, but this section has illustrated other possible outcomes. Likewise, in politics, stability-producing mechanisms may sometimes produce something other than a Pareto optimum.

The major factor that inhibits democracies from producing Pareto optimal results is that some individuals are automatically given the right, by being in the majority, to coerce others. It certainly should not be surprising, then, that majority rule does not always produce optimal outcomes.

Bureaucracy as a Stability-Producing Mechanism

The universalism and reciprocity that exist in a representative democracy produce stability, but there are other types of stability-producing mechanisms in government as well. One is the bureaucracy that is characteristic of twentieth-century governments. Most of those who study bureaucracy conclude that it is an inefficient allocator of resources.[15] This naturally leads to the question of why bureaucracy would ever be used to allocate

resources. The first response to the claim of bureaucratic inefficiency is that the efficiency of bureaucracy in the real world is
being compared to a theoretical ideal of efficiency, and that no
real-world institutional structure can be expected to live up to a
theoretical ideal. There is at least some truth to this claim. Bureaucracies are often used where market arrangements are not
feasible, suggesting as a first line of defense that bureaucracy is
the best available alternative.

Even here, though, bureaucracies are relied on more than is
necessary in modern governments. The arguments for public
sector provision of police and fire protection, education, mail
delivery, and garbage pickup, to name a few, are not arguments
that prevent the government from contracting with private sector firms for provision rather than producing the services
itself.[16] One answer might be that the employees in an industry
would be better off working for the government rather than a
private sector firm. Government mail carriers, for example,
seem to be much better paid than private sector couriers who
have almost the same job. This answer has some merit, for it
explains why a government bureaucracy, once establshed, would
tend to perpetuate itself. The individuals in the bureaucracy are
earning rents, and this gives them an incentive to act as an interest group and lobby for the perpetuation of the bureaucracy.[17]

In fact, there are many reasons why a government bureaucracy, once established, will tend to act as an interest group.
Perhaps the most significant is, as just mentioned, that rent-
earning bureaucrats have an incentive to try to maintain the job
that provides the rents. In addition, bureaucracies are not pro-
fit-making entities but have incentives for budget maximization
instead.[18] Thus, the incentives faced by bureaucrats lead them,
as if by an invisible hand, to try to expand their bureaucracies.
Another factor is that people tend to seek jobs in areas that they
believe are interesting and important. Thus, individuals in bureaucracies naturally will be those people who believe most
strongly that the bureaucracy has an important mission to ac-
complish. For all of these reasons, a bureaucracy can be expected to act as a special interest group that will lobby to expand
its budget and its sphere of influence.

Another factor that increases the government bureaucracy's

ability to lobby in its own behalf is that the bureaucracy is the government's own in-house source of information about its activities. Special interest groups in the private sector may have to compete among themselves (and, perhaps, government agencies) for favors, but the government bureaucracy is in the position of acting as its own expert witness. Thus, the bureaucracy is in an ideal position to be an especially effective special interest group. There are many reasons why a government bureaucracy, once established, will tend to become a permanently established and growing entity. Perhaps the most dramatic example of this is the Federal Energy Office. Established by the president in 1974 as a temporary agency to deal with the OPEC oil embargo, it grew to become the Federal Energy Administration, and finally the cabinet level Department of Energy, in less than five years.

Government bureaucracies, once established, tend to remain. Before a bureaucracy is established, however, it cannot act as a special interest group, because it does not exist. The next question, then, is why a bureaucracy would be established in the first place. The alternatives would be to rely on the private sector through contracting or even simply to distribute cash to a private sector interest group in lieu of establishing the bureaucracy the interest group requests. While the alternatives may appear more efficient, the answer lies in the permanence of the bureaucracy, once established. An interest group may win a cash transfer, or services produced in the private sector, but perpetuating the transfer year after year may be a formidable political task. However, if a bureaucracy is established, it will tend to perpetuate itself and to grow. Thus, to an interest group, the present value of establishing a small bureaucracy to provide it with benefits will outweigh the value of a larger cash transfer, because the establishment of a bureaucracy is the establishment of a permanent and growing source of benefits. Bureaucracies may be inefficient payment to an interest group in a static sense, but their permanence makes them more desirable than say, a cash transfer, since the cash transfer will require more effort to retain year after year.

When representatives convey distributions to interest groups by bureaucracy, the interest group can view that as a mechanism for enforcing the multi-year promises of representatives.[19] Even if the representative is voted out of office, the bureaucracy will remain to continue the flow of benefits. Seen in this light, bureaucracy is a method for reducing the transactions costs of bargaining in the game of distributive government. By imposing stability on the distributive game, the entire government budget cannot seriously be viewed as subject to negotiation each year. Much of the budget will be assigned to the same bureaucracies in the same proportions as in the previous year. This is an additional factor that helps produce the solution of universalism that was developed earlier. Bureaucracy tends to be a stability-producing device, and one that reinforces the earlier conclusions of the book.

Incentives toward Efficiency

Resource allocation by representative democracy is inherently inefficient, as argued throughout the book, because of the incentive structure implied in the institutions of representative democracy. A majority has the right to impose its will on a minority in any democratic setting, and representative democracies are designed in order to emphasize the desires of special interests over the general public interest. Any time resources are allocated inefficiently, there are incentives to produce more efficient resource allocation, because more efficiency will create an economic gain which could be appropriated by the entrepreneur proposing the improvement. The beginning of this chapter argued that the incentives in a representative democracy are such that no individual has the incentive to take on an entrepreneurial role and propose an efficiency gain. This is the case largely because the entrepreneur in a democracy must appeal to individuals as a group large enough to be a majority, rather than to individuals singly as in the market. This makes the costs of entrepreneurship high. In addition, the entrepreneur runs the risk of being in the potentially exploitable minority, again increasing the cost of political entrepreneurship.

Still, these costs do not take away the incentive for efficiency gains. They only have the effect of making the costs exceed the benefits in most cases. This does not eliminate the possibility of cases where the benefits exceed the costs, and political entrepreneurship leads democratic decision making to the efficient outcome. Such cases undoubtedly exist. The argument of the book is simply that the cases are much less frequent than when the special interest outcome occurs. Nevertheless, it is still worthwhile to examine the cases that produce efficient outcomes.

Consider the following simple hypothetical example. A firm has won a government contract to construct an experimental water treatment plant at a location to be determined by a majority vote of a three-person legislature. Where the locations are designated by letters, the three individuals have preferences ABC, BCA, and CAB, which produces a cyclical majority. At first glance, it would appear than the location of the plant is indeterminate—indeed it is with the information given. However, the information given also makes it unclear which location would be the most efficient. To imbed efficiency conditions in the problem, assume that the three locations have different water conditions, so that the payoff to individuals 1, 2, and 3, respectively, for alternative A is $1,000, $1, $2; for alternative B is $2, $3, $1; and for C is $1, $2, $3. Thus, despite the cyclical preferences, the social values of A, B, and C, respectively, are $1,0003, $6, and $6. In this case, there is every reason to believe that outcome A will be chosen. The preferences in this case are summarized in table 9.1.

The reason why the efficient outcome is so likely in this case is that project A is worth so much more to the first individual than any other project is worth to anyone else is that there is a large profit that individual 1 could share with the others in exchange for their votes. An explicit cash payment would be possible, or an exchange of votes in some future issue. With so much entrepreneurial profit available, the efficient outcome is both likely and likely to be stable. Such an example clearly is at odds with the book's main hypothesis, because stability has been an important issue. Here is an example of a stable outcome that is optimal. The book's model does not deny the possibility of this case, however, and will concede that when it arises the efficient outcome will probably be chosen.

Even this case requires some qualification, though. Alternative A is superior to B and C, but may not be superior to doing

TABLE 9.1   CYCLICAL PREFERENCES WITH A POSSIBLE EFFICIENT
OUTCOME

Dollar Value of Project to Individual		Individual		
		1	2	3
	A	$1,000	$1	$2
	B	$2	$3	$1
	C	$1	$2	$3

nothing. If the cost of the project were $500, then the project is worthwhile, and the efficient alternative will be chosen. If the cost is $5,000, then the project is not worthwhile, and it is only a small consolation that the least inefficient alternative is selected. Another possibility is that all three projects will be undertaken. This is outside the bounds of the original problem, where one of the three was to be selected, but it must be considered as a real-world possibility. In politics, economic efficiency often takes a back seat to other criteria, and it might be decided that in the interest of fairness, if project A is undertaken which is the most preferred alternative for individual 1, the projects B and C should also be undertaken, since they are the favorites of 2 and 3.

It is easy to see that many things can stand in the way of producing the most efficient outcome. Nevertheless, there may be circumstances under which the efficient alternative is chosen. In the original example depicted in table 9.1, where one of the three alternatives is to be chosen, it is most likely that the efficient outcome, A, will be selected. This example shows the possibility of efficiency in government, in response to the entrepreneurial incentive. The example is fairly straightforward, though, and the complexities that are normally associated with the call for government action are absent.

Spillovers and Public Goods

A usual economic justification for governmental action is the existence of spillovers or public goods. These conditions,

TABLE 9.2   CYCLICAL PREFERENCES WITH SIGNIFICANT SPILLOVERS

Dollar Value of Project to Individual		Individual		
		1	2	3
	A	$1,000	$1	$2
	B	$300	$600	$200
	C	$200	$300	$600

which are normally cited as problem areas for market allocation of resources, also complicate the political decision-making process. In the example in table 9.1, the likely outcome in a more complex political setting would be that individual 1 would favor project A, but the other two individuals have no strong incentive to be concerned about any of the projects, so their political interests would be likely to fall elsewhere.

An example of a more likely scenario is depicted in table 9.2. Project A in table 9.2 is the same as in table 9.1, but the other two projects now are projects that offer more significant benefits to individuals 2 and 3 and also are characterized by significant spillover benefits. Once again, a simple ranking of the projects produces a cyclical majority, leaving the question open regarding which alternative actually will be chosen by a majority.

Projects B and C both have total values greater than project A, so there is the potential for a set of side payments that would produce an efficient allocation of resources, as in the earlier example. The likely stumbling block to this outcome, though, is that in a representative government, one representative cannot claim the credit for another representative's project. If a mosquito control project in one district lowers the number of mosquitos in another district, the credit for the benefit will go to the representative in the district with the project, not to the representative of the district that receives the spillover benefit. The constituents in the district that receives the spillover may actually place blame on their representative for not getting a project in their own district. As a result, spillover benefits are not likely to be included in the cost/benefit calculus when representatives engage in political bargaining. Spillovers will benefit the representative's constituents, but since the representative is unlikely to receive credit for the spillovers, they are likely to be ignored in the political process.

There is a definite parallel here between spillovers in government and spillovers in the market. In the market, transactions costs may be low enough that the Coase theorem may apply, but if not (and sometimes, even if so), there will be a call for a government intervention. It may be that externalities in the market may be contained inside political boundaries, but this is unlikely for significant externalities, in which case the problem of ignoring the spillovers will occur in government just as in the market.

In the problem summarized in table 9.2, this means that the absence of accounting for spillovers, project A will be worth $1,000 to individual 1, while B and C will be worth only $600 to 2 and 3. The outcome will be like that in table 9.1, where individual 1 is in a position to offer more substantial side payments than the other two individuals, and project A will be the likely outcome in a representative democracy. Of course, this does not have to be the case, and sophisticated constituents may be able to entice their representatives to engage in a logrolling scheme that provides the high spillovers inherent in projects B and C along with side payments. This is less likely when the rational ignorance of constituents is accounted for, since it is unclear that the representative deserves credit for the spillovers of others' projects, but it is very clear that the representative deserves credit for projects that benefit the home district primarily. The efficient outcome is possible, and there are potential gains from trade to be shared from the efficiency, but the incentives in a representative democracy are set up such that when significant spillovers exist, they will be ignored in the political decision-making process.

What is true for spillovers is even more true for public goods. A public good can be viewed as the most extreme example of a spillover, where the benefits of the project are shared equally among everyone. An example is depicted in table 9.3. Here, there is a cyclical majority in the preferences for projects A, B, and C, where each of these projects has a value of $1,003.

TABLE 9.3   CYCLICAL PREFERENCES WITH A PUBLIC GOOD

Dollar Value of Project to Individual		Individual		
		1	2	3
	A	$1,000	$1	$2
	B	$2	$1,000	$1
	C	$1	$2	$1,000
	D	$500	$500	$500

Project D has a value of $1,500 spread equally over the three individuals. The question now is which project will be selected by majority rule. Projects A, B, and C appear very similar, with the only difference being who prefers what. Thus, there would be a difficult political battle involved in making a democratic choice among those three alternatives. This being the case, project D would not be likely to receive much support. Any support given to project D by one individual would reduce the support that individual could make to the project the individual values most highly. Even though project D is in the public interest, the political battle will be fought among projects A, B, and C.

This example is significant because it is precisely this type of case that is used to justify the use of government to allocate economic resources in the first place.[20] When public goods problems exist, the government is called upon to intervene, yet an examination of the incentives facing those in government show the government to be inefficient as well.[21] This does not mean that the government is more or less efficient than the market; the situation may vary from case to case. It does show, however, that representative democracy does not solve the problem of efficiently allocating resources for public goods. Without evidence in a particular case, the government cannot be assumed to be more efficient than the market.

A look back at the example shows why this is the case. Representatives must spend their political IOUs carefully in order to maximize the likelihood of reelection. This means supporting the programs that benefit their constituents the most. Every representative in the example in table 9.3 will have good reason to support the program that provides the highest benefit to the representative's district, which leaves the public good with no support. If public-spirited individual 3, for example, decided to allocate some political capital for the support of project D, this would lower the amount of support available for project C, which would increase the likelihood of A or B being chosen. Representatives who try to act in the public interest do not act in the best interests of the special interests who support them. The next election is never far away, reinforcing the general conclusion that representatives will cater to special interests while ignoring the general public interest.

Representative government may at times act in the public interest, but this is more likely in the clear cut cases that do not involve spillovers of public goods. Even in the clear-cut cases there may be problems, but even larger impediments to efficiency exist when there are spillovers and public goods—the very kinds of problems that the government is trying to solve. All things considered, the government does not allocate resources very efficiently.

Conclusion

There are some activities that governments almost naturally find themselves involved in. These generally involve the protection of individual rights.[22] These activities of government seem to be efficient virtually by definition, since there is no viable private sector alternative.[23] Even here, of course, there are choices as to how the governmental activity is to be organized. However, all modern governments have gone well beyond these minimal activities of government, so for most governmental activity it is very appropriate to evaluate it compared to the private sector alternative. This has been done frequently.[24] In the absence of readily observable private sector alternatives, the efficiency of public sector activities can be compared with a Pareto optimal allocation as a benchmark. This benchmark is a demanding standard, but one that is frequently used to measure the efficiency of private sector activities.[25] In addition, any allocation that falls short of the ideal of Pareto optimality has at least the potential for improvement.

In this regard, it was noted that the kind of inefficiency

analyzed in this book is a small subset of the total possibilities for inefficiency in the public sector. Scholars have identified a wide range of public sector inefficiencies that fall outside the scope of the present analysis, yet are significant in their own right. The most obvious type of public sector inefficiency arises when the same output could be produced with fewer inputs. Niskanen has called this process inefficiency, and it is the most frequently cited type. An important cause of process inefficiency in the public sector is an incomplete specification of property rights that produces no residual claimant, and so no incentive for process efficiency. Another important type of inefficiency frequently analyzed by economists is the excess burden or welfare loss of taxation. This inefficiency arises due to the reallocation of resources in an effort to avoid taxation. Closely related is the inefficiency due to rent seeking that has received much attention from economists recently. In addition, the tendency of bureaucracies to be budget maximizers rather than profit maximizers also causes inefficiency. This partial list of the origins of public sector inefficiency identifies many significant problems with allocating resources in the public sector, but these are outside the scope of the present analysis.

The analysis in this book focuses on the incentive structure inherent in a representative democracy. Representative democracies tend to serve special interests while ignoring the general public interest, which is another source of public sector inefficiency. The analysis here is complementary with other sources of inefficiency; but even if the public sector were process efficient, it would still misallocate resources. Niskanen's budget-maximizing bureaucracies will tend to reinforce the efforts of special interest groups, but in a larger context, the budget maximization occurs in programs that serve special interests rather than the general public interest. In addititon, the gains to special interests may be competed away by rent seeking anyway.

Combining these source of inefficiency creates a picture even bleaker than looking at them in isolation, because all of the sources can apply to any public sector activity. Farm subsidies, for example, may be inefficient due to rent seeking, the excess burden of taxation, process inefficiency, and budget maximizing-bureaucracies in addiiton to the special interest effects of representative government. Contrast this with the market failure literature in which only one source of inefficiency usually applies to each case, and in which multiple effects may sometimes cancel each other out.[26] The overall picture makes the government look very inefficient next to the market.

This being the case, the economic theorist might observe that large inefficiencies imply large gains to be reaped by repairing the inefficiency. A political entrepreneur could structure a remedy such that everybody could gain (or at least be made no worse off), and the entrepreneur could design the remedy to provide a substantial entrepreneurial reward. Because of this potential, one would expect political entrepreneurs to follow up on the incentives for efficiency, and for inefficient institutions to be replaced by efficient ones. An important part of this chapter has been addressing this issue.

One element that has been observed by many economists regarding the public sector is that in most cases no individual has residual claimant status. It is difficult to claim a property right in government profits, so any gain in efficiency will usually go to someone other than the initiator of the efficient action. The general institutional conditions make it difficult for individuals, even when they are willing, to accept the risks of profit and loss in the public sector. Also, individuals in the government may reap in-kind benefits, such as easier working conditions, automatic promotions, government travel, and so forth, from inefficiency, so that a move toward efficiency may be objected to by those in the government. These reasons, which fall into the general category of incompletely defined property rights, are often cited as sources of public sector inefficiency that inhibit political entrepreneurs from initiating efficiency gains.

The reasons behind the model in this book are somewhat different, although complementary. They have to do with the incentive structure inherent in a representative democracy. One of the most important factors is that in any democracy, a majority has the right to impose its will on a minority. This factor alone is a source of inefficiency that cannot be eliminated from democratic decisions, and so automatically produces an institutional structure that is antagonistic toward Pareto improvements. In economic exchange, and with a political rule of unanimity, the guiding principle is to make changes that make everybody better off. With majority rule, the guiding principle is to choose an alternative favored by some (the majority) but opposed by others (the minority). Under such a system, inefficiencies should not be surprising, and the scope of government was limited by the U.S. Constitution for just this reason.

The inefficiencies of majority rule are compounded in a representative government because representatives have the incentive to cater to special interests rather than to pursue the general public interest. The incentive structure is such that no individual has an incentive to act as a political entrepreneur and propose a more efficient allocation of resources. A representative's constituents will be rationally ignorant about most political activities but will be more aware of the special benefits concentrated on them. Special interests find it more profitable to pursue highly concentrated special interest benefits rather than public interest programs that dilute the benefits across an entire nation. Representatives, accounting for these facts, produce special interest benefits in exchange for political support. Constituents credit their representative for special interest benefits but cannot fault their representative for the high taxes used to pay for everyone else's programs, since the taxes would continue no matter what their representative did.

Here, the problem of majority rule is very clear. Either a representative can join the majority coalition and participate in the logrolling that produces special interest benefits for everyone, or the representative can refuse to cooperate in the inefficiency produced by the coalition and become a member of the exploited minority. The majority votes that the minority must pay taxes to finance the special interests of the majority, but the minority receives no benefits in return. Faced with this choice, the incentives inherent in majority rule force everyone to try to become a member of the majority rather than the potentially exploitable minority. No one representative can change this situation because no single representative's vote is necessary under majority rule.

Economically efficient outcomes are possible in a democracy. An example illustrated this. However, the incentive structure in a representative democracy is oriented to produce economically inefficient results.

10 / The Growth of Government

The United States was founded as a nation in which its citizens could escape the tyranny of government. The world political climate at that time was more oriented toward laissez-faire than at any time in history, but still the basic premise of government was that its citizens are the subjects of government. Britain, the most laissez-faire nation of the time, was a kingdom, and it would not be difficult to speculate that rights granted by such a government to its citizens could some day be taken back. The premise of American government was entirely different. The government did not grant rights to its citizens; rather, its citizens had rights that the government was legally prohibited from violating. The government was created as a vehicle for protecting the inalienable rights of its citizens. If ever there was a chance for the government to be contained, this would have seemed to be it.

The government of the United States has changed immensely in the intervening centuries; indeed, all Western governments have changed. They have become larger, both in the scope of their activities and in their economic size relative to the private sector.[1] The growth was gradual at first and has accelerated in recent decades. This chapter will consider that growth within the context of the theory set forth in the book.

Republics and Democracies

The material in this book has been about democratic government, so it is worthwhile to reflect on the fact that the government of the United States was not set up primarily to be a democratic government. It was established as a republic. The distinction is important, although sometimes obscure.[2] The Constitution of the United States clearly is a document that limits the scope of government and recognizes the rights of individuals, rather than giving the government rights or having the government allow individuals to have rights. In order to emphasize and clarify this, the Bill of Rights was appended to be a part of the original document. The government was established as a mechanism for protecting individual rights, and it was explicitly recognized that the government had the potential to violate those rights just as did other individuals or foreign nations. The United States was established as a republican government. A republican government is one that explicitly recognizes and protects the rights of the individual.

A government can protect individual rights because government is the institution that has a legal monopoly on the use of force in a society.[3] The challenge in designing a republican government is in limiting the government's actions to those intended by the founders. This is the role of democracy. Democracy means majority rule, but in the case of a republic, the majority does not have the right to make any decision. Rather, the role in the United States has been to use democracy to choose those who will be in charge of administering the government and of legislating within the constitutionally allowed bounds. The democratic aspect of the government is severely limited— limited to choosing who will oversee the government's activities as it protects individual rights.

This stands in great contrast to a pure democracy, where a majority has the right to make decisions that impose their will on a minority. A pure democracy is a type of dictatorship, but the dictatorial power rests with the majority rather than with a single individual. Over time, the United States and other Western governments have been moving away from a republican form of government toward a more purely democratic form of government. Today, the government is generally viewed not as an institution that protects individual rights but as an institution that carries out the will of the majority. Nowhere is this more clear than in distributive issues. The Founding Fathers would have been appalled at a government that allowed a majority to dictate that money be taken from some and redistributed to others, yet today this is a generally accepted function of modern government.

The scope of governmental activity has increased over the centuries, and this is largely because of a change in national political philosophy. Over the centuries, the political climate has changed from republican to democratic. The terms here apply to types of government, although there is a similarity between these types and the contemporary political parties that bear their names.

Governments seem to grow constantly, but the shift in political philosophy seems to have taken place in the 1930s. In the 1920s, laissez-faire was the accepted way of running an economy, although the enactment and enforcement of antitrust laws, the establishment of a Federal Reserve Bank, and so forth, illustrate the enlarging scope of government before the 1930s. But the Great Depression ushered in an era of growing government intervention. Income redistribution was started in earnest, government projects sprung up in areas formerly restricted to the private sector, and deficit finance became acceptable in peacetime. Intellectually, Keynesian economics blossomed from the necessary remedy in the 1930s to a dominant political force in the 1960s.[4] The 1930s, 1940s, and 1950s were, perhaps, a transitional period, but by the 1960s, the United States had been transformed from a republic to a democracy.

The change in the scope and philosophy of government brought with it a change in the way that economists view government activity as well. The subdiscipline of public choice was born after World War II, undoubtedly as a response to growing government. Economists have been more interested in analyzing government activity as the government's economic activity has grown. A part of this is evaluating how certain government actions affect the economy. Anoher part is evaluating how individual preferences can be aggregated into a collective expression of social choice. It is this social choice which motivates government activity.

A pioneering work in this area is Kenneth Arrow's *Social Choice and Individual Values*. Arrow's thought-provoking analysis has never been far from the central issues of public choice, and this chapter now will turn to a discussion of some of his ideas.

Arrow Problems

Perhaps the most significant of Arrow's findings regarding collective choice is his impossibility theorem. Briefly, Arrow argued that any acceptable method of making social choices would have to have five characteristics. First, the method would have to be capable of ranking all possible configurations of individual preferences. Second, if every person preferred one option, the social choice system would have to choose that option. Third, the relative rankings of any pair would have to be independent of irrelevant alternatives. Fourth, the system must be able to compare all possible alternatives, and fifth, the ranking of alternatives must be transitive.[5] These five conditions seemed reasonable to Arrow and to others considering the problems of finding a good system of collective decision making, yet Arrow proved that the only social choice rule that would satisfy all five conditions is a dictatorship. If nondictatorship is added as a sixth condition, then it is impossible to find a rational collective choice mechanism, where rational means that all of Arrow's conditions are met.

Public choice theorists have addressed Arrow's finding in a number of different ways. One way is to weaken Arrow's conditions and search for a system of social choice that adheres to some of Arrow's conditions. Another way is to avoid the problem by analyzing only those preferences or alternatives that do not violate Arrow's conditions. Still another method is to examine Arrow's findings more deeply to analyze the causes for there being no possible method of optimal social choice. Arrow's findings on social choice are all the more interesting in light of his contribution in proving the uniqueness and stability of competitive equilibrium. Resources can be allocated rationally in the market; the market chooses a unique allocation of resources, and the allocation of resources in Pareto optimal. Why is it no possible for a collective choice mechanism to do the same?

Some insight on this question can be gained by looking at the example of the cyclical majority given in chapter 9, table 9.1.

TABLE 10.1 PREFERENCE
RANKINGS THAT ESCAPE THE
CYCLICAL MAJORITY

	Individuals		
	1	2	3
	A	D	D
Rankings	D	B	C
	B	C	A
	C	A	B

In that example, a simple majority rule election would result in A defeating B, but C defeating A, and B defeating C. Thus, a cycle is established where the social choice rule says C is preferred to A, B is preferred to C, and A is preferred to B. This violates the condition of transitivity, so majority rule is not a rational social choice rule, using Arrow's conditions as a guide. In searching for a rational choice rule, Arrow ultimately decided that there are none. Yet, in chapter 9, it was argued that a representative democracy would choose alternative A. How was the illustration in chapter 9 able to escape Arrow's impossibility theorem?

The illustration in chapter 9 escaped the impossibility theorem by stepping outside of Arrow's framework. In the example in table 9.1, the total social value of alternative A was $1,003, while alternatives B and C were worth only $6 each. The problem of cycles was avoided by creating a new possibility that the largest beneficiary of alternative A would pay the other individuals in order to get them to vote for A. With the side payments included, the new alternative would be worth more to everybody than B or C, so A would be chosen. In effect, the choice of A with the side payment is a new alternative, D. This new alternative is ranked higher than any other by the second and third individuals, and is ranked below A only for the individual making the payment. This is illustrated in table 10.1.

Now, the question is why introducing another alternative in the example makes the model stable. The obvious answer, in a political framework, is that the new alternative is preferred by a majority to any other alternative. Looking at the model from more of an economic perspective, though, the new alternative reduces the number of Pareto optimal allocations, and this reduction in the number of Pareto optimal allocations is the key to understanding the difference between political and economic equilibrium. In the model, the economically efficient allocation requires alternative A to be chosen (or D, of which A is a subset). Without D as a contender, however, alternatives A, B, and C are all Pareto optimal, because a move from any one to any other one would make some people better off, but some people worse off. In politics, the lack of opportunity for side payments will greatly expand the Pareto optimal set, but many Pareto optimal allocations will not be economically efficient, like B and C in the example. When side payments are possible, the economically efficient alternative will have to be a part of any Pareto optimal choice. The only difference between A and D in this example is distributional, and since a majority prefers the distribution in D, it will be chosen by majority rule.

The key fact to see here is the important difference between the notions of a Pareto optimum in economics and in politics. In economics, Pareto optimality is synonymous with economic efficiency. In political choices when side payments are not allowed, this may not be so. There may be many more Pareto optimal allocations, and many may not be economically efficient. When preferences are aggregated only by ranking, and when individual rankings are the only available information from utility functions, a host of Pareto optimal allocations that are not economically efficient will probably exist. The reason why the Arrow impossibility theorem can coexist with the unique, stable, efficient, competitive equilibrium is that individuals in the competitive equilibrium are allowed to make payments to each other to change the allocation. This requires the resulting allocation to be economically efficient.

The whole question is not yet answered, though. In the example, there were two Pareto optimal outcomes, both economically efficient. Only the distribution of wealth differed, and since a majority preferred D, it was chosen. In reality, there are many possible distributions to go with any allocation. If the example were not restricted to only one set of side payments, the allocation would have been efficient, but there would have been cycles in the various motions regarding the distribution of the gains. The problem is this: a move toward efficiency creates a surplus, and somehow that surplus must be divided among the participants. In absence of some predetermined rule, there will not be a unique outcome.

Chapter 4 established the plausibility of a rule of even division for distributive political games. Other rules would be possible as well.[6] Regarding the Arrow problem, the main point is that once an economically efficient allocation can be generated by side payments, a method for sharing the gains must be devised to produce a unique solution. In the competitive model, individuals are paid their marginal products, and purchase output at its marginal cost. This is the distributional rule in the competitive model that produces a unique, stable, efficient equilibrium.

In this sense, the Walrasian model of competitive equilibrium can be viewed as a model of collective choice. With the auctioneer running the election system, all individuals declare their excess demands at the announced price vector. When a price vector is announced that produces unanimous agreement (i.e., the sum of excess demands for each good is zero), the collective choice is made. With an auctioneer acting as chairman, and with all individuals casting ballots at the central market-place, Walras's model seems like more of a political decision than an economic decision anyway. Thus, the conclusions of the Arrow impossibility theorem can be avoided if, first, side payments are possible (to produce an efficient allocation), and second, there is a predetermined rule on how the gains from efficiency are to be divided. In an economy with production, these side payments may be payments to entice producers to produce, in which case the payments may themselves produce a unique distribution; but at any rate, the Walrasian model of competition can easily be viewed as a model of collective choice with a unique and optimal outcome.

Arrow was able to generate the impossibility theorem because preferences in his model were only rank orderings of alternatives, with no side payments allowed to produce economic efficiency. However, many people may view it as fair that economic wealth not be a criterion for all social decisions.[7] This is part of the motivation for trying to allocate resources through the public sector. Another part, stemming from the experience of the 1930s, and continuing in the intellectual arena in economics, is the idea that markets are less than perfectly efficient allocators of resources in reality, and that the government should assist. There may be ways in which the public sector could efficiently allocate resources by considering the value of various options to individuals,[8] but it is clear that a democratic government, which relies on majority rule, cannot allocate resources efficiently.

In the immediate case of democracy, the reason is that a democracy is inherently coercive, forcing a minority to abide by the will of the majority. Viewed in this way, it is apparent that democracy has the potential for tyranny unless its power is restricted. In a larger perspective, though, Arrow's theorem illustrates the futility of trying to design a social choice system that is able to make rational choices. Except in cases of unanimous approval, any system of social choice has a coercive element, and one should not be surprised at the impossibility theorem for this reason. Why would anyone expect that a system of social choice that forces some people to abide by the will of others to be optimal, rational, or desirable in any sense? It would appear simply from an ethical standpoint that a social choice mechanism that forces some to abide by the will of others is undesirable.[9] Arrow and a host of other public choice theorists have found that from an economic standpoint such social choice mechanisms have their drawbacks as well. The theme of this book is concerned primarily with the special drawbacks inherent in decision making by representative democracy.

Given these problems, resource allocation by majority rule appears undesirable. As noted earlier, the Founding Fathers of the United States did not intend for the government to allocate resources by democracy. The economic philosophy was laissez-faire, and the government was established to protect individual rights. Democracy was not intended as a mechanism of social choice for the activities of government. Democracy was simply a method of choosing governmental officials, and of easily replacing them if their performance was not satisfactory. The Founding Fathers seemed to be quite aware of the dangers of unlimited democracy, and the Constitution was written in order to constrain the government and limit the power of the majority. Since that time the government has grown, despite the limits intended by the nation's founders. That growth can be explained within the interest group model in this book.

The Development of a Limited Democracy

At this point, the argument in the book has traveled a full circle, because in chapter 2 a contractarian model established the principle of a limited democracy, where majority rule would be the system used to select the legislators and administrators of a government with constitutionally limited powers. If the reasons for constraining the power of the majority were not clear in chapter 2, they certainly should be now. The American government seemed to be established with this in mind, because after the Constitution enumerates the powers and responsibilities of the government, it expressly prohibits the government from undertaking any activity not explicitly allowed by the Constitution. The Tenth Amendment to the Constitution reads, "The powers not delegated to the United States by the Constitution nor prohibited by it to the States, are reserved to the States respectively, or to the people." It would seem that such an explicit limitation on the powers of the federal government should have prevented the great increase in the government's scope of activity. When compared to the rest of the world, the United States has relatively little government activity, but when compared with the nation at its founding, the government has expanded greatly.

The expansion of government is the result of economic growth and special interest politics. The way in which government grows can be illustrated in a framework similar to that of Buchanan[10] or Rawls,[11] in which the constitutional rules of a society are agreed upon. This type of framework was used in chapter 2 to establish some principles of representative democracy.[12] The general purpose behind establishing a constitution is to organize individuals in a society through government in such a way that the government enhances the well-being of its citizens. Buchanan's conception of the process can be outlined

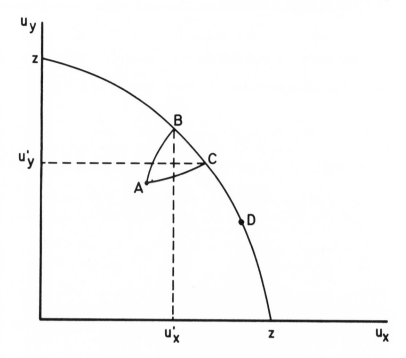

Fig. 10.1   The adoption of a constitution

with the aid of figure 10.1. Without a government uniting individuals, they live in a condition of anarchy. Using a government as a collective method of protecting individual rights and perhaps engaging in other activities can increase the well-being of everybody. Cooperation enables specialization and gains from trade.[13] Within the context of figure 10.1, there is some utility possibilities frontier, ZZ, that can be attained through cooperation, but in an anarchistic situation individuals find themselves at point A, inside the boundary. In this two-person representation, the horizontal axis measures the utility of individual X and the vertical axis measures the utility of individual Y. From point A, where anarchy prevails, individuals expect that the cooperation through the collective adoption of some constitutional rules could move them to the production possibilities curve. While there is some uncertainty about how much each individual could gain through cooperation, there is a range of expectations represented by the arc BC within which individuals could expect the outcome to fall.

In establishing the constitutional rules for a society, there are two general considerations. One is efficiency. The constitution should be written in order to place the society on the utility possibilities frontier. The other is equity. A point such as point D is on the utility possibilities frontier, but it makes Y worse off than in a situation of anarchy at point A. Individuals like Y would never agree to this situation. This raises the question of what it means to be in agreement with a society's constitution, since most individuals find themselves governed by one set of rules or another by accident of birth rather than explicit agreement to live under those rules.

Buchanan develops a notion of conceptual agreement in this way. If the society were returned to a state of anarchy like point A, and a new constitution were to be drawn up, people, while uncertain about its exact terms, would expect for the outcome to fall within the range BC. As long as the existing constitution places the society within this range, there is conceptual agreement with the rules of society. Rawls looks at the situation in a similar way. If individuals were to draw up the rules of society without knowledge of what role they would play in the society, the rules could be expected to be fair. To use the terminology of Rawls, the rules of society would be agreed upon behind a veil of ignorance. This model can be used to describe the concept behind the writing of the American Constitution. The government's powers were explicitly limited, and since governmental officials would be chosen democratically after the adoption of the Constitution, there was a veil of ignorance at least with regard to who would administer the government. This was more true due to the provision for periodic elections.

This model provides a framework within which the development of a representative democracy can be analyzed, both with regard to the American case and with regard to the model developed in earlier chapters. It is apparent from that model that the use of unrestrained majority rule to make governmental decisions leads to an inefficient use of resources and the neglect of the public interest to further the desires of special interests.

In light of this, it would be desirable to explicitly limit the powers of government to those items which will be in the public interest. The theory explains why government should be limited in this way, and the Founding Fathers seemed to be well aware of the dangers when they wrote the Constitution in a way to try to limit the powers of government to those areas where it would act in the public interest.

Special Interests and Government Growth

Once the machinery of government is put into place, it develops in a way that makes it more difficult to control over time. In an important sense the writing of an actual constitution is done behind a veil of ignorance. That sense is that before the organization of an elected government, nobody knows who will be elected to government positions and who will be outside the government. This will continue to be true over time when periodic elections are held, but over time the terms of the social contract—the constitutional rules—must change, and herein lies the problem.

For a government to endure over time, it must have a provision for changing its operation to respond to new and unforeseen circumstances. Conditions today are certainly different from two hundred years ago, and because many important changes cannot be foreseen, a government must have the flexibility to be able to respond to new conditions. Legislation is the mechanism for adaptation. The administrative and judicial branches are designed to work within the existing rules,[14] but the legislative branch of government exists explicitly to create new rules and modify old ones.[15] Legislation is the mechanism created by the constitution to modify a society's rules, and as such is a very powerful tool. For this reason, its applicability was severely limited in the U.S. Constitution, with the hope that laws would be made as if behind a veil of ignorance, to use Rawl's model, or as if the social contract were being continually renegotiated, to use Buchanan's model, even though the veil has been lifted and the contract is not continually being renegotiated.

The problem with legislation in a representative democracy

is that some individuals are chosen to be the legislators, and even the most well-meaning individuals will tend to implement changes that benefit themselves, or that at least will not harm themselves. The result is that as changes in the rules occur, they tend to favor the rule makers. This is unavoidable, since it is always easier for one to see one's own interest more clearly than the interests of others. When the government alters the rules, they will tend to be biased to favor those in government. People outside government might recognize this and want to do something about it, but in order to change the rules, one first must become a part of the group that has the power to change them, namely the government. Becoming a member of the government changes the perspective of the potential rule changer, so the problem persists. Over time, the rules of society naturally evolve to favor the government.

The establishment of a minimal government that protects individual rights provides a foundation that will build a productive society, but also one that will have an increasing amount of surplus that can be gathered by any group that gets the power to do so. A productive nation will have an increasing production possibilities frontier, which could be represented on figure 10.1 as a shift outward in the utility possibilities frontier. Figure 10.1 and a new utility possibilities frontier Z'Z' are shown together in figure 10.2. Adam Smith's first lesson in *The Wealth of Nations* is that increasing productivity comes with increasing specialization, making everyone in a society more dependent on each other. It is conceivable that in 1776 most Americans could survive in family units without interacting with others, since the nation then was composed largely of self-sufficient farming households. Today, most of the nation could not survive without cooperation, because specialization has caused everyone to become so interdependent. The result is that at the same time that the utility frontier shifts out, the point representing anarchistic equilibrium shifts in, as in the movement from A to A' in figure 10.2.

Thus, as a nation grows, the range within which a new constitution could be expected to be renegotiated grows as well, from BC to B'C' in figure 10.2. For a nation of people who are close to self-sufficient, there is a relatively small bargaining

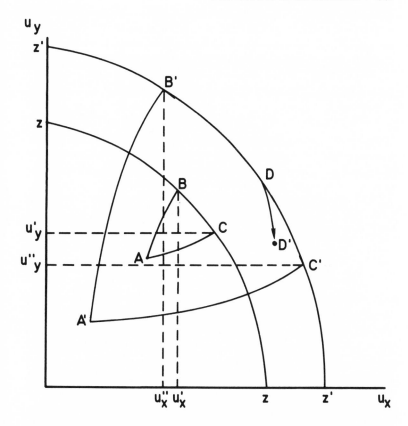

Fig. 10.2   The evolution of a constitution

range within which the terms of a voluntarily negotiated constitution could fall. For a more interdependent nation, this range is
considerably larger, both because the interdependent nation is
more productive and because each individual would have a
harder time surviving without the others. In an advanced nation, a completely unbiased constitution might be expected to
fall within the range from B′C′, but likely near D at the center of
the range. However, as a nation progresses, the inherent bias
favoring the government makes an outcome near D less likely. If
U represents the well-being of those in government and U_x represents those outside the government, over time the rules can be

expected to change such that the outcome migrates from D to D', favoring those in the government. D' is likely to be inside the frontier as a result of the inefficiency generated in the process.

How does this bias develop? The interest group theory presented in earlier chapters explains. Legislators have an incentive in catering to special interests rather than to the general public interest, but their ability to respond to this incentive is limited severely at first by the constitution. Over time, changes in the rules slowly alter them to be more biased toward the interest of the legislators, allowing more special interest legislation. Representatives can purchase political support with the government budget they control. Indeed, the standard political model has representatives evaluated by their actions in office. It stands to reason that the larger the budget is that representatives control, the more political support they can buy. Thus representatives would want the government to grow, and since they make the rules, they have the power to see that it happens. This bias toward government growth seems to be an inherent characteristic of representative government.

The Demand for Special Interest Legislation

When an explicitly limited government is established, there will be a limited amount of special interest legislation that can be passed, and this is by design. As the rules change over time, more special interest legislation will be passed, which provides an incentive for special interest groups to form and seek special interest legislation. There is a loop here, where more special interest legislation encourages the formation of more special interest groups, and the existence of more special interest groups encourages more special interest legislation.[16]

When a government is small, it can provide very limited benefits to special interest groups, so there is a small incentive for special interest groups to lobby the government. The successes of those that do lobby the government will cause the government to grow. This occurs because the great majority of voters and taxpayers are rationally ignorant about most government activity, making it easy to increase everybody's taxes a small amount to provide a sizable benefit to a few. Most people do not have an incentive to investigate in detail the allocation of their tax dollars, but the special interest with the sizable benefit will repay the representatives with political support. Thus, special interest groups cause government growth.

The growth of government, in turn, raises the payoff available to special interest groups. With a higher potential payoff to special interest groups, this encourages the formation of new special interest groups to share in the payoff. A larger government can support a larger number of special interest groups. Thus, as government grows, more special interest groups form. The formation of special interest groups in turn increases the demand for special interest legislation, causing a further growth in government spending.

The role of the government itself as an interest group has already been mentioned, and is relevant at this point. The establishment of a government program brings with it the establishment of a government bureaucracy, and the growth of a program brings with it the growth of bureaucracy. Those in the bureaucracy have every incentive to see the bureaucracy continue to grow. Furthermore, the bureaucracy is the government's source of expertise in the area that the bureaucracy works, virtually ensuring that expert opinion will always favor an increase in that area of government. This factor makes government programs much easier to start than to stop. If a certain potential program has just enough interest group support to be established, the mere act of establishing the program creates another interest group in the bureaucracy, which then is more than enough to keep the program underway. Any move to abolish the program must then contend not only with the original interest group that favored the program but also with the bureaucracy created after the program was established.

Special interest legislation has a way of perpetuating itself, and of fostering more special interest legislation. It perpetuates itself by establishing a bureaucracy that supports the demands of special interests for continued legislation. It fosters more special interest legislation because as the amount of special interest legislation increases, the potential benefit to seeking special interest legislation increases. This encourages more special interests to lobby for more legislation. The increased demand for special interest legislation is met by an increased supply, as Congress exchanges benefits to well-organized groups for political support. The increased supply in turn causes increased interest group formation and lobbying, and so the process continues. In the terminology used earlier, the process is one of continually expanding the feasible majority set to allow additional special interest legislation. If the process continues, the logical conclusion is that government expenditures will be constrained only by the amount of revenue the government can raise. Some have argued that modern governments have already reached that point.

Conclusion

The theory presented here and the evidence of the last century appear to arrive at the conclusion that governments, once established, inevitably grow. Indeed, in the American case, the government that was established explicitly as a limited government has continuously grown in size and in scope since its establishment. Yet in the British case, the government at the time of the industrial revolution evolved into an institution of smaller scope. The notion of evolution, rather than revolution, here is critical. Mancur Olson[17] has attributed the postwar industrial successes of Japan and West Germany to the war that eliminated established institutions and interest groups that were responsible for rigidities and inefficiency. The industrial revolution in Britain may have had the same effect, but even so it shows the possibility for evolution toward a more laissez-faire government without political revolution. In the rapidly changing economy today, there is, perhaps, the same potential.

One way in which the potential for positive reform can arise is through changes in governmental rules and procedures. Several possibilities have been suggested throughout the book, especially at the end of chapter 8. Some possibilities deal with budgetary procedures. A return to the balanced budget would eliminate a politically easy revenue source from Congress. More appropriate would be to approve an aggregate spending limit that cannot be exceeded without the explicit approval of Congress. Even better would be to require each spending bill to specify its source of revenue. This way, taxes and spending would be considered as a package. Under such a system, spending on a program could not exceed its revenue source without Congress voting the program additional funds, again from an earmarked revenue source. While such budgetary procedures would help, their approval is not likely. Congress would have to initiate the rule change, and Congress is unlikely to pass rules that constrain its behavior.

Another possibility is to decentralize government activity as much as possible. Interest group legislation is profitable to interest groups because it takes resources from a large, poorly organized group and transfers them to a small, well-organized group. By decentralizing government, the large group becomes smaller, immediately lowering the profitability of special interest legislation, and the small group also becomes a more significant fraction of the large group. Wherever possible, governmental activities should be undertaken at smaller levels of government.

Another reform that would reduce the influence of special interests would be to give the president more power relative to Congress. The president, elected at large, is more likely to represent the general public interest than Congress, which is explicitly elected to represent specific subgroups of the population. One way that the president's power could be increased would be to allow an item veto on bills, rather than allowing only a veto of an entire bill. Often, a bill favored by the president will contain unrelated items providing special interest benefits to some group. Currently, the president cannot veto that item without vetoing the entire bill. An item veto would help. Since the president represents the entire nation, increased presidential power has the potential of reducing the influence of special interests. There are drawbacks to this, as well, however. The Constitution explicitly limits the power of the president to keep him from usurping too much power, and the threat of unchecked presidential power must be balanced against the influence of special interests.

These suggestions are, in a sense, overly idealistic, for they are asking the system that has created the problems to reform itself. The incentives facing the potential reformers will lead them to continue, as in the past, creating legislation that favors special interests at the expense of the general public interest.

The real hope lies in a developing and dynamic economy that will displace established special interests with new groups and industries that are less well organized, and that rely less on collective action to produce economic benefits. In the United States, older established industries like automobiles, steel, and textiles are becoming less significant, and as this occurs the special interest legislation providing quotas, tariffs, regulations, and subsidies becomes less of a burden on the society. At the same time, and often for the same reasons, unionized labor is becoming a smaller percentage of the work force, and a less organized work force is less able to lobby for specialized legislation to benefit themselves. Meanwhile, new industries are growing, today often in highly technological areas, that are not looking for government protection but for laissez-faire policies that will allow rapid growth. This process of economic evolution counteracts the political influence of special interests by replacing old, well-organized industries with new industries that are relatively poorly organized.

Whether rapid technological change can reverse the trend of government growth remains to be seen. It appears to have been a significant influence during the industrial revolution. If so, then some of the earlier suggested reforms may become politically feasible. Indeed, economic change may be an important ingredient in preserving a government from being controlled by special interests, because economic change replaces well-organized established groups with new groups that are less well organized.

Another factor that has influenced government growth since World War II has been the economic and intellectual history dating from the 1930s. With the free world in a Great Depression, the leading scholars of the era mapped a course whereby the government could guide the nation to prosperity. Keynesian economists viewed World War II as the injection of government expenditures called for by the theory, and by 1960, economists viewed themselves more as social engineers than as mere observers of economic events.[18] The perceived power of economic theory to engineer a stable and productive economy was also accompanied by the desire to deliberately design a more humane social system. The composition of government expenditures at all levels composed about 28 percent of GNP in 1960, but more than one-third of those expenditures were for national defense. Thus, nondefense expenditures accounted for less than twice the amount of defense expenditures. By 1980, nondefense expenditures were more than five times as great as defense expenditures.[19] Considering the many activities of governments, especially at the state and local level, the government budget has changed in those two decades from being a predominantly defense-oriented institution. This dramatic shift may be explained by the interest group theory of legislation, but undoubtedly there were other catalysts that allowed this shift to take place. The intellectual climate of the time was an important ingredient.

Armed with powerful, if new untested, economic theories, the United States was growing in wealth and was recognized as the world's most powerful nation, both in economic and in military terms. The reigning political ideals of the time were to put some of that wealth to work for social causes, which at the time meant to allow the government to collect more taxes and then spend that money where it could best be used. The weak link in the theory was that although there were many (often conflicting) ideas about how the money should be spent, there was not a well-developed positive theory about how the money actually would be spent. There was an asymmetry in the theory of private and public sector behavior, for in the private sector it was assumed that individuals would follow their own self-interests, but in the public sector it was assumed that individuals would act for the public benefit. There is no reason to believe that public sector employees are any different from those in the private sector, and more recent theoretical work—of which this book is a part—has investigated the actual pattern of resource allocation in the public sector, taking into account the incentives facing the participating individuals.

The result of this new willingness to spend money in the public sector is that as more money becomes available, it becomes more profitable for interest groups to try to organize and have some of that money diverted for their own special interests. Since the general public interest is poorly represented in politics, the outcome is the distributive government that caters to special interests, as explained in the theory of this book. The catalysts that allowed for the rapid increase in special interest legislation were the particular intellectual and historical conditions present in the 1960s.

If this is the case, then there is some cause for optimism that the trend may reverse itself. In the 1960s, the realities of market capitalism were being compared with the ideal welfare state. Proponents of large-scale social programs had limited experience on which to base their claims. After several decades, it is obvious to all the promises of the great society, produced through government, have not been kept. The simple history of the intervening decades has made voters more reluctant to accept uncritically the notion that government programs can solve the society's problems. Experience over those decades has made voters skeptical of the notion that the government can effectively allocate resources.

The theoretical work done during those decades has provided explanations for the poor actual performance of government in solving social problems. Many specific studies, such as this one, cite problems inherent in the existing incentive structure embedded in political institutions. The suggestion is that existing political institutions are not well suited for allocating economic resources. More far-reaching are general studies, such as Arrow's that show the general inappropriateness of any political institution as a mechanism for choosing social conditions. Arrow showed that under reasonable conditions, collective decision making in any form is not capable of making rational choices among alternative social states. Work like this has provided an intellectual foundation beneath the general observation that governments are not effective allocators of resources.

Just because democracy cannot provide a rational ranking of various states of the world is no reason to abandon democratic choice altogether. For some purposes, such as selecting representives in a representative government, it may be the ideal institution. But just because representatives are chosen by majority rule does not mean that the representative government should be charged with carrying out the will of the majority. In a republic, the role of the elected representative is specified in, and carefully limited by, the Constitution, and the role is primarily to protect the rights of individuals, not to further the will of the majority. Problems arise when people want their governments to do more for them than is even theoretically possible. Over time, majority rule has become not only the method by which representatives are elected but also the central principle of government. The scope of governmental activity has been predicated not on constitutional limitations but on the desires of the majority. If there is a demand for a certain government program, that becomes the reason for supplying the program.

The theoretical and historical evidence of the past several decades suggests that people have been asking too much of their governments. In the democratic governments of the last century, majority rule was a method of selecting political leaders. Today, it has become a method of making social decisions. Majority rule is a good method for selecting representatives, but a poor method for directing social policy. If the recent historical evidence is not convincing enough, there is a growing body of theoretical literature to buttress the claim.

There is an inherent problem with the democratic allocation of resources. In a democracy, some individuals, in the majority, have a right to coerce those in the minority. The potential tyranny inherent in an unbridled democracy must be dealt with. Herein lies the origins of limited democracy. In a democratic society, it is, perhaps, natural for citizens to turn to their government to deal with social problems, but what constitutes a problem is a matter of degree. Certainly, the world will never arrive at a state where nobody can imagine any possible improvements. But rather than seeing the world's problems and asking the government to intervene, it is appropriate to ask whether government intervention would be beneficial. As economists understand more about how the government allocates resources, it becomes obvious that there are some problems that the government cannot deal with effectively. This is partly due to limitations on the abilities of representive democracies, but in a larger sense it is due to the limitations inherent in the types of choices that can rationally be made by collective decision making. It is becoming increasingly clear that the citizens of democratic countries have been expecting their governments to give them more than the governments could possibly deliver.

Notes
Bibliography
Index

Notes

1
Introduction

1. *Democracy in America* (New York: Geo Dearborn & Co., 1838), p. 153.

2. See Leon Homo, *Roman Political Institutions* (London: Routledge & Keagan Paul, 1962), esp. pp. 174–97. Also see Randall G. Holcombe, "The Origin of the Legislature," *Social Science Review* (forthcoming).

3. To avoid excessive footnoting, the ideas in this section are not footnoted in this overview section. Footnotes and references to these ideas appear in the chapters where the ideas are discussed in detail.

4. Harold Hotelling, "Stability in Competition," *Economic Journal* 39 (Mar. 1929): 41–57.

5. Howard R. Bowen, "The Interpretation of Voting in the Allocation of Economic Resources," *Quarterly Journal of Economics* 58 (Nov. 1943): 27–48; Duncan Black, *The Theory of Committees and Elections* (Cambridge: Cambridge University Press, 1958); and Anthony Downs, *An Economic Theory of Democracy* (New York: Harper and Row, 1957).

6. By Bowen, Black, and Downs, respectively.

7. Three examples are Thomas E. Borcherding and Robert T. Deacon, "The Demand for Services of Non-Federal Governments," *American Economic Review* 62 (Dec. 1972): 891–901; Theodore Bergstrom and Robert Goodman, "Private Demand for Public Goods," *American Economic Review* 63 (June 1973): 280–96; and Robin Barlow, "Efficiency Aspects of Local School Finance," *Journal of Political Economy* 78, no. 5 (Sept./Oct. 1970): 1028–40.

8. There was some reason for skepticism even before, however. Duncan Black had illustrated the possibility of cycles in *The Theory of*

Committees and Elections, and Kenneth J. Arrow's pioneering *Social Choice and Individual Values* (New Haven and London: Yale University Press, 1951) questioned the ability of any collective choice mechanism to make rational choices.

9. William A. Niskanen, *Bureaucracy and Represenative Government* (Chicago and New York: Aldine-Atherton, 1971).

10. See James M. Buchanan and Marilyn Flowers, "An Analytic Setting for a Taxpayer's Revolution," *Western Economic Journal* 7 (Dec. 1969), pp. 249–59.

11. See, e.g., Thomas Romer and Howard Rosenthal, "Political Resource Allocation, Controlled Agendas, and the Status Quo," *Public Choice* 33, no. 4 (1978): 27–43; Romer and Rosenthal, "Bureaucrats Versus Voters: On the Political Economy of Resource Allocation by Direct Democracy," *Quarterly Journal of Economics* 93, no. 4 (Nov. 1979): 563–87; and Randall G. Holcombe, "An Empirical Test of the Median Voter Model," *Economic Inquiry* 18, no. 2. (Apr. 1980): 260–4.

12. The concept is described more fully in chap. 3. The brief description here probably is not sufficient to describe the concept of agenda control to someone not already familiar with it.

13. R. D. McKelvey, "Intransitivities in Multi Dimensional Voting Models and some Implication for Agenda Control," *Journal of Economic Theory* 12, no. 3 (June 1976): 472–82.

14. See William H. Riker, "Implications from the Disequilibrium of Majority Rule for the Study of Institutions," *American Political Science Review* 74, no. 2 (June 1980): 442–46.

15. See, e.g., Barry R. Weingast, Kenneth A. Shepsle, and Christopher Johnsen, "The Political Economy of Benefits and Costs: A Neoclassical Approach to Distributive Politics," *Journal of Political Economy* 89, no. 4 (Aug. 1981): 642–64; and Gordon Tullock, "Why So Much Stability," *Public Choice* 38, no. 1 (1982): 189–202.

2
The Origins of Democracy

1. The Peloponnesian War was extended from 431 to 404 B.C. See Russell Meigs, *The Athenian Empire* (Oxford: Clarendon Press, 1972), for a history of the period, and also Hugh Thomas, *A History of the World* (New York: Harper & Row, 1979), pp. 157–58, for some insights on Athenian democracy.

2. Milton Friedman, in *Capitalism and Freedom* (Chicago: University of Chicago Press, 1962), points to the right of those who oppose democratic institutions to argue against them in a free society. More directly,

Joseph Shumpeter, *Capitalism, Socialism, and Democracy*, 3d ed. (New York: Harper & Row, 1950), makes the same argument and states explicitly that he does not believe that capitalism can survive.

3. Such a framework is useful from a theoretical standpoint, but may also be important in reality. A century and a half ago, Alexis de Tocqueville, in *Democracy in America* (New York: Geo. Deardorn & Co., 1838), noted, "I am well aware of the influence which the nature of a country and its political precedents exercise upon a constitution" (p. 311). While a development of this idea is beyond the scope of this book, it is interesting to speculate on the effects of how a democracy orginated on how democratic institutions will evolve.

4. Scott Gordon, "The New Contractarians," *Journal of Political Economy* 84, no. 3 (June 1976): 573–90.

5. James M. Buchanan, *The Limits of Liberty: Between Anarchy and Leviathan* (Chicago: University of Chicago Press, 1975); Robert Nozick, *Anarchy, State, and Utopia*, (New York: Basic Books, 1974); and John Rawls, *A Theory of Justice* (Cambridge, Mass.: Belknap, 1971).

6. See also Ayn Rand, "Man's Rights" and "The Nature of Government," in her *The Virtue of Selfishness* (New York: New American Library, 1961), for a similar view of government.

7. For example, individuals might be ignorant of their positions in society and still have disagreements over the best rules to promote the social welfare. This raises the question of how identical individuals must be in the model to secure unanimous agreement. If they are identical in every respect, then it appears that the problem of agreement is simply assumed away, and the model becomes one of benevolent dictatorship.

8. Sir Ernest Barker, in his introduction to *Social Contract* (New York & London: Oxford University Press, 1960), notes that in England, "the house of Lords, as a part of the Convention Parliament, had agreed by 55 votes to 46 that there was an original contract between the King and the people (p. xxii)."

9. Special interests have, of course, influenced American politics from the beginning. See, e.g., Jonathan R. T. Hughes, *The Governmental Habit* (New York: Basic Books, 1977). The point here, though, is that it would be hard to imagine circumstances where a government could be established more free of special interests and outside constraints than the American case.

10. Gordon, in "The New Contractarians," assumes that Rawls presents a normative theory but notes that there is some ambiguity.

11. This line of reasoning is explored in more depth in Randall G. Holcombe, *Public Finance and the Political Process* (Carbondale and Edwardsville: Southern Illinois University Press, 1983), chap. 8.

12. On the issue of fairness, see William J. Baumol, "Applied Fairness Theory and Rationing Policy," *American Economic Review* 72, no. 4 (Sept. 1982): 639–51; and for another view, Randall G. Holcombe, "Applied Fairness Theory: Comment," *American Economic Review* 73, no. 5 (Dec. 1983): 1153–56.

13. The opening pages of Ludwig von Mises' *Human Action*, 3d rev. ed. (Chicago: Henry Regnery Company, 1966), provide a superb analysis of the origins of economic thinking and the development of economic man in intellectual history.

14. Murray Edelman, *The Symbolic Uses of Politics* (Urbana: University of Illinois Press, 1964), provides explanations of the role of fictions in society, within a model in which political activity has consequences because of its symbolic nature.

15. See Randall G. Holcombe, "The Origin of the Legislature," *Social Science Review* (forthcoming), for a discussion of the origin, nature, and evolution of legislative institutions.

16. Perhaps this should be qualified, since the checkoff is taken by many taxpayers. Reflecting on the issue, though, the dangers of giving additional control over the electoral process to those who already have political power must be viewed as a danger, since the government in existence then has more power to perpetuate itself.

17. This might be considered the first lesson of economics, if for no other reason than that it is the first lesson in Adam Smith's *The Wealth of Nations* (New York: Modern Library, 1937). Friedrich A. Hayek, "The Use of Knowledge in Society," *American Economic Review* 35, no. 4 (Sept. 1945): 519–30, notes, however, that as a member of a society becomes more dependent upon the rest of the society in general, the individual's dependence upon any particular member of the society is reduced.

18. Still others claim that government cannot be justified on efficiency grounds. See, e.g., Murray N. Rothbard, *For A New Liberty* (New York: Macmillan, 1973), for a description of how an orderly anarchy would outperform governments on efficiency grounds.

19. Nozick, *Anarchy, State, and Utopia*, and Rand, "Nature of Government," both cited above.

20. Recall the arguments of Rothbard, briefly noted above.

21. The classic statement of these conditions is Francis Bator's "The Anatomy of Market Failure," *Quarterly Journal of Economics* 72 (Aug. 1958): 351–79.

22. Buchanan has explored this theme extensively. See, e.g., James M. Buchanan, "Public Finance and Public Choice," *National Tax Journal* 28 (Dec., 1975): 383–94.

23. Paul A. Samuelson's classic articles on the subject are "The Pure

Theory of Public Expenditure," *Review of Economics and Statistics* 36 (Nov. 1954): 387–89, and "A Diagrammatic Exposition of a Theory of Public Expenditure," *Review of Economics and Statistics* 37 (Nov. 1955): 350–56.

24. This idea is developed in Holcombe, *Public Finance and the Political Process*, chap. 2.

25. See Arthur T. Denzau and Robert J. Mackay, "Benefit Shares and Majority Voting," *American Economic Review* 66 (Mar. 1976): 69–76, for a full development of this argument.

26. James M. Buchanan and Gordon Tullock, *The Calculus of Consent* (Ann Arbor: University of Michigan Press, 1962), chap. 6.

27. With more than two candiates, a more inclusive rule might appear to be optimal, but even here, a minority would impose its candidate on a majority. Thus, with equally intense preferences, a simple majority can still appear optimal even with many candidates. The question of how a single candidate would be selected from many if no one received a majority is a difficult one, though. T. Nicolaus Tideman and Gordon Tullock, "A New and Superior Process for Making Social Choices," *Journal of Political Economy* 84 (Dec. 1976): pp. 1145–60, give one possible answer.

3
The Median Voter

1. Duncan Black, *The Theory of Committees and Elections* (Cambridge: Cambridge University Press, 1958).

2. Some circumstances can be envisioned where an individual would not necessarily prefer closer alternatives to those further away. Take the example of public education. Individual 3 might like a high level of expenditures Q_3 to produce quality schools, but if a lower level is chosen, like Q_2, will send his or her children to private schools. Thus, the individual could prefer Q_1 to Q_2 as a way of minimizing taxes for public schools, even though the individual's most preferred level is Q_3. Throughout the book, however, the assumption that individuals prefer outcomes closer to their ideal levels, than to those farther away, will be retained. These issues are discussed in Yoram Barzel, "Private Schools and Public School Finance," *Journal of Political Economy* 81, no. 1 (Jan./Feb. 1973): 174–86, written in response to Robin Barlow's "Efficiency Aspects of Local School Finance," *Journal of Political Economy* 78, no. 5 (Sept./Oct. 1970): 1028–40. See also the comment by Theodore Bergstrom, "A Note of Efficient Taxation," *Journal of Political Economy* 81, no. 1 (Jan./Feb. 1973): 187–91, and Barlow's reply, "Efficiency As-

pects of Local School Finance: Reply," *Journal of Political Economy* 81, no. 1 (Jan./Feb. 1973): 199–202.

3. Howard R. Bowen, "The Interpretation of Voting in the Allocation of Economic Resources," *Quarterly Journal of Economics* 58 (Nov. 1943): 27–48. The presentation here is slightly different from Bowen's, but keeps the spirit of Bowen's model.

4. Harold Hotelling, "Stability in Competition," *Economic Journal* 39 (Mar. 1929): 41–57; and Anthony Downs, *An Economic Theory of Democracy* (New York: Harper & Row, 1957).

5. Francis M. Bator, "The Anatomy of Market Failure," *Quarterly Journal of Economics* 72 (Aug. 1958): 351–79.

6. However, see T. Nicolaus Tideman an Gordon Tullock, "A New and Superior Process for Making Social Choices," *Journal of Political Economy* 84 (Dec. 1976): 1145–60. The title of that article illustrates the authors' views that a better social choice rule is possible.

7. This view is close to the Austrian concept of economic activity. See, e.g., Israel M. Kirzner, *Competition and Entrepreneurship* (Chicago: University of Chicago Press). See also Ronald Coase's classic, "The Problem of Social Cost," *Journal of Law & Economics* 3 (Oct. 1960): 1–44. The concept of economic activity as attempts to lower information and transactions costs are also explored in Coase's "The Nature of the Firm," *Economica* 4 (Nov. 1937): 386–405; Armen A. Alchian and Harold Demsetz, "Production, Information Costs, and Economic Organization," *American Economic Review* 62, no. 5 (Dec. 1972): 777–95; and Louis De Alessi, "Property Rights, Transaction Costs, and X-Efficiency: An Essay in Economic Theory,"*American Economic Review* 73, no. 1 (Mar. 1983): pp. 64–81.

8. The term, "agenda control," was used by Thomas Romer and Howard Rosenthal, "Political Resources Allocation, Controlled Agendas, and the Status Quo," *Public Choice* 33, no. 4 (1978): 27–43. See also their "Bureaucrats versus Voters: On the Political Economy of Resource Allocation by Direct Democracy," *Quarterly Journal of Economics* 93, no. 4 (Nov. 1979): 563–87. While the agenda control has gained some recent notice, the basic concept has some intellectual antecedents. See, e.g., James M. Buchanan and Marilyn Flowers, "Analytic Setting for a Taxpayers' Revolution," *Western Economic Journal* 7 (Dec. 1969): 349–59; and Raymond Jackson, "A 'Taxpayers' Revolution' and Economic Rationality," *Public Choice* 10 (Spring 1971): 93–96.

9. These issues are discussed in the author's *Public Finance and the Political Process*, chap. 3.

10. The following examples step slightly outside the model in this chapter and anticipate some of the material on cycles that appears in

chap. 9. The problem of cycles is sometimes referred to as the Arrow problem, since Kenneth J. Arrow begins his book, *Social Choice and Individual Values* (New Haven and London: Yale University Press, 1951), with a description of the problem.

11. Some other issues regarding the order of issues on the agenda appear in Charles R. Plott and Michael E. Levine, "A Model of Agenda Influence on Committee Decisions," *American Economic Review* 68, no. 1 (Mar. 1978): 146–60. Another interesting perspective on cycles is developed in Ronald A. Heiner, "The Collective Decision Problem, and a Theory of Preference," *Economic Inquiry* 19, no. 2 (Apr. 1981): 297–331. See also R. D. McKelvey, "Intransitivities in Multi Dimensional Voting Models and Some Implications for Agenda Control," *Journal of Economic Theory* 12 (1976): 472–82.

12. The model originally appeared in William A. Niskanen, "The Peculiar Economic Bureaucracy," *American Economic Review* 58 (May 1968): 293–305, and was further developed in *Bureaucracy and Representative Government* (Chicago and New York: Aldine-Atherton, 1971) and "Bureaucrats and Politicians," *Journal of Law Economics* 18 (Dec. 1975): 617–43.

13. The reader interested in more detail is referred to the author's *Public Finance and the Political Process*, chap. 3 and 4, as well as in the earlier referenced articles by Romer and Rosenthal.

14. James L. Barr and Otto A. Davis, "An Elementary Political and Economic Theory of the Expenditures of State and Local Governments," *Southern Economic Journal* 33 (Oct. 1966): 149–65.

15. Robert P. Inman, "Testing Political Economy's 'as if' Assumption: Is the Median Income Voter Really Decisive?" *Public Choice* 33, no. 4 (1978): 45–65.

16. Thomas Romer and Howard Rosenthal, "The Elusive Median Voter," *Journal of Public Economics* 12, no. 2 (Oct. 1979): 143–70.

17. Romer and Rosenthal, "The Elusive Median Voter," p. 144.

18. Even this assertion is open to question. For a discussion, see Mario J. Rizzo, "Praxeology and Econometrics: A Critique of Positivist Economics," in Louis M. Spadaro, ed., *New Directions in Austrian Economics* (Kansas City, Kans.: Andrews & McMeel, 1978).

19. Romer and Rosenthal note some studies that do so.

20. Thomas Romer and Howard Rosenthal, "Median Voters or Budget Maximizers: Evidence from School Expenditure Referenda," *Economic Inquiry* 26, no. 4 (Oct. 1982): 577.

21. Romer and Rosenthal, "The Elusive Median Voter," mention the study in a footnote on p. 162, where they relate, "Deacon (1977) refers to unpublished work by Holcombe (1976), saying that it conducts a

direct test, yielding 'evidence that strongly supports the median voter outcome' [Robert T. Deacon, "Private Choice and Collective Outcomes: Evidence from Public Sector Demand Analysis," *National Tax Journal* 30 (1977): 386]. Our reading of Holcombe's paper leads us to regard Deacon's characterization as unduly optimistic." Needless to say, I tend to agree with Deacon's characterization rather than Romer and Rosenthal's. The unpublished 1976 paper was subsequently published as "An Empirical Test of the Median Voter Model," *Economic Inquiry* 18, no. 2 (Apr. 1980): 260–74, and was later included, with some revision and additional material, as chap. 4 in *Public Finance and the Political Process.* Outside of this footnote, the empirical test presently being discussed was not analyzed by Romer and Rosenthal.

22. William A. McEachern, "Collective Decision Rules and Local Debt Choice: A Test of the Median Voter Hypothesis," *National Tax Journal* 31, no. 2 (June 1978): 129–36. This article was not referenced by Romer and Rosenthal in their critique of empirical tests of the model.

23. Footnote 21 gives the direct evidence of the two very different appraisals of the author's article. For an extension of this idea, see David Friedman, "Many, Few, One: Social Harmony and the Shrunken Social Choice Set," *American Economic Review* 70, no. 1 (Mar. 1980): 225–32.

24. The seminal article on intergovernmental competition is Charles M. Tiebout, "A Pure Theory of Local Expenditure," *Journal of Political Economy* 64 (Oct. 1956): 416–24.

25. See, e.g., Robert J. Mackay and Carolyn L. Weaver, "Monopoly Bureaus and Fiscal Outcomes: Deductive Models and Implications for Reform," in Gordon Tullock ad Richard E. Wagner, eds., *Policy Analysis and Deductive Reasoning* (Lexington, Mass.: Lexington Books, 1978): 141–65.

26. This issue is discussed in more detail in the author's *Public Finance and the Political Process,* chap. 6.

27. Arthur T. Denzau and Robert J. Mackay analyze this case, using an example of locating a fire station, in "Benefit Shares and Majority Voting," *American Economic Review* 66 (Mar. 1976): 69–76.

28. This same example is extended to the case of fifteen voters in the author's *Public Finance and the Political Process,* chap. 6.

29. This assumes that marginal and average benefits change in the same direction. Denzau and Mackay illustrate a case where this is not true in "Benefit Shares and Majority Voting."

30. Two prominent median voter studies that looked at goods not provided by referendum are Theodore C. Bergstrom and Robert

Goodman, "Private Demand for Public Goods," *American Economic Review* 63 (June 1973): 280–96; and Thomas E. Borcherding and Robert T. Deacon, "The Demand for Services of Non-Federal Governments," *American Economic Review* 62 (Dec. 1972): 891–901. These studies used the median voter model as an assumption in the model rather than providing a test, however.

4
Coalitions and Stability in Multidimensional Issues

1. Even though voters are forced to rank alternatives, forcing the issue into a single dimension for each voter, there is not necessarily a continuum where the preferences of all voters will be single peaked, so a cyclical majority problem may arise in single-dimensioned issues as well as multidimensional issues. The cycle problem is discussed later in the chapter, but mention is made here because the recent public choice literature has related cycles to multidimensional issue space. The reader should observe that just because an issue can be collapsed into a single-dimensioned issue space, there is no guarantee of a stable majority rule outcome.

2. Mancur Olson, *The Logic of Collective Action* (New York: Shocken Books, 1965), makes the distinction between large and small number settings in politics.

3. One might anticipate that when several dimensions of political issues are bundled, as in a presidential election, some aspects of the agenda control model could apply. In fact, some of the models later in the book may apply to this case, since coalitions can form to determine combinations of output in several dimensions that could be feasible. Still, this type of problem—analogous to determining the platform of a presidential candidate—is not the type of problem that is the main concern of the book.

4. This prompted Gordon Tullock, "Why So Much Stability," *Public Choice* 37, no. 2 (1981): 189–202, to observe that while many public choice models predict that political processes would be unstable, a look at the real world shows them to be stable. Tullock challenged readers to account for this discrepancy between theory and reality and, at the same time, offered some explanations of his own. A discussion of these issues is carried on by Willian H. Riker, "Implications from the Disequilibrium of Majority Rule for the Study of Institutions," *American Political Science Review* 74, no. 2 (June 1980): 432–46, and in the same journal, Peter C. Ordeshook, "Political Disequilibrium and Scientific Inquiry" (pp. 447–50), and Douglas Rae, "An Altimeter for Mr. Escher's Stair-

way" (pp. 451–55), both comment on Riker's article and Riker's reply (pp. 456–58.). In Kenneth A. Shepsle's "Institutional Arrangements and Equilibrium in Multidimensional Voting Models," *American Journal of Political Science* 23, no. 1 (Feb. 1979): 27–59, is an example of a model that explicitly recognizes the institutional constraints used to generate an equilibrium.

5. Examples are Theordore Bergstrom and Robert Goodman, "Private Demand for Public Goods," *American Economic Review* 63 (June 1973): 280–96, and Thomas E. Borcherding and Robert T. Deacon, "The Demand for Services of Non-Federal Governments," *American Economic Review* 62 (Dec. 1972): 891–901. These studies are certainly not being cited as an example of low-quality work; on the contrary, they are some of the better articles of that vintage and are cited as representative of the application of public choice models at that time.

6. Economists who have examined some of the foundations of the social structure, as e.g., in James M. Buchanan's *The Limits of Liberty* (Chicago: University of Chicago Press, 1975), are an exception, but in other works Buchanan assures voluntary exchange without analysis. This is not a criticism, as will be made apparent, but an observation. Murray N. Rothbard, *For a New Liberty* (New York: Macmillan, 1973), looks at the institutional structure of voluntary exchange and concludes that it could emerge without governmentally protected rights, taking a new look at the theory of anarchistic societies. While other social philosophers have examined similar questions, Rothbard's and Buchanan's attempts are noteworthy because of their backgrounds as economists.

7. This is what Thomas S. Kuhn called a paradigm in *The Structure of Scientific Revolutions* (Chicago: University of Chicago Press, 1962).

8. William J. Baumol, "Contestable Markets: An Uprising in the Theory of Industry Structure," *American Economic Review* 72, no. 1 (Mar. 1982): 1–15, looks at these aspects and concludes that ease of entry is the primary determinant of market structure. Bammol's conclusion is of less interest here than the observation that the theory of market structure is still developing. By analogy, the theory of political structures, being much younger, ought to have much room for development.

9. Yoram Barzel, "Private Schools and Public School Finance," *Journal of Political Economy* 81, no. 1 (Jan./Feb. 1973): 174–86, gives an example with public school finance, suggesting that the model has some generality.

10. See Richard D. McKelvey, "Intransitivities in Multi Dimensional Voting Models and Some Implications for Agenda Control," *Journal of Economic Theory* 12, no. 3 (June 1976): 472–82, and his "General Condi-

tions for Global Intransitivities in Formal Voting Models," *Econometrica* 47, no. 5 (Sept. 1979): 1085–1112.

11. Charles R. Plott, "A Notion of Equilibrium and Its Possibility under Majority Rule," *American Economic Review* 62, no. 4 (Sept. 1967): 787–806. James M. Enelow and Melvin J. Hinich, "Ideology, Issues, and the Spatial Theory of Elections," *American Political Science Review* 76, no. 3 (Sept. 1982): 493–501, consider the effects of ideology in a multidimensional model, suggesting that ideological differences may either reduce or magnify differences in spatial positions. See also Enelow and Hinich, "On Plott's Pairwise Symmetry Condition for Majority Rule Equilibrium," *Public Choice* 40, no. 3 (1983): 317–21, where they argue that the symmetry condition is sufficient, but not necessary.

12. A contract curve is the locus of points where one individual in the pair can be made better off only by making the other individual worse off.

13. Gordon Tullock, "The General Irrelevance of the General Impossibility Theorem," *Quarterly Journal of Economics* 81, no. 2 (May 1967): 256–70, and chap. 3 of *Toward a Mathematics of Politics* (Ann Arbor: University of Michigan Press, 1967).

14. However, James M. Buchanan, "The Economics of Earmarked Taxes," *Journal of Political Economy* 71 (Oct. 1963): 457–69, illustrates that the mix of programs is a determinant of the level of spending most preferred by the median voter.

15. This same game was analyzed at length by James M. Buchanan and Gordon Tullock, *The Calculus of Consent* (Ann Arbor: University of Michigan Press, 1962), chap. 11.

16. Chap. 5 suggests that even if there were, the income distribution would not be affected much. The skeptical reader may skip ahead to examine the argument.

17. This observation, made by Tullock in "Why So Much Stability," was in response to the apparent discrepancies between theoretical models of instability and the real-world appearance of stability.

18. This formulation of the distributional problem follows along the lines of Randall G. Holcombe and Asghar Zardkoohi, "On the Distribution of Federal Taxes and Expenditures and the New War between the States," *Public Choice* 40 (1983): 165–74.

19. An early statement of this idea was made by David Klingaman, "A Note on a Cyclical Majority Problem," *Public Choice* 6 (Spring 1969): 99–101.

20. See Barry R. Weingast, Kenneth A. Shepsle, and Christopher Johnsen, "The Political Economy of Benefits and Costs: A Neoclassical Approach to Distributive Politics," *Journal of Political Economy* 89, no. 4

(Aug. 1981): 642–64. This is also consistent with Stephen A. Hoenack, "On the Stability of Legislative Outcomes," *Public Choice* 41, no. 2 (1983): 251–60. Richard G. Niemi, "Why So Much Stability? Another Opinion," *Public Choice* 41, no. 2 (1983): 261–70, argues that stability is generated because of the limited number of real-world alternatives available, but this argument seems to lose its persuasiveness when it is recognized that cyclical majorities are often represented in a three alternative illustration.

21. A very confident participant might accept the cyclical outcome in exchange for the knowledge that the participant would be in the initial majority, if the participant's rate of time discount were high enough. The higher payoff in the first period could conceivably compensate the player for a higher variance later.

22. William H. Riker, *The Theory of Political Coalitions* (New Haven: Yale University Press, 1962).

23. Anthony Downs, *An Economic Theory of Democracy* (New York: Harper & Row, 1957).

5
Taxes and Redistribution

1. This tends to be true for income taxes at the federal level, anyway. State income taxes are frequently proportional, and sales and property taxes are usually considered to be regressive with respect to income. Even for federal income taxes, average tax payments (as opposed to marginal tax rates) are largely proportional, with very low-income individuals paying less and very high-income individuals paying more. The argument that taxes are not as progressive as they appear will only serve to strengthen the arguments in this chapter.

2. This literature was begun with a two-part essay, Peter A. Diamond and James A. Mirrlees, "Optimal Taxation and Public Production: I and II," *American Economic Review* 61 (Mar. 1971): 8–27, (June 1971): 261–78. Some examples of the continuation of the optimal tax literature are James A. Mirrlees, "An Exploration in the Theory of Optimum Taxation," *Review of Economic Studies* 38 (Apr. 1971): 175–208, and his "Optimal Tax Theory—A Synthesis," *Journal of Public Economics* 6 (Nov. 1976): 327–58. Much of the optimal tax literature appeared in the *Journal of Public Economics:* e.g., A. B. Atkinson and J. E. Stiglitz, "The Design of the Tax Structure: Direct versus Indirect Taxation," *Journal of Public Economics* 6 (July–Aug. 1976): 55–75; Michael Allingham, "Inequality and Progressive Taxation: An Example," *Journal of Public Economics* 11 (Apr. 1979): 273–74; Avinash Dixit,

"Price Changes and Optimum Taxation in a Many-Consumer Economy," *Journal of Public Economics* 11 (Apr. 1979): 143–57; Jannus A. Ordover, "Distributive Justice and Optimal Taxation of Wages and Interest in a Growing Economy," *Journal of Public Economics* 5 (Jan.–Feb., 1976): 130–60; Agnar Sandmo, "Optimal taxation—An Introduction to the Literature," *Journal of Public Economics* 6 (July–Aug., 1976): 37–54; and J. K. Seade, "On the Shape of Optimum Tax Schedules," *Journal of Public Economics* 7 (Apr. 1977): 203–35. That so much of this literature appears in the *Journal of Public Economics* may be due to the views of the editor, A. B. Atkinson, on issues of income redistribution and social welfare maximization. For examples, see Atkinson's "On the Measurement of Inequality," in A. B. Atkinson, ed., *Wealth, Income, and Inequality: Selected Readings* (Baltimore: Penguin, 1973), pp. 46–68; *The Economics of Inequality* (Oxford: Clarendon Press, 1975); and "Housing Allowances, Income Maintenance, and Income Taxation," in Martin S. Feldstein and Robert P. Inman, eds., *The Economics of Public Services* (London: Macmillan, 1977), pp. 3–16. The essence of the optimal tax literature is that a social welfare function exists where interpersonal utility comparisons are possible, and social welfare is maximized by redistributing income through the tax system.

3. See, e.g., James M. Buchanan, "Taxation in Fiscal Exchange," *Journal of Public Economics* 6 (July–August 1976): pp. 17–29; Martin Feldstein, "On the Optimal Progressivity of the Income Tax," *Journal of Public Economics* 2 (Nov. 1973): 357–76; and Martin Ricketts, "Tax Theory and Tax Policy," in Alan Peacock and Francesco Forte, eds., *The Political Economy of Taxation* (New York: St. Martin's Press, 1981), pp. 29–46.

4. Rawls, in *A Theory of Justice*, goes a step further and argues that individuals would so agree.

5. See Harold M. Hochman and James D. Rogers, "Pareto Optimal Redistribution," *American Economic Review* 59 (Sept. 1969): 542–57, for this argument. Although there may not be unanimous agreement, the ideas in Buchanan and Tullock, *The Calculus of Consent*, chap. 6, discussed in chap. 2 of this book, might justify less than unanimous approval.

6. Adam Smith, *The Wealth of Nations* (New York: Modern Library, 1937 [1776]), p. 772.

7. Earl A. Thompson, "Taxation and National Defense," *Journal of Political Economy* 82, no. 4 (July/Aug. 1974): 755–83.

8. Notes 2 and 3, above, list numerous articles regarding optimal taxation.

9. Joseph E. Stiglitz and Michael J. Boskin, "Some Lessons from the

New Public Finance," *American Economic Review* 67 (Feb. 1977): 295–301, have remarked that "this literature probably represents the most significant body of work in 'second best economics' " (p. 295).

10. However, Ordover, "Distributive Justice and Optimal Taxation of Wages and Interest in a Growing Economy," p. 158, suggests a confiscatory tax on interest incomes: "Our analysis indicates that the optimal rule of interest tax is high. In many or perhaps most cases it equals one hundred percent."

11. Here, there is a similarity between the minimax criterion of Rawls and the optimal tax literature, although there are differences as well.

12. See Buchanan, "Taxation and Fiscal Exchange."

13. See Ricketts, "Tax Theory and Tax Policy," for an excellent critique of the optimal tax literature in this vein.

14. See the author's *Public Finance and the Political Process*, chap. 2, and particularly pp. 18–21, for a fuller discussion of optimal taxes in this context.

15. Quoted from Atkinson, *The Economics of Inequality*, p. 161.

16. Martin Bronfenbrenner, *Income Distribution Theory* (Chicago: Aldine-Atherton, 1971), pp. 1–2, notes the importance of the determination of income distribution to Ricardo by quoting the following passage from p. 5 of Ricardo's *Principles:* "The produce of the earth—all that is derived from its surface by the united application of labour, machinery, and capital, is divided among three classes of the community. . . . To determine the laws which regulate this distribution is the principal problem in Political Economy." Harry G. Johnson's *The Theory of Income Distribution* (London: Gray-Mills, 1973) is representative of the neoclassical theory of income distribution that continues the Ricardian tradition.

17. Feldstein's "On the Optimal Progressivity of the Income Tax" is an exception.

18. The general principle here is that the more elastic the demand or supply schedule is, the greater will be the amount of the tax shifted to the other side of the market. Thus, a perfectly elastic supply schedule places the entire burden of the tax on demanders. Richard A. Musgrave, *The Theory of Public Finance* (New York: McGraw-Hill, 1959), esp. chaps. 10–16, provides a thorough analysis of tax shifting and the excess burden of taxation.

19. The empirical findings of Morgan Reynolds and Eugene Smolensky, *Public Expenditures, Taxes, and the Distribution of Income* (New York: Academic Press, 1977), suggest that the results of this model are descriptive of reality. They show (p. 74, table 5.5) that there has not

been a statistically significant change in the postfisc distribution of income from 1950 to 1970 despite increasingly progressive taxes. They also find, as this model suggests, a statistically significant increase in the inequality of the prefisc distribution of income during the same period.

20. *Public Expenditures, Taxes, and the Distribution of Income*, cited above.

21. Robert Nozick, *Philosophical Explanations* (Cambridge, Mass.: Belknap, 1981), has some interesting observations on the way that one develops theories and uses evidence to support theories. Nozick observes that often individuals will have prior notions about what would be a correct answer to a question. If the inquirer arrives at a conclusion at odds with the prior concept, more research can be undertaken to find flaws in methodology or conflicting evidence. The search continues until the expected conclusion is produced. This procedure, even though it may not be conscious, tends to lead investigators toward conclusions with which they feel comfortable. Of course, it is possible for one to change his or her mind in light of new evidence, but the point is that it is never necessary. Through continued search, one can almost always find support for one's currently held ideas, and then can quit searching.

22. In another empirical examination, Edgar K. Browning, "The Trend toward Equality in the Distribution of Net Income," *Southern Economic Journal* 43, no. 1 (July 1976): 912–23, concludes that the distribution of net income became more equal from the period 1952 to 1972. Browning's methodology differs from Reynolds and Smolensky because Browning does not seek a prefisc distribution of income for comparison but uses census data which includes transfers in gross income.

23. Henry Hazlitt, *Economics in One Lesson* (New York: Harper, 1946).

24. See Gordon Tullock's review of Mancur Olson, *The Rise and Decline of Nations* (New Haven: Yale University Press, 1982), in *Public Choice* 40, no. 1 (1983): 111–16, where this possibility is mentioned.

6
Distributive Government

1. Kenneth Arrow, *Social Choice and Individual Values.*

2. Howard Bowen, "The Interpretation of Voting in the Allocation of Economic Resources". Duncan Black, *The Theory of Committees and Elections;* and Anthony Down, *An Economic Theory of Democracy.*

3. This conclusion, discussed in chap. 4, is proven by R. D. McKelvey, "Intransitivities in Mulit Dimensional Voting Models and Some Implications for Agenda Control."

4. Agenda control was discussed in chap. 3.

5. Chap. 4 discussed the relationship between single and multidimensional issues at length.

6. This theme is explored in James M. Buchanan, "Politics, Policy, and the Pigouvian Margins," *Economica*, n.s., 29 (Feb. 1962): 17–28. Even in some unanimous agreements democratic decision making may in a sense coerce minorities into joining a majority coalition. This idea is discussed later in the chapter.

7. See Plott and Levine, "A Model of Agenda Influence on Committee Decisions," for a discussion of this issue.

8. Along these lines, see Armen A. Alchian, "Uncertainty, Evolution, and Economic Theory," *Journal of Political Economy* 58 (1950): 211–21.

9. Riker's *The Theory of Political Competition* raises this objection to Downs's *An Economic Theory of Democracy*.

10. Baumol's "Contestable Markets: An Uprising in the Theory of Industry Structure" makes a similar point regarding economic competition.

11. This material draws on the insight of Downs, *An Economic Theory of Democracy*, and has also been discussed at length by Gordon Tullock, "Political Ignorance," chap. 7 of *Toward a Mathematics of Politics*.

12. Thomas C. Schelling, *A Strategy of Conflict* (Cambridge, Mass.: Harvard University Press, 1960), presents a most insightful analysis of this type of situation.

13. Kenneth J. Koford, "Centralized Vote-trading," *Public Choice* 39, no. 2 (1982): 245–68, develops a model where political entrepreneurs set up a market for vote trading, capturing the surplus for themselves. The result is Pareto optimal. The argument is ingenious, but the question remains about how entrepreneurs can maintain their positions when votes can be more cheaply traded directly. Could competing entrepreneurs start cycles?

14. Ronald Coase, "The Problem of Social Cost," *Journal of Law & Economics* 3 (Oct. 1960): 1–44.

15. Here, the argument might be made that if transactions costs are too high for improvement, then the existing state of the world is optimal. The problem with this argument is that once the transactions costs are recognized, there may be institutional changes that could be made to lower transactions costs, making Pareto improvements possible.

16. Waterway operators, e.g., compare themselves with the railroad industry, arguing that much larger subsidies are made to rails. The lobbyists are not arguing for less rail support but for more waterway funding.

17. See Bruce L. Benson, "Logrolling and the High Demand Review Committee," *Public Choice* 41, no. 3 (1983): 427–34.

18. This description of the process seems to encompass (and perhaps unify) arguments made by Tullock, "Why So Much Stability," and Kenneth A. Shepsle and Barry R. Weingast, "Structure Induced Equilibrium and Legislative Choice," *Public Choice* 37, no. 3 (1981): 503–19.

19. Except where externalities affect those not participating in the exchange. This exception does not apply to the rule of unanimity because everyone must approve of the measure.

20. Buchanan, "Politics, Policy, and the Pigouvian Margins."

21. *Newsweek,* 20 Dec. 1982, ran its cover story on the inefficiency of military budgeting procedures and competition among the services.

22. This observation is based in part on classified documents exchanged between the services while the author was employed at the Center for Naval Analyses. A general observation regarding classified documents from the Pentagon, CIA, and other sources is that many documents are classified not for national security reasons but to keep poor analysis and political maneuverings out of the sight of the general public.

7
Interest Groups and Distributional Activity

1. This insight is discussed by James M. Buchanan, "Politics, Policy, and the Pigouvian Margins." Peter Bernholz, "Externalities as a Necessary Condition for Cyclical Social Preferences," *Quarterly Journal of Economics* 97, no. 4 (Nov. 1982): 699–705, argues, as his title suggests, that externalities are a necessary condition for cyclical social preferences.

2. This is the theme of Armen Alchian's insightful article, "Uncertainty, Evolution, and Economic Theory."

3. Richard A. Posner, "Taxation by Regulation," *Bell Journal of Economics and Management Science* 2 (Spring 1971): 22–50, and George J. Stigler, "The Theory of Economic Regulation," *Bell Journal of Economics and Management Science* 2 (Spring 1971): 3–21.

4. In a study done for the state of Alabama by the author, Alabama was found to benefit from federal inland waterway subsidies. The subsidies are not cost-effective because the waterway improvements cost more than the benefits they generate. However, the residents of the state pay a small fraction of the federal taxes used for waterway improvements, and the benefits to Alabama exceed Alabama's share of the taxes used to finance the benefits. The residents of Alabama are better off with the subsidies and should support their representatives' efforts

to continue them. However, it is obvious that if every state had similar programs, the total cost of all programs will exceed the total benefits. Waterway subsidies are a good example of the special interest legislation generally referred to here.

5. Growth in government may cause an absolute growth in interest group politics, but the causation may also go the opposite way, as Mancur Olson, *The Rise and Decline of Nations* (New Haven: Yale University Press, 1982), p. 71, suggests, so that growing interest groups cause larger government as well.

6. Harold Demsetz, "Why Regulate Utilities?" *Journal of Law and Economics* 11 (1968): 55–65, uses this concept to suggest that utilities could compete for the right to be a monopoly supplier for a specified period of time. The idea has obvious parallels in politics, and the parallels are discussed by Gordon Tullock, "Entry Barriers in Politics," *American Economic Review* 55, no. 2 (Mar. 1965): 458–66; and W. Marke Crain, "On the Structure and Stability of Political Markets," *Journal of Political Economy* 85, no. 4 (Aug. 1977): 829–42.

7. Gordon Tullock makes this argument in his review of Mancur Olson's book, *The Rise and Decline of Nations*.

8. See, e.g., Buchanan's "Taxation in Fiscal Exchange." Another interesting conception is found in Thompson's "Taxation and National Defense."

9. A possible counterargument is that the subsidies are insurance, and the expected cost of an insurance premium is always more than the expected payout. This is unlikely to be true in the case of farm subsidies, since the risks are so widely distributed. It is rare to see insurance against price fluctuations sold on the private market; however, contracts agreeing to future delivery at a fixed price may serve this role.

10. Richard A. Musgrave, *The Theory of Public Finance* (New York: McGraw-Hill, 1959). Musgrave also includes stabilization as a third function of government.

11. *Newsweek*, 20 Dec. 1982, devoted its cover story to this subject, as noted in the previous chapter.

8
The Government Budget Constraint

1. James M. Buchanan, "The Economics of Earmarked Taxes."

2. Douglas R. Hofstadter, "Metamagical Themas," *Scientific American* 248, no. 6 (June 1983), p. 14. Hofstadter's reasoning on the problem is quite Rawlsian. He reasoned essentially that when playing the game with other intelligent people who understand the game (which

presumably eliminates a random selection of an alternative), everybody will select the same option. Any individual will be better off if everybody chooses to cooperate rather than to not cooperate. Therefore, the individual should choose to cooperate and assume that everyone else's reasoning will lead them to the identical choice. This solution seems to me to omit the final step in the reasoning. Now that the individual knows that everyone else will cooperate, the individual can do still better by not cooperating, but the point here is that someone well informed about the nature of the prisoners' dilemma can still argue that the cooperate solution is the optimal choice for the individual. The reader might also be interested in Hofstadter's "Metamagical Themas," *Scientific American* 248, no. 5 (May 1983): 16 for a very insightful discussion of the prisoners' dilemma game, and his *Godel, Escher, Bach: An Eternal Golden Braid* (New York: Basic Books, 1979), for an insight into the recursive type of reasoning that leads Hofstadter to argue that cooperation can be the individual optimum.

3. Some implications of this are explored by Geoffrey Brenan and James Buchanan, "Predictive Power and the Choice of Regimes," *Economic Journal* 93 (Mar. 1983): 89–105.

4. For an explanation of how an economy could choose tax rates this high, see James M. Buchanan and Dwight R. Lee, "Politics, Time, and the Laffer Curve," *Journal of Political Economy* 90, no. 4 (Aug. 1982): 816–19; and Lee and Buchanan, "Tax Rates and Tax Revenues in Political Equilibrium: Some Simple Analytics," *Economic Inquiry* 20, no. 3 (July 1982): 344–54.

5. The classic article on intergovernmental competition is Tiebout's "A Pure Theory of Local Expenditures."

6. See, e.g., James M. Buchanan and Charles J. Geotz, "Efficiency Limits of Fiscal Mobility: An Assessment of the Tiebout Model," *Journal of Public Economics* 1 (1972): 25–43.

7. See Richard B. McKenzie and Robert J. Staaf, "Revenue Sharing and Monopoly Government," *Public Choice* 33, no. 3 (1978): 93–97.

8. Knut Wicksell, "A New Principle of Just Taxation" (1896), in Richard A. Musgrave and Alan T. Peacock, eds., *Classics in the Theory of Public Finance* (New York: St. Martin's Press, 1976): 72–118.

9. Stanley L. Winer, "Some Evidence on the Effect of the Separation of Spending and Taxing Decisions," *Journal of Political Economy* 91, no. 1 (Feb. 1983): 126–40, provides some evidence along these lines and observes that the political structure may cause voters to feel that they are getting something for nothing when general revenues pay for their special interest programs.

10. Several essays in Alan Peacock and Francesco Forte, eds., *The*

Political Economy of Taxation (New York: St. Martin's Press, 1981), deal with taxes and tax bases in less developed countries. In particular, see "Taxes on International Transactions and Economic Development," by David Greenaway; "Leading Issues of Tax Policy in Developing Countries: The Economic Problems," by G. K. Shaw; and "Leading Issues of Tax Policy in Developing Countries: The Administrative Problems," by Leif Muten. One theme is that low income and the difficulty of monitoring transactions make taxes on international transactions a major source of revenue in developing nations, while the income tax is used in developed nations.

11. James M. Buchanan and Richard E. Wagner, *Democracy in Deficit: The Political Legacy of Lord Keynes* (New York: Academic Press, 1977).

12. John Maynard Keynes, *The General Theory of Employment, Interest, and Money* (New York: Harcourt, Brace, 1936).

13. See Randall G. Holcombe, "Deficits, Savings, and Capital Formation," *Federal Reserve Bank of Atlanta Review* 67, no. 8 (Aug. 1982): 38–44; and Randall G. Holcombe, John D. Jackson, and Asghar Zardkoohi, "The National Debt Controversy," *Kyklos* 34, no. 2 (1981): 186–202.

14. One might appeal to an argument like Robert J. Barro's, "Are Government Bonds Net Wealth?" *Journal of Political Economy* 82 (Nov./Dec. 1974): 1095–1117, that taxes and borrowing are equivalent in their real effects; but as Geoffrey Brennan and James M. Buchanan, "The Logic of the Ricardian Equivalence Theorem," *Finanzarchiv* 38 (1980): 1–16, note, Barro's argument ignores the excess burden of taxation, which Barro also notes in "On the Determination of Public Debt," Part 1, *Journal of Political Economy* 87, no. 5, (Oct. 1979): 940–71. When considering fiscal constraints on government, the excess burden is the crucial issue.

15. Posner, "Taxation by Regulation," and Stigler, "The Theory of Economic Regulation," are the two seminal pieces on the subject.

16. See Jonathon R. T. Hughes, *The Governmental Habit* (New York: Basic Books, 1977).

17. Anthony Downs, "Why the Government Budget Is Too Small in a Democracy," *World Politics* 12 (July 1960): 541–64.

9
Cycles, Stability, and Economic Efficiency

1. The concept of entrepreneurship used here is the same as Kirzner's, in *Competition and Entrepreneurship*, where entrepreneurs find and exploit previously unexploited profit opportunities.

2. Ronald Coase, "The Problem of Social Cost."

3. Freidrich A. Hayek gave this title to chap. 6 in his *Studies in Philosophy, Politics, and Economics* (Chicago: University of Chicago Press, 1969). It is a recurring theme throughout his other work as well.

4. Olson, *The Logic of Collective Action*, emphasizes the large group-small group dichotomy in organizing to act collectively.

5. See James M. Buchanan, "The Relevance of Pareto Optimality," *Journal of Conflict Resolution* (Nov. 1962): 341–54.

6. See Buchanan, "Public Finance and Public Choice," for an elaboration of the theme in this paragraph.

7. This insight motivated Niskanen's insightful analysis in *Bureaucracy and Representative Government*.

8. See Armen A. Alchian, "Some Economics of Property Rights," *Il Politico* 30, no. 4 (1965): 816–29.

9. See, e.g., W. Mark Crain and Asghar Zardkoohi, "A Test of the Property-Rights Theory of the Firm: Water Utilities in the United States," *Journal of Law & Economics* 21, no. 2 (Oct. 1978): 395–408; David G. Davies, "The Efficiency of Public versus Private Firms: The Case of Australia's Two Airlines," *Journal of Law & Economics* 14 (Apr. 1971): 149–65; Cotton M. Lindsay, "A Theory of Government Enterprise," *Journal of Political Economy* 84 (Oct. 1976): 1061–77; and Roger D. Blair, Paul B. Ginsberg, and Ronald J. Vogel, "Blue Cross-Blue Shield Administration Costs: A Study of Non-Profit Health Insurers," *Economic Inquiry* 13 (June 1975): 237–51.

10. The seminal papers on rent seeking are Gordon Tullock, "The Welfare Costs of Tariffs, Monopolies, and Theft," *Western Economic Journal* 5 (June 1967): 224–32; Anne O. Krueger, "The Political Economy of the Rent-Seeking Society," *American Economic Review* 64 (June 1974): 291–302; and Richard A. Posner, "The Social Costs of Monopoly and Regulation," *Journal of Political Economy* 83 (Aug. 1975): 807–27. Many subsequent works on the subject appear in James M. Buchanan, Robert D. Tollison, and Gordon Tullock, eds., *Toward a Theory of the Rent-Seeking Society* (College Station: Texas A&M University Press, 1980). See also Robert B. Ekelund, Jr., and Robert D. Tollison, *Mercantilism as a Rent-Seeking Society* (College Station: Texas A&M University Press, 1981).

11. This is the basis of criticism of neoclassical economics by some writers, such as Ludwig von Mises, in *Human Action*, and Israel Kirzner, in *Competition and Entrepreneurship*.

12. See Ronald Heiner, "The Collective Decision Problem, and a Theory of Preference," for an insightful and unusual discussion.

13. See Thomas Schwartz, "The Universal-instability Theorem," *Public Choice* 37, no. 3 (1981): 487–501.

14. A figure similar to this appears in Schwartz's "The Universal-instability Theorem."

15. Note 9 above cites case studies. See also Alchian, "Some Economics of Property Rights," Niskanen, *Bureaucracy and Representative Government*, and Gordon Tullock, *The Politics of Bureaucracy* (Washington, D.C.: Public Affairs Press, 1965).

16. Again, the reader is referred to note 9 above for studies comparing public and private production of similar services.

17. See Gordon Tullock's review of Mancur Olson's *The Rise and Decline of Nations* for a brief argument on the government as an interest group.

18. This has been noted earlier and is drawn from the arguments made in Niskanen's *Bureaucracy and Representative Government*.

19. See Paul H. Rubin, "On the Form of Special Interest Legislation," *Public Choice* 21 (Spring 1975): 79–90, for a supporting argument.

20. Francis Bator's title, "The Anatomy of Market Failure," certainly conveys this idea.

21. It is interesting to note that television and radio broadcasts fit the Samuelsonian definition of public goods very well, yet are successfully produced in the private sector.

22. See Ayn Rand's "Man's Rights," in her *The Virtue of Selfishness*. Also see Robert Nozick's *Anarchy, State, and Utopia* for a theory of the state that naturally develops as a protector of individual rights.

23. See, however, Murray Rothbard's *For a New Liberty* for an excellent counterargument to this statement.

24. Some examples are listed in note 9 above.

25. Bator's "The Anatomy of Market Failure" can again be cited as a seminal work.

26. See James M. Buchanan, "External Diseconomies, Corrective Taxes, and Market Structure," *American Economic Review* 59 (Dec. 1969): 873–85.

10
The Growth of Government

1. J. R. T. Hughes, *The Governmental Habit*, argues that the government has always intervened into the private sector, however.

2. *The American College Dictionary* (New York: Random House, 1968), lists almost identical definitions for republic and democracy.

3. This is the definition given by Ayn Rand in "The Nature of Government," an essay in her *Virtue of Selfishness*.

4. See Buchanan and Wagner, *Democracy in Deficit: The Political Legacy of Lord Keynes.*

5. This is a simple explanation. For more elaboration, a good source is Douglas H. Blair and Robert A. Pollack, "Rational Collective Choice," *Scientific American* 249, no. 2 (Aug. 1983): 88–95. Blair and Pollack also provide a simple proof of the impossibility theorem.

6. See Earl A. Thompson and Roger L. Faith, "A Pure Theory of Strategic Behavior and Social Institutions," *American Economic Review* 71, no. 3 (June 1981): 366–80, for an insightful analysis of solutions to game theoretic problems.

7. See, e.g., Baumol, "Applied Fairness Theory and Rationing Policy," and Holcombe's comment, followed by Baumol's reply.

8. Tideman and Tullock, "A New and Superior Process for Making Social Choices," gives an example.

9. It seems worthy of note that while Arrow and others object to dictatorship of a single individual as a way out of the impossibility theorem, they do not seem to mind the coercive element of democracy.

10. James M. Buchanan, *The Limits of Liberty: Between Anarchy and Leviathan.*

11. John Rawls, *A Theory of Justice.*

12. See also Holcombe, *Public Finance and the Political Process*, chap. 8, for an analysis along these lines.

13. Some, like Rothbard, *For a New Liberty*, would argue that a government is neither necessary nor desirable for these purposes.

14. Even this is somewhat of an idealistic view, of course, because the executive and judicial branches do have the power to modify rules. See Holcombe, *Public Finance and the Political Process*, chap. 9, for a discussion of the common law in this regard.

15. See Holcombe, "The Origin of the Legislature."

16. See Mancur Olson, *The Rise and Decline of Nations*, p. 71, for a similar point.

17. *The Rise and Decline of Nations.*

18. See, e.g., Paul A. Samuelson and Robert M. Solow, "Analytical Aspects of Anti-Inflation Policy," *American Economic Review* 50, no. 2 (May 1960): 177–94. Their figure 2, p. 192, of a Phillips curve, is captioned, "This shows the menu of choice between different degrees of unemployment and price stability, as roughly estimated from the last twenty-five years of American data," showing that element of social engineering inherent in the Keynesian economics of that day.

19. Data are from the *Statistical Abstract of the United States*, 1980 edition.

Bibliography

Alchian, Armen A. "Some Economics of Property Rights." *Il Politico* 30, no. 4 (1965): 816–29.

———. "Uncertainty, Evolution, and Economic Theory." *Journal of Political Economy* 58 (1950): 211–21.

Alchian, Armen A., and Harold Demsetz. "Production, Information Costs, and Economic Organization." *American Economic Review* 62, no. 5 (Dec. 1972): 777–95.

Allingham, Michael. "Inequality and Progressive Taxation: An Example." *Journal of Public Economics* 11 (Apr. 1979): 273–74.

Arrow, Kenneth J. *Social Choice and Individual Values.* New Haven and London: Yale University Press, 1951.

Atkinson, A. B. *The Economics of Inequality,* Oxford: Clarendon Press, 1975.

———, ed. *Wealth, Income, and Inequality: Selected Reading.* Baltimore: Penguin, 1973.

Atkinson, A. B., and J. E. Stiglitz. "The Design of the Tax Structure: Direct versus Indirect Taxation." *Journal of Public Economics* 6 (July–Aug. 1976): 55–75.

Barker, Sir Ernest. *Social Contract.* New York & London: Oxford University Press, 1960.

Barlow, Robin. "Efficiency Aspects of Local School Finance." *Journal of Political Economy* 78, no. 5 (Sept./Oct. 1970): 1028–40.

———. "Efficiency Aspects of Local School Finance: Reply." *Journal of Political Economy* 81, no. 1 (Jan./Feb. 1973): 199–202.

Barr, James L., and Otto A. Davis. "An Elementary Political and Economic Theory of the Expenditures of State and Local Governments." *Southern Economic Journal* 33 (Oct. 1966): 149–65.

Barro, Robert J. "Are Government Boards New Wealth?" *Journal of Political Economy* 82 (Nov./Dec. 1974): 1095–1117.

————. "On the Determination of the Public Debt," *Journal of Political Economy* 87, no. 5. (Oct. 1979): 940–71.

Barzel, Yoram. "Private Schools and Public School Finance." *Journal of Political Economy* 81, no. 1 (Jan./Feb. 1973): 174–86.

Bator, Francis M. "The Anatomy of Market Failure." *Quarterly Journal of Economics* 72 (Aug. 1958): 351–79.

Baumol, William J. "Applied Fairness Theory and Rationing Policy." *American Economic Review* 72, no. 4 (Sept. 1982): 639–51.

————. "Contestable Markets: An Uprising in the Theory of Industry Structure." *American Economic Review* 72, no. 1 (Mar. 1982): 1–15.

Benson, Bruce L. "Logrolling and the High Demand Review Committee." *Public Choice* 41, no. 3 (1983): 427–34.

Bergstrom, Theodore. "A Note on Efficient Taxation." *Journal of Political Economy* 81, no. 1 (Jan./Feb. 1973): 187–91.

Bergstrom, Theodore, and Robert Goodman, "Private Demand for Public Goods." *American Economic Review* 63 (June 1973): 280–96.

Bernholtz, Peter. "Externalities as a Necessary Condition for Cyclical Social Preferences." *Quarterly Journal of Economics* 97, no. 4 (Nov. 1982): 699–705.

Black, Duncan. *The Theory of Committees and Elections.* Cambridge: Cambridge University Press, 1958.

Blair, Douglas H., and Robert A. Pollack. "Rational Collective Choice." *Scientific American* 249, no. 2 (Aug. 1983): 88–95.

Blair, Roger D., Paul B. Ginsberg, and Ronald J. Vogel. "Blue Cross-Blue Shield Administration Costs: A Study of Non-Profit Health Insurers." *Economic Inquiry* 13 (June 1975): 237–51.

Borcherding, Thomas E., and Robert T. Deacon, "The Demand for Services of Non-Federal Governments." *American Economic Review* 62 (Dec. 1972): 891–901.

Bowen, Howard R. "The Interpretation of Voting in the Allocation of Economic Resources." *Quarterly Journal of Economics* 58 (Nov. 1943): 27–48.

Brenan, Geoffrey, and James Buchanan. "The Logic of the Ricardian Equivalence Theorem." *Finanzarchiv* 38 (1980): 1–16.

———. "Predictive Power and the Choice of Regimes." *Economic Journal* 93 (Mar. 1983): 89–105.

Bronfenbrenner, Martin, *Income Distribution Theory* Chicago: Aldine-Atherton, 1971.

Browning, Edgar K. "The Trend toward Equality in the Distribution of Income." *Southern Economic Journal* 43, no. 1 (July 1976): 912–23.

Buchanan, James M. "The Economics of Earmarked Taxes." *Journal of Political Economy* 71 (Oct. 1963): 457–69.

———. "External Diseconomies, Corrective Taxes, and Market Structure." *American Economic Review* 59 (Dec. 1969): 873–85.

———. *The Limits of Liberty: Between Anarchy and Leviathan.* Chicago: University of Chicago Press, 1975.

———. "Politics, Policy, and the Pigouvian Margins." *Economica*, n.s., 29 (Feb. 1962): 17–28.

———. "Public Finance and Public Choice." *National Tax Journal* 28 (Dec. 1975): 383–94.

———. "The Relevance of Pareto Optimality." *Journal of Conflict Resolution* (Nov. 1962): 341–54.

———. "Taxation in Fiscal Exchange." *Journal of Public Economics* 6 (July–Aug. 1976): 17–29.

Buchanan, James M., and Marilyn Flowers. "An Analytic Setting for a Taxpayer's Revolution." *Western Economic Journal* 7 (Dec. 1969): 349–59.

Buchanan, James M., and Charles J. Goetz. "Efficiency Limits of Fiscal Mobility: An Assessment of the Tiebout Model." *Journal of Public Economics* 1 (1972): 25–43.

Buchanan, James M., and Dwight R. Lee. "Politics, Time, and the Laffer Curve." *Journal of Political Economics* 90, no. 4 (Aug. 1982): 815–19.

Buchanan, James M., and Gordon Tullock. *The Calculus of Consent.* Ann Arbor, University of Michigan Press, 1962.

Buchanan, James M., and Richard E. Wagner. *Democracy in Deficit: The Political Legacy of Lord Keynes.* New York: Academic Press, 1977.

Buchanan, James M., Robert D. Tollison, and Gordon Tullock, eds. *Toward a Theory of the Rent-Seeking Society.* College Station: Texas A&M University Press, 1980.

Coase, R. H. "The Nature of the Firm." *Economica* 4 (Nov. 1937): 386–405.

———. "The Problem of Social Cost." *Journal of Law & Economics* 3 (October 1960), p. 1–44.

Crain, W. Mark. "On the Structure and Stability of Political Markets." *Journal of Political Economy* 85, no. 4 (Aug. 1977): 829–42.

Crain, W. Mark, and Asghar Zardkoohi. "A Test of the Property-Right Theory of the Firm: Water Utilities in the United States." *Journal of Law & Economics* 21, no. 2 (Oct. 1978): 395–408.

Davies, David G. "The Efficiency of Public versus Private Firms: The Case of Australia's Two Airlines." *Journal of Law & Economics* 14 (Apr. 1971): 149–65.

Deacon, Robert T. "Private Choice and Collective Outcomes: Evidence from Public Sector Demand Analysis." *National Tax Journal* 30 (1977): 371–86.

De Alessi, Louis. "Property Rights, Transactions Costs, and X-Efficiency: An Essay in Economic Theory." *American Economic Review* 73, no. 1 (Mar. 1983): 64–81.

Demsetz, Harold, "Why Regulate Utilities?" *Journal of Law & Economics* 11 (1968): 55–65.

Denzau, Arthur T., and Robert J. Mackay. "Benefit Shares and Majority Voting." *American Economic Review* 66 (Mar. 1976): 69–76.

Diamond, Peter A., and James A. Mirrlees. "Optimal Taxation and Public Production: I and II." *American Economic Review* 81 (Mar. 1971): 8–27, (June 1971): 261–78.

Dixit, Avinash. "Price Changes and Optimum Taxation in a Many-Consumer Economy." *Journal of Public Economics* 11 (Apr. 1979): 143–57.

Downs, Anthony, *An Economic Theory of Democracy.* New York: Harper & Row, 1957.

———. "Why the Government Budget Is Too Small in a Democracy." *World Politics* 12 (July 1960): 541–64.

Edelman, Murray. *The Symbolic Uses of Politics.* Urbana: University of Illinois Press, 1964.

Ekelund, Robert B., Jr., and Robert D. Tollison, *Mercantilism as a Rent-Seeking Society.* College Station: Texas A&M University Press, 1981.

Enelow, James M., and Melvin S. Hinich. "Ideology, Issues, and the Spatial Theory of Elections." *American Political Science Review* 76, no. 3 (Sept. 1982): 493–501.

———. "On Plott's Pairwise Symmetry Condition for Majority Rule Equilibrium." *Public Choice* 46, no. 3 (1983): 317–21.

Feldstein, Martin. "On the Optimal Progressivity of the Income Tax." *Journal of Public Economics* 2 (Nov. 1973): 357–76.

Feldstein, Martin, and Robert P. Inman, eds., *The Economics of Public Services.* London: Macmillan, 1977.

Friedman, David. "Many, Few, One: Social Harmony and the Shrunken Choice Set." *American Economic Review* 70, no. 1 (Mar. 1980): 225–32.

Friedman, Milton. *Capitalism and Freedom.* Chicago: University of Chicago Press, 1962.

Gordon, Scott. "The New Contractarians." *Journal of Political Economy* 84, no. 3 (June 1976): 573–90.

Hayek, Friedrich A. "The Use of Knowledge in Society." *American Economic Review* 35, no. 4 (Sept. 1945): 519–30.

———. *Studies in Philosophy, Politics, and Economics.* Chicago: University of Chicago Press, 1967.

Hazlitt, Henry. *Economics in One Lesson.* New York: Harper, 1946.

Heiner, Ronald A. "The Collective Decision Problem, and a Theory of Preference." *Economic Inquiry* 19, no. 2 (Apr. 1981): 297–31.

Hochman, Harold M., and James D. Rogers. "Pareto Optimal Redistribution." *American Economic Review* 59 (Sept. 1969): 542–57.

Hoenack, Stephen A. "On the Stability of Legislative Outcomes." *Public Choice* 41, no. 2 (1983): 251–60.

Hofstadter, Douglas R. *Gödel, Escher, Bach: An Eternal Golden Braid.* Basic Books, 1979.

———. "Metamagical Themas," *Scientific American* 248, nos. 5, 6 (May, June 1983): 16, 14.

Holcombe, Randall G. "Applied Fairness Theory: Comment." *American Economic Review* 73, no. 5 (Dec. 1983): 1153–56.

———. "Deficits, Savings, and Capital Formation." *Federal Reserve Bank of Atlanta Review* 67, No. 8 (Aug. 1982): 38–44.

———. "An Empirical Test of the Median Voter Model." *Economic Inquiry* 18, no. 2 (Apr. 1980): 260–74.

———. "The Origin of Legislature." *Social Science Review*, forthcoming.

———. *Public Finance and the Political Process.* Carbondale & Edwardsville: Southern Illinois University Press, 1983).

Holcombe, Randall G. and Asghar Zardkoohi. "On the Distribution of Federal Taxes and Expenditures, and the New War between the States." *Public Choice* 40 (1983): 165–74.

Holcombe, Randall, G., John D. Jackson, and Asghar Zardkoohi. "The National Debt Controversy." *Kyklos* 34, no. 2: 186–202.

Hotelling, Harold. "Stability in Competition." *Economic Journal* 39 (Mar. 1929): 41–57.

Hughes, Jonathan R. T. *The Governmental Habit.* New York: Basic Books, 1977.

Inman, Robert P. "Testing Political Economy's 'as if' Assumption: Is the Median Income Voter Really Decisive? *Public Choice* 33, no. 4 (1978): 45–65.

Jackson, Raymond. "A 'Taxpayers' Revolution' and Economic Rationality." *Public Choice* 10 (Spring 1971): 93–96.

Johnson, Harry G. *The Theory of Income Distribution.* London: Gray-Mills, 1973.

Keynes, John Maynard. *The General Theory of Employment, Interest, and Money.* New York: Harcourt, Brace, 1936.

Kirzner, Israel M. *Competition and Entrepreneurship.* Chicago: University of Chicago Press, 1973.

Klingaman, David. "A Note on a Cyclical Majority Problem." *Public Choice* 6 (Spring 1969): 99–101.

Koford, Kenneth J. "Centralized Vote-trading." *Public Choice* 39, no. 2 (1982): 245–68.

Krueger, Anne O. "The Political Economy of the Rent-Seeking Society." *American Economic Review* 64 (June 1974): 291–303.

Kuhn, Thomas S. *The Structure of Scientific Revolutions.* Chicago: University of Chicago Press, 1962.

Lee, Dwight R., and James M. Buchanan. "Tax Rates and Tax Revenues in Political Equilibrium: Some Simple Analytics." *Economic Inquiry* 20, no. 3 (July 1982): 344–54.

Lindsay, Cotton M. "A Theory of Government Enterprise." *Journal of Political Economy* 84 (Oct. 1976): 1061–77.

McKelvey, R.D. "General Conditions for Global Intransitivities in Formal Voting Models." *Econometrica* 47, no. 5 (Sept. 1979): 1085–1112.

———. "Intransitivities in Multi Dimensional Voting Models and Some Implications for Agenda Control." *Journal of Economic Theory* 12, no. 3 (June 1976): 472–82.

McKenzie, Richard B., and Robert J. Staaf. "Revenue Sharing and Monopoly Government." *Public Choice* 33, no. 3 (1978): 93–97.

Meigs, Russell. *The Athenian Empire.* Oxford: Clarendon Press, 1972.

Mirrlees, James A. "An Exploration in the Theory of Optimum Income Taxation." *Review of Economic Studies* 38 (Apr. 1971): 175–208.

———. "Optimal Tax Theory—A Synthesis." *Journal of Public Economics* 6 (Nov. 1976): 327–58.

Mises, Ludwig von. *Human Action.* 3d rev. ed. Chicago: Henry Regnery Company, 1966.

Musgrave, Richard A. *The Theory of Public Finance.* New York: McGraw-Hill, 1959.

Niemi, Richard G. "Why So Much Stability? Another Opinion." *Public Choice* 41, no. 2 (1983): 261–70.

Niskanen, William A. "Bureaucrats and Politicians." *Journal of Law & Economics* 18 (Dec. 1975): 617–43.

———. *Bureaucracy and Representative Government.* Chicago and New York: Aldine-Atherton, 1971.

———. "The Peculiar Economics of Bureaucracy." *American Economic Review* 58 (May 1968): 293–305.

Nozick, Robert. *Anarchy, State, and Utopia.* New York: Basic Books, 1974.

———. *Philosophical Explanations.* Cambridge, Mass.: Belknap, 1981.

Olson, Moncur, Jr. *The Logic of Collective Action.* New York: Shocken Books, 1965.

———. *The Rise and Decline of Nations.* New Haven: Yale University Press, 1982.

Ordeshook, Peter C., "Political Disequilibrium and Scientific Inquiry: A Comment on William Riker's "Implications from the Disequilibrium of Majority Rule for the Study of Institutions." *American Political Science Review* 74, no. 2 (June 1980): 447–50.

Ordover, Jannus A. "Distributive Justice and Optimal Taxation of Wages and Interest in a Growing Economy." *Journal of Public Economics* 5 (Jan.–Feb. 1976): 139–60.

Peacock, Alan, and Francesco Forte. *The Political Economy of Taxation.* New York: St. Martin's Press, 1981.

Plott, Charles R. "A Notion of Equilibrium and Its Possibility under Majority Rule." *American Economic Review* 62, no. 4 (Sept. 1967): 787–806.

Plott, Charles R., and Michael E. Levine. "A Model of Agenda Influence on Committee Decisions." *American Economic Review* 68, no. 1 (Mar. 1978): 146–60.

Posner, Richard A. "The Social Costs of Monopoly and Regulation." *Journal of Political Economy* 83 (Aug. 1975): 807–27.

———. "Taxation by Regulation." *Bell Journal of Economics and Management Science* 2 (Spring 1971): 22–50.

Rae, Douglas, "An Altimeter for Mr. Escher's Stairway: A Comment on William H. Riker's "Implications from the Disequilibrium of Majority Rule for the Study of Institutions." *American Political Science Review* 74, no. 2 (June 1980): 451–55.

Rand, Ayn. *The Virtue of Selfishness*, New York: New American Library, 1961.

Rawls, John. *A Theory of Justice*. Cambridge, Mass.: Belknap, 1971.

Reynolds, Morgan, and Eugene Smolensky. *Public Expenditures, Taxes, and the Distribution of Income*. New York: Academic Press, 1977.

Ricketts, Martin. "Tax Theory and Tax Policy." In Alan Peacock and Francesco Forte, eds., *The Political Economy of Taxation*. New York: St. Martin's Press, 1981, pp. 29–46.

Riker, William H. "Implications from the Disequilibrium of Majority Rule for the Study of Institutions." *American Political Science Review* 74, no. 2 (June 1980): 432–46.

———. "Reply to Ordeshook and Rae." *American Political Science Review* 74, no. 2 (June 1980): 456–58.

———. *The Theory of Political Coalitions*. New Haven: Yale University Press, 1962.

Rizzo, Mario J. "Praxeology and Econometrics: A Critique of Positivist Economics." In Louis M. Spadaro, ed., *New Directions in Austrian Economics*. Kansas City, Kans.: Andrews & McMeel, 1978.

Romer, Thomas, and Howard Rosenthal. "Bureaucrats versus Voters: On the Political Economy of Resource Allocation by Direct Democracy." *Quarterly Journal of Economics* 93, no. 4 (Nov. 1979): 563–87.

———. "The Elusive Median Voter." *Journal of Public Economics* 12, no. 2 (Oct. 1979): 143–70.

———. "Median Voters or Budget Maximizers: Evidence from School Expenditure Referenda." *Economic Inquiry* 26, no. 4 (Oct. 1982): 556–78.

———"Political Resource Allocation, Controlled Agendas, and the Status Quo." *Public Choice* 33, no. 4 (1978): 27–43.

Rothbard, Murray N. *For a New Liberty*. New York: Macmillan, 1973.

Rubin, Paul H. "On the Form of Special Interest Legislation." *Public Choice* 21 ((Spring 1975): 79–90.

Samuelson, Paul A. "A Diagrammatic Exposition of a Theory of Public Expenditure." *Review of Economics and Statistics* 37 (Nov. 1955): 350–56.

———. "The Pure Theory of Public Expenditure." *Review of Economics and Statistics* 36 (Nov. 1954): 387–89.

Sandmo, Agnar, "Optimal Taxation—An Introduction to the Literature." *Journal of Public Economics* 6 (July–Aug. 1976): 37–54.

Schelling, Thomas C. *The Strategy of Conflict*, (Cambridge, Mass.: Harvard University Press, 1960).

Schwartz, Thomas. "The Universal-instability Theorem." *Public Choice* 37, no. 3 (1981): 487–501.

Seade, J. K., "On the Shape of Optimum Tax Schedules." *Journal of Public Economics* 7 (Apr. 1977): pp. 203–35.

Shepsle, Kenneth A. "Institutional Arrangements and Equilibrium in a Multidimensional Voting Model." *American Journal of Political Science* 23, no. 1 (Feb. 1979): 27–59.

Shepsle, Kenneth A., and Barry R. Weingast. "Structure-Induced Equilibrium and Legislative Choice." *Public Choice* 37. no. 3 (1981): 503–19.

Shumpeter, Joseph A. *Capitalism, Socialism and Democracy*. 3d ed. New York: Harper & Row, 1950.

Smith, Adam. *The Wealth of Nations*, New York: Modern Library, 1937.

Stigler, George D. "The Theory of Economic Regulation." *Bell Journal of Economics and Management Science* 2 (Spring 1971): 3–21.

Stiglitz, Joseph E., and Michael J. Boskin. "Some Lessons from the New Public Finance." *American Economic Review* 67 (Feb. 1977): 295–301.

Thomas, Hugh. *A History of the World*. New York: Harper & Row, 1979.

Thompson, Earl A. "Taxation and National Defense." *Journal of Political Economy* 82, no. 4 (July/August 1974): 755–83.

Thompson, Earl A., and Roger L. Faith. "A Pure Theory of Strategic Behavior and Social Institutions." *American Economic Review* 71, no. 3 (June 1981): 366–80.

Tideman, T. Nicolaus, and Gordon Tullock. "A New and Superior Process for Making Social Choices." *Journal of Political Economy* 84 (Dec. 1976): 1145–60.

Tiebout, Charles M. "A Pure Theory of Local Expenditures." *Journal of Political Economy* 64 (Oct. 1956): 416–24.

Tocqueville, Alexis de, *Democracy in America*, New York: Geo. Deardorn & Co., 1838.

Tullock, Gordon. "Entry Barriers in Politics." *American Economic Review* 15, no. 2 (Mar. 1965): 458–66.

―――. "The General Irrelevance of the General Impossibility Theorem." *Quarterly Journal of Economics* 81, no. 2 (May 1967): 256–70.

―――. *The Politics of Bureaucracy.* Washington, D.C.: Public Affairs Press, 1965.

―――. Review of Mancur Olson, *The Rise and Decline of Nations.* In *Public Choice* 40, no. 1 (1983): 111–16.

―――. *Toward a Mathematics of Poltics.* Ann Arbor: University of Michigan Press, 1967.

―――. "The Welfare Costs of Tariffs, Monopolies, and Theft." *Western Economic Journal* 5 (June 1967): 224–32.

―――. "Why So Much Stability." *Public Choice* 37, no. 2 (1982): 189–202.

Weingast, Barry R., Kenneth A. Shepsle, and Christopher Johnsen. "The Political Economy of Benefits and Costs: A Neoclassical Approach to Distributive Politics." *Journal of Political Economy* 89, no. 4 (Aug. 1981): 642–64.

Wicksell, Knut, "A New Principle of Just Taxation." In Richard A. Musgrave and Alan T. Peacock, eds., *Classics in the Theory of Public Finance.* New York: St. Martin's Press, 1967, pp. 92–118.

Winer, Stanley L. "Some Evidence on the Effect of the Separation of Spending and Taxing Decisions." *Journal of Political Economy* 91, no. 1 (Feb. 1983): 126–40.

Index

RANDALL G. HOLCOMBE is a member of the economics department at Auburn University, where he has taught since 1977. He has also been on the faculty of Texas A & M University. His research has been published in such journals as the *American Economic Review, Southern Economic Journal, Economic Inquiry, National Tax Journal, Journal of Public Economics,* and *Public Choice.* He is author of the book *Public Finance and the Political Process.*